Both Sides

of Then

Finding Love After Abandonment

JENNIFER GRIFFITH

A REGALO PRESS BOOK
ISBN: 979-8-88845-514-2
ISBN (eBook): 979-8-88845-515-9

Both Sides of Then:
Finding Love After Abandonment
© 2024 by Jennifer Griffith
All Rights Reserved

Cover Design by theBookDesigners.com

Publishing Team:
Founder and Publisher – Gretchen Young
Editorial Assistant – Caitlyn Limbaugh
Managing Editor – Caitlin Burdette
Production Manager – Alana Mills
Production Editor – Rachel Hoge
Associate Production Manager – Kate Harris

As part of the mission of Regalo Press, a donation is being made to Concerned United Birthparents, as chosen by the author. Find out more about this organization at https://concernedunitedbirthparents.org/.

All people, locations, events, and situations are portrayed to the best of the author's memory. While all of the events described are true, many names and identifying details have been changed to protect the privacy of the people involved.

Regalo Press
New York • Nashville
regalopress.com

Published in the United States of America
1 2 3 4 5 6 7 8 9 10

For Mom and Drake

There are no secrets that time does not reveal.

—Jean Racine

TABLE OF CONTENTS

PART THREE - RECKONING

AUTHOR'S NOTE

This is my memoir.

It is also my mother's memoir written by me, her daughter. I've painted my mother's story based on the vignettes she shared with me throughout her life; relying on creativity to recreate the scenes and events where I was not present.

In our history, when we lived in tribes, there were story keepers responsible for holding on to narratives for the next generation. They were passed down orally in simple anecdotes or drawings. Eventually, the practice evolved into the complex form of writing. One cannot be completely accurate when telling someone else's story. For various reasons, my mother doesn't remember many of the details of her young life. With her blessing, I've recreated her story to the best of my ability relying on conversations, letters, interviews, photos, and her fractional moments of clarity.

Some names and events were altered to protect the privacy of others.

PREFACE

I always knew my mother was different from other moms. She was shy and intimidated at social gatherings. Even though she encouraged me to have friends, she rarely spent time with any of her own. When she found out we were playing spin the bottle at boy-girl parties, she forbade me to play, or I would be grounded for a month. I sat to the side watching my friends. I was meant to avoid boys at all costs.

My father was the center of her existence. Her days were spent getting ready for him to come home from work. She stripped and made their bed, changing the sheets daily. Even if it was freezing outside, she opened the windows to "air out the house" and release the smell of my father's cigarettes from the night before. She turned on the potpourri pot and let the aroma of cinnamon and orange flow through the rooms. Her final touch was to vacuum perfect lines in the carpet to show her work. Once the definition was in place, I was told not to walk in the room.

She had no family except for her sister and three brothers. Hints of her past lived in framed black-and-white family photos. It took decades for me to understand their significance. One was of her parents, two people I would never meet, but who held celestial importance in my mother's life. I saw the image daily, tucked in the corner shelf of her dresser. Her parents are leaning into each other while sitting on the hood of a large, old automobile. When I was a young girl, they reminded me of ghosts.

"It's the only picture I have of them together," she would say to me throughout my childhood. Both her parents had died, separately, by the time my mother was ten years old.

Another picture was of a beautiful brick building surrounded by maple trees. On the bottom printed in white it read, "Rohrman Cottage. Baptist Orphanage. Philadelphia. PA."

These were the first clues I had into the tragedy that surrounded my mother during her young life. She and her four siblings were raised in an orphanage. No family wanted to adopt all five children, which had been her father's wish, so they were destined to live in the children's home until they were eighteen years old.

For countless nights, while her head lay on a pillow that smelled of starch, my mother struggled with the memories of what it was like to have a family and have it suddenly torn apart. What it felt like to be loved by parents who were now gone. My mother dreamed of changing her destiny and creating a family of her own. Eventually, she would create the family she had longed for—but not until she had experienced one terrible loss after another.

There begins my journey with the enigma that is my mother. A woman who still bleeds from the wounds of the little girl who lost so much. A woman in search of a conventional life, even though she had tasted it only for brief moments in her childhood.

Anyone who has met my mother has told her she should write her life story. Every time she is encouraged to do so, she blushes and brushes it off with a nervous laugh and a biting comment that instantly pushes both the person and idea away. She has a way of distancing people when they get too close to the sorrow she carries within her.

"I'm not that interesting. I don't know why anyone would want me to write about all of that. I don't want people's pity."

Throughout the years, I encouraged her to write her story. She entertained the idea but never put words to paper. Eventually, as her sister was dying, she sat down at her computer and wrote a page and a half, single-spaced. Months later, she reluctantly shared what she wrote with me. She had done her best to remember the details of her childhood, but so many of the memories were elusive. What she recalled most was that it was painful losing her mother, but losing her father two years later was a tragedy that defined her life.

The voice that emerges in her writing differs from the woman I know her to be. She is wise, funny, and insightful. The memories she wrote down read as if a little girl's soul is trapped in her body.

Occasionally, she opens up to me about her life—typically after a few glasses of wine or on a long drive—and when she does, I can piece together her story. There have always been gaps, things she never wanted to talk about. Moments when she stops herself short, holding back tears. "Maybe one day I will be able to tell you about that. Not now."

These moments—revelations that cause her to choke on tears and stop her breath—are the richest. They are the most overwhelming and enchanting stories for me and others to comprehend. Her recollections carve a harsh reality. Being an orphan was the one truth that took her through the peaks and valleys of her life and ultimately led to the decision she would always regret.

I always wondered, *How did she bring herself to do that? How was that the only option?*

It's a peculiar trait my mother has displayed throughout her life. She has faced the most difficult of life's challenges and survived, but there are moments where she has frozen in the face of adversity, unable to accept a painful truth.

As her daughter, there were moments in my adolescence that filled me with a sense of emptiness and disorientation and made it difficult to clearly see my reflection. My mother's response then was to dismiss both the concern and my pain as if they weren't real.

"Oh, do I know pain! My life has been full of it," she would say.

By the time I was a teenager, remnants from my mother's early life started to appear. When her past collided with our present, I began to feel an overwhelming sense of isolation from the woman raising me. I wondered what terrible things had happened to her and why it felt as if her pain mattered most. Was there something about my mother's past haunting not only her but haunting me?

When I became a mother, I realized my childhood could influence the kind of mother I would be to my son. The stakes had become higher. I had to find a way to address painful parts of my adolescence to release my son from the legacy of my burdens.

It led me to question: If I imagined what it was like to live my mother's childhood, would I truly get to know my mother? Would I see my own life more clearly?

Perhaps in reliving my mother's story, I would reveal something about myself. Then I could be set free from the pain of the past, and so could she.

The nagging questions led to a single pursuit: to understand how my mother's experience lay at the root of what happened to me when I was young.

This story is about why my mother's life should be written and shared. It is also a story about why I was meant to write it for her.

PART ONE

WHAT CAME BEFORE

CHAPTER ONE

YOU HAVE A BROTHER

Jennifer, 1987

I was thirteen when my mother told me she gave up her firstborn, my brother, for adoption.

In the dark room lit by colorful Christmas lights on the tree and the yellow hue of the fire next to me, I sat waiting. A few minutes before, my mother knocked rapidly on my bedroom door. I opened it to see her large golden eyes were wide and anxious, darting around my face in sudden movements. "Can you come to the living room for a few minutes?" she said. "There is something important I need to share with you."

Up until this moment, everything in my world existed like any average teenager. A month before my fourteenth birthday, the year was 1987, and a poster of Johnny Depp from *21 Jump Street* hung on the wall above my bed. To support my obsession with the show, mostly with Johnny, I recorded episodes on VHS so I could watch them over and over again. Wearing my favorite white sweatshirt with Esprit written in rainbow colors across the front, I wore a surplus of blue eye shadow and used enough Aussie Scrunch Spray to ensure my bangs created a wave above my forehead. My friends and I spent our days writing notes and passing them to each other in class and talking on the phone for hours every day after school. Life appeared simple, with minor teenage complications emerging.

I found my mother waiting for me in our perfectly clean living room, which appeared like a showroom. She kept it immaculate and had recently purchased new pillows she liked to fluff and reposition throughout the day. Shopping lifted my mother's spirit. Her days were filled with housework and running errands to buy everything from groceries to furniture, wallpaper, and my clothes. When my father grumbled about her frequent shopping, she responded, "Well, it was on sale—twenty percent off."

I walked into the living room and took my father's chair tucked next to the fireplace. If he was around, we left the seat open for him, but my mother motioned for me to take it. She sat across from me on our large sofa with fabric that scratched the back of your legs. Her chestnut hair feathered like waves against her cheeks. Her eyebrows pinched, and her knees were pressed together tightly with her hands resting on top of them. A large coffee table sat between us; holding a glass of wine, she nervously sipped as we remained in silence.

Fidgeting with one of the tree ornaments while I waited for her to speak, my dad poked his head into the living room and looked at both of us, stopping to stare in my mom's direction and giving her a knowing look. "I'll be back," he said, looking at her intently and making it clear he knew the trouble my mother held secret. I concluded he took the short walk to our neighbor's house for a smoke and a drink. He made the trip often.

I let him leave the room without saying goodbye. I began to accept my dad was a man of few words, slowly relinquishing my little girl hope he might become the type of father to have long discussions with his daughter. Good at the quick catch-up, he kept hugs and expressions of love brief. He wasn't home often, and from my teenaged perspective, he always appeared to be working, golfing, or doing his own thing. I heard him walk down the steps and shut the front door behind him, followed by my mother's voice.

"Jenny, do you remember asking for a baby brother or sister over the years?"

What a confusing question. My two sisters lived three thousand miles away; they were my father's daughters from his first marriage. Beth was my eldest sister by twelve years, and my middle sister, Linda, a closer six years older than me. As I learned to walk, Beth listened to Aerosmith, and Linda did backflips in gymnastics. I rarely saw them but adored them from afar. I coveted the clothes they gave me, the letters they wrote me, and my pictures of them. Framed school photos hung next to our front door. My mother inserted a new photo of us each year, and the longing to be closer to my siblings ran deeper. My sisters came for short visits, and I fell into a puddle of tears every time they left. Often, in the boredom and solitude as the only child growing up in our home, I would ask my mom for a brother or sister. After a day of playing outside, I always envied my friends who went home to have dinner with their siblings and parents. Instead, I entered a quiet house. My mom cooking from her place at the stove while my dad sipped vodka poured over ice while answering the telephone that rang nonstop with demands from his work.

"Are you pregnant?" I asked, feeling somewhat excited but embarrassed.

"No, no, dear, I'm not pregnant." She bit her lip and gave me a huge smile. "Jenny, you have a brother. I just found him."

My ears filled with the sensation of being on a plane descending. My face burned, and my heart pulsed in fear.

You have a brother. Is that what she just said?

I dug my nails into the sides of the chair, the velour fabric mushing under my fingernails. A long, awkward pause. *Perhaps this new brother is Johnny Depp,* I mused and experienced a surge of excitement run through my veins. In my mind, my arms were linked with my new brother as we walked the red carpet and appeared in *Sassy* magazine.

Until then, I was my mother's only child. There wasn't a day I didn't know how much my mother wanted to be a mom. Wanted to be *my* mom.

"Is this Dad's kid?"

"No, he is not your dad's child. He's eighteen years old."

The hopes of my new brother being Johnny Depp sank to the pit of my already queasy stomach.

"Who's the father?" I didn't know what else to ask.

"The father's name is Harry. It's a long story."

"And where's Harry?"

"I haven't talked to Harry in years. We never married. Another family raised your brother." She let out a sound which sounded like a giggle. "Would you like to see a picture of him?"

My eyes focused intently on my mother as I tried to comprehend her words.

Was I really going to meet my new brother by looking at a photo?

Like a roller coaster, my body absorbed the sensation of gaining and losing something at the same time.

Finally, she got up and extended her arm as if she were going to put it around my shoulder.

I motioned for her to keep walking as she took eager steps toward her bedroom, turning around to ensure I followed. I walked slowly and felt the foundation of my life as I knew it shift. Of course, I wanted a brother; I always longed for a sibling in the house. This wasn't the truth rattling my core, robbing me of a calm throat and steady air. It was my mother. Walking through her open bedroom door, she was changing before my eyes.

My parents' bedroom colors were blue and white with loud, flowery wallpaper lit up by the lone lamp hanging in the middle of the ceiling where bugs would collect. As we walked down the hallway, the floorboards creaked. I always found the noises under the carpet a comforting sound, as if the house spoke to you. Dad said he liked the home to make noise, so he knew where people were at all times. I wondered why he wasn't with us. I envisioned him drinking his second martini and smoking his fifth cigarette.

Then, like a brick hitting me hard in the chest, a new truth entered my life. *My mother isn't who she said she is.*

She stopped at her brown dresser with stacked drawers and a hutch attached to the top. The shelves hosted figurines, photos from her past, and vases. Neatly tucked behind one of her ceramics was an envelope with unfamiliar handwriting on it. She turned to me with the paper in her hand and a slight smile.

"I know this is hard, Jenny, but it will be a good thing." She continued to hold the letter in her hand, asking if I had any other questions.

"Where does he live?"

"He lives in Florida. In Miami." Another layer of confusion washed over me.

Miami? How did he end up in Miami?

I was born in Philadelphia, my parents' hometown, and moved to Tacoma, Washington with my mother and father when I was four years old, and my sisters stayed with their mom on the East Coast. How did my brother end up in Florida?

My hand reached for the envelope clutched in my mother's hands. I knew his photo was in there. I wanted to get the reveal over with; I didn't want to be around this version of my mom anymore. She held the letter more tightly to her chest.

"What's his name?"

"His name is Jack."

"Did you name him?"

"No." I could tell the question hurt her, but I didn't mind hurting her.

She took out the photo and handed it to me, her fingers close to mine in anticipation of taking it back again. I snatched the picture with a sudden jerk. I looked down and saw my brother's face for the first time. Dressed in a tuxedo with a silver cummerbund and tie, he matched the dress of the girl his arm wrapped around. A palm tree stood tall in the background and my brother, tan and happy, smiled back at me.

There he was—the eighteen-year-old brother I never knew. I had just heard his name for the first time. I looked at the picture quickly and noticed the young man looked a lot like my mother.

I handed the photo back to her, and she took it with care. An awkward silence hung in the air, heavy and quiet. My mind racing, I thought of my friends wondering how I would explain this news to them.

"It is nice, isn't it? The fact you have a brother now. And guess what? He's coming next month for your birthday. He was born in January, too."

"Neat," I said.

"It's a good present, isn't it?"

"I guess." I moved toward the hallway, down the stairs to our rec room and shut the door with a slam telling my mom to leave me the hell alone for a long time. I heard the front door open as Dad came in from his martini-laden visit next door.

Soon my parents were arguing in the kitchen. My mother's voice rising, trying to get my dad to understand what she wanted. His stern voice telling her she was wrong. She wanted to come to me, but my father said, "Leave her alone." I wanted both. I wanted to be held and comforted after this strange revelation, and I wanted them to leave me alone forever.

I picked up our heavy rotary phone and dialed one of my best friends. I watched the dial go around as the numbers returned to their resting place. The phone rang on the other end, and I heard, "Hello."

"Hey, Lynnette, it's Jenny. You won't believe this. I just got a brother for my birthday."

~

My brother would arrive a month later. I stayed home playing Atari while my parents went to the airport. My father's job was to keep my mother together, to ensure she didn't come undone and embarrass herself, which seemed highly probable. Prior to the night of my brother's arrival, she became a total basket case in my critical teenage view. She cleaned the house twice a day; not a speck of dust survived. She bought new furniture and several outfits. She counted and recounted silverware. Our refrigerator and cabinets were overflowing with food as if ten new brothers were coming.

The day my brother landed she spent hours getting ready. I watched as my mom shook her head several times, letting her newly rolled curls bounce as if shooing away the harsh reality that she would be meeting her son for the first time. In the weeks leading up to his visit, I felt myself slowly pulling away from her. Something about her scared me now; how different her behavior seemed, the long-kept secret, the hiding of a sibling, and the unknowns related to her new story.

Two hours later, I heard the garage door open, and in walked my brother. He came down our narrow basement hallway and greeted me at the door to our rec room. A yellow light shone on his head, and our family pictures hung on the wall behind him. I wondered how it must have felt to see our memories staring back at him. My mother stood to his side smiling excitedly.

My tan, affable new brother, opened his arms for a hug. "Hi, Jen," he said. "I'm Jack."

I leaned in to loosely hug him back. My body quivered, and I didn't know what to say. On the other hand, my brother seemed to be handling the stress of meeting his birth mom well. After a brief introduction, I went back to playing my game while my parents and brother went upstairs.

Sometime later, my mother summoned me upstairs with an enthusiastic, "Dinner!"

During our meal, the conversation revolved around Jack's life in college. My mother gulped her wine in between bites of food, and my brother sipped a beer. I pushed my food around my plate and tried to find questions to ask him, but my mind was blank.

Later, my brother and I were seated together on the sofa, getting to know one another. He gave me a sweatshirt from his school, Florida State University. Then, my mother walked into the room with her camera in hand.

"Smile, let me take your picture. Brother and sister," she said as the flash went off.

I curled against the armrest leaning as far away from him as I could. I didn't find him repulsive—in fact, he was intriguing—but in the moment, I didn't know how to respond. How do you behave when you meet your eighteen-year-old brother for the first time, I wondered. Seeing my mother standing before us, her frantic energy spilling over, I knew she couldn't help me. I existed alone in the experience.

As my brother left for his flight the next week, rather than saying goodbye, I told him, "Don't crash."

I remained bratty and difficult towards him, but I didn't know how to express that while I gained something extraordinary, he had been stolen from me as well. The sudden news of his presence surprised me like a scare that turns to tears. Most of all, I felt disappointed in my mother for her secret and in myself for not knowing what to do with it. Not only did she no longer look the same in my eyes, but everything she told me about her life shifted. There were caverns in her story.

Months after meeting my brother, my father made an explosive announcement of his own. On a chilly, sunny day, as I walked up our dead-end street from the bus stop, I looked at my house—like I always did—and felt a sudden shift. Walking through the front door, I made my way up the narrow stairs to the kitchen and heard my mother in the back bedroom. I decided to startle her—something my father and I enjoyed doing because she scared easily. I crept up behind her and yelled, "Boo!" She dropped the laundry basket in her hands and began to cry.

A wave of guilt washed over me, "Are you okay, Mom?"

"No, no, I'm not. Go get your father."

Ten minutes later, the three of us were seated together in the living room, an ominous feeling in the air. My father was in his chair, the same seat I'd sat in when my mother sprang my new brother on me.

"Go ahead, you tell her." My mother wasn't speaking; she was sneering.

"I don't want to be here anymore," I heard him say.

I could feel my mother's anger as she scowled at the man sitting across from us. He wore a navy-blue jacket and his favorite sailor hat. His eyes were on our beige carpet in front of him, his head tilted in a type of sadness or regret. The room became hollow, void of love, as I absorbed my parents' state; they looked nothing like they did months before. Something changed and, in an instant, I had, too.

Their marriage was over; I could taste the staleness in the air. I didn't need my father to explain his words. With a jolt straightening my spine, I realized I was anticipating his departure, I'd felt his disillusion for some time.

I wondered why my father didn't love my mother, or me, anymore. Why didn't he want to live with me? What did I do wrong?

I ran to the phone in their bedroom and called my friend Lynnette. When she answered, my breath disappeared, and what remained were gasps heavy and deep. My father grabbed the piece from my hand and slammed it on the receiver. He hugged me for the first time in a very long while. I could feel him crying and realized it was only the third time I saw him weep.

For a moment we embraced, then my hands went to his chest and pushed him away.

After my father's declaration that he no longer wanted to be part of our family, a strange thing happened. Stranger than gaining an adult brother you've never met. Stranger than your father announcing he no longer wants to be married to your mother and live with you.

My father stayed.

CHAPTER TWO

WHERE HOME BEGAN

Anna, 1948

W e lived with Mommy and Daddy in a row house on Stafford Street in Manayunk. The home stood narrow like a railroad car. Each house on our block was built directly against the next, giving the neighborhood the appearance of a giant loaf of bread sliced into many pieces. Four narrow stairs led up to a white metal screen door with a brass knocker. The front door was encased with a screened gate that slammed when shut. That sound would always bring me back to our place in Manayunk throughout my life.

The melodies of our neighborhood started early. Before the sun peeked over the houses, tired men like my daddy rose from their beds and made their breakfasts in silence. Most of the workers were employed in the local steel factories. Five days a week, they walked or drove several miles across the Schuylkill Bridge and over the canal wrapping around our town like a scarf.

When I heard the faint sounds of Daddy getting dressed and making breakfast, I would sneak down to the kitchen to see him, startling him with my presence. Silently he invited me to sit in his lap. He ate methodically but quickly. I enjoyed the sound of him chewing and slurping his last bit of coffee. Once he finished eating, he led me to our old worn couch and laid a blanket over me, giving me a kiss on the cheek before gathering his things. He carefully opened the front door, and a wave of fresh air chilled my face. I loved those moments with Daddy before everyone else awoke. They were my moments. He was mine then, all mine and only mine. I would close my eyes and fall asleep to the faint memories of his warmth, the scratchiness of his wool clothing, and the bitter smell of coffee on his breath.

There were five of us crammed into our house. My older sister, Eve, was seven. I was nearly six, and my brother, Howard, was a year younger than me. A picture of each of us hung on the living room wall, as well as a picture of Mommy and Daddy leaning into each other as they sat on the hood of a car. They wore confident smiles on their faces, young adults about to take on the world. It would eventually be the only picture I had of them together. A photo of Eve taken before Howard and I were born showed a beautiful, smiling cherub of a baby propped up in a chair, her hands clasped together, her cheeks spread wide in a smile, and her hair curled around her face. As adults, whenever we looked at that picture, we joked she was happiest then—before we were all born.

Mommy stayed home with us while Daddy worked. Eve floated at Mommy's skirt, helping her in small ways or just getting in the way. She made sure we knew her place as Mommy's closest companion, standing by her side as if she were guarding her.

Mommy and Daddy were in stark contrast to each other. Daddy was tall and lanky, while Mommy was small and thin. Frequently in motion, she resembled a bird looking for a place to land. We spent our days watching her glide through the house. Any time of day, she was either cooking in the kitchen or running up and down the stairs with laundry she washed in our dark and terrifying basement. Occasionally, she would sit at the bottom of the stairs, place her head in her hands, and close her eyes. I wanted to sit next to her and rest my head on her shoulder, but as quickly as the thought crossed my mind, Eve stood there.

When Daddy came home, we ran to him and nestled into any available spot on his lap until dinner appeared on the table. He ate his meal as if he hadn't eaten all day. Whether morning or night, he wore a strained expression causing his face to wrinkle and large lines to appear across his forehead. His fingers rolled against the tabletop in a strange rhythm as he ate, Mommy's voice being the only thing capable of breaking his concentration. A warm smile would relax his expression as his eyes moved toward her. Daddy reminded me of a cat watching a butterfly float by, tempted to try to catch her, but choosing to be still as she drifted past. It was May, spring emerged, and the windows were open. Mommy made me a cake, filling the house with the smell of butter and sugar. Six flames danced on the candles. Just the five of us together around the table like most nights, but on this occasion, it was about me. Moments before, she'd placed the cake in front of me, a beautiful smile on her face. I'd blushed and reveled in the attention as my family sang "Happy Birthday."

Daddy sliced the cake, and we fell silent, gobbling our pieces in a hurry as if it were a race. There were no gifts as we had little money. Instead, Mommy made everyone paint cards for me. Later, I taped them on the wall in the room I shared with Eve.

After we ate, Daddy cleared his throat and looked at Mommy with a serious expression. His forehead creased in his familiar, worried look. Mommy glanced down and gently placed her fork on the plate, letting out a sigh as she dabbed her mouth with her napkin. I loved watching how gracefully she moved.

"Your mother and I have something to tell you," Daddy said and paused. "We are having another baby! Another wonderful life to add to our beautiful family."

Howard let out a sound similar to "Bay-bee."

"How exciting, Daddy. I like being a big sister," I said. Eve let out a sound like a loud yawn. Her fork crashed loudly on her plate as she burst into tears. Our heads turned toward her with identical shocked expressions.

"Eve," Mommy said, resting her right hand on my sister's trembling arm. "It will be an adjustment, but any baby is a gift from God."

Mommy's other thin hand reached up and touched her rosary. Her fingers wrapped around the cross and squeezed tightly, the blue veins appearing sharp against her pale skin. Eve pulled away and folded her arms across her chest. My mouth dropped open. It was unlike Eve to treat Mommy in such a way.

Why is she upset about another baby?

Excitement swirled in my belly, but the news transformed Eve's mood. I wondered if she reacted like this when I was born, my heart pinching at the thought.

Eve's spirit remained melancholy, and just as Eve changed immediately, slowly—very slowly at first—many things began to change.

Mommy transformed before our eyes. She became fatigued as her belly grew. As she strained to go about her day the way she used to, our family slowed down with her.

I knew the baby was coming when Mommy's suitcase sat by the front door. One brisk fall night, Mommy moaned in pain and woke us up with her cries. Daddy let in a neighbor who shuffled us back to bed as our parents rushed out the door to the hospital.

We awoke the next morning to our neighbor in the kitchen and breakfast on the table. We sat down in front of three bowls of lumpy oatmeal. Too excited to eat, we peppered our neighbor with questions about the baby.

"Your mommy delivered twin boys. Their names are Jim and John."

"Two babies?!" Eve squealed.

"It sure makes sense how tired your mom was in the end," the neighbor said, shaking her head and reaching for her rosary. I recognized the woman as someone my mother went to church with every Sunday while Daddy stayed home with us. Seeing the woman grasp for the beads wrapped around her neck—like Mommy often did—made me long for her.

How was it such exciting news about the twins was wrapped in a feeling of sadness and longing as well? In the moment, the only thing I wanted was to set eyes on Mommy, but it would be weeks before we would see her again.

Slowly, at the young age of six, I started to grasp that often, when you're given something, you could easily lose something in return.

CHAPTER THREE

DEEP END OF THE POOL
Jennifer, 1980

I remember two things from second grade. When asked what I wanted to be when I grew up, I wrote, "A secretary for my dad at his company so I can see him more often."

The other memory is nearly dying in a friend's pool until my father saved my life.

I grew up in Tacoma, Washington—a city in the Pacific Northwest—where few people had pools since the weather was gray and overcast most of the year. When the sun emerged in the summer months, people left work early and basked in the hot days that stayed light until ten o'clock. Inevitably, I would get a lobster-red sunburn as we were out of practice on how to use sunscreen. With the sun's emergence, everyone purchased sunglasses, only to lose them later when the clouds reappeared.

The morning I nearly drowned, my mother drove me to Kmart to buy a swimsuit and a pool toy. As we rode to the store in our silver Chrysler LeBaron, I barely contained my excitement. To me, Kmart might as well be a local Disneyland. The store's interior contained thrilling sale details blasted through loudspeakers, and flashing blue lights indicated discounted items. My mother's ears perked up when she heard, "Attention Kmart shoppers."

"You'll need something for the pool since you don't know how to swim yet," my mother said.

We walked the aisle full of float toys, sunglasses, sunscreen, and beach toys. My eyes went toward a floaty shaped like a duck. The picture on the front showed white plastic with accents of primary colors and a face adorned with a giant smile. I grabbed it, and my mother nodded.

Leaving the store, I pulled the package close to my chest. I breathed in the warm air of summer mixed with the scent of plastic clenched in my hands.

"I'm going to name him Ducky," I told her.

Hours later, we arrived at our friends' pool; my mother brought deviled eggs, one of her signature dishes. The adults sat in lounge chairs, drinking and talking while I committed to the shallow end steps. I watched as my father used all his available lung capacity to blow up Ducky. He handed him to me and then rewarded himself with a cigarette.

I placed myself in the middle of my new friend and let my arms hang over Ducky's sides.

"Good job, Jenny," my mother said as I coasted into the water. I listened as the adults laughed, and their voices filled the air like the sound of seagulls.

Even though I didn't know how to swim, with Ducky wrapped around me I was fearless. We ventured to the deep end, where the water felt cooler against my legs. My body slipped through the half-circle, and I was sinking, no longer in the inflatable toy's embrace. Eyes submerged but open, I faced the side of the pool and could see my dark reflection floating downward against the sunlit blue wall. The light above showed the slow ripple of waves. I didn't see Ducky anywhere, my body slippery in the water heading downwards.

Then the world went dark.

My father was conversing with someone when he turned to see Ducky at the deep end of the pool without me in it. He ran across the lawn, dived in, and pulled me out of the water by my pigtails. Then, we were both out of the pool, exhausted, and resting on the concrete.

I awoke from the moment in the arms of someone warm and comforting. I heard myself crying loudly until another voice emerged, "It's okay, honey. You're okay." I realized the woman holding me wasn't my mother; it was our family friend. I appreciated the softness of her embrace and the warmth of her voice, but as the cold cement beneath me brought me back to reality, I wondered where my mother went.

"I saved your life. Your mother was supposed to be watching you," my father declared often.

"I only turned my head away for one second, and you were gone," my mom replied in defense.

"You *never* take your eyes off a child in the pool," he retorted, emphasizing *never*.

As my father retold the story, my mother's lips would purse, and she would repeat, "I turned my head for a second." Eventually, she would resort to silence as he retold the story countless times throughout my life. I watched my mother's face turn crimson, and her head bowed in a turn of shame. I sensed my father blamed my mother for my near drowning while he felt like a hero and reveled in saving my life on a hot summer day.

As I witnessed the story unfold over the years, I wondered whether my mother was upset about the accident or consumed with disappointing my father.

My mother's insistence we get rid of Ducky soon overshadowed the terrifying day.

"That toy almost killed you," she declared.

"Please, please don't give him away. I won't use him in a pool ever again. I'll keep him in my room like my stuffies." I cried hysterically.

My bedroom was various shades and patterns of pink with a small zoo of stuffed animals. Ducky was on my hutch, still smiling at me from the corner in my room.

"No! That thing caused the accident. It's not safe. He has to go," she said adamantly.

I pleaded with her, but nothing was going to change her mind. She grabbed the plastic floaty and tossed him on a pile of unwanted things in the garage.

My mother regularly purged items in our home. She frequently left heaps of bags at the top of our driveway for Goodwill to pick up. In time, she gave away all of my baby clothes, not even keeping a pair of shoes.

Ducky remained with her pile of donations in the garage. As we walked past the mass to get in her car, my impulse was to save him. One day, I snuck him back into my room with the hope my mother wouldn't notice. Within twenty-four hours, he appeared back on the pile. Several mornings later, I heard the roar of a truck backing up our steep driveway. The burly driver got out and opened the back gate. The slam of the door rattled my bones. I could see the interior of the truck partially full of other people's discards. He began tossing our bags one by one. I watched as he grabbed Ducky and callously added him to the pile.

My knees buckled as I wailed.

"Mommy, please, I don't want to get rid of him. Just let me keep him." My voice rising, my tears overwhelming.

She remained stoic. Ducky lay on top of the pile of debris, smiling back at me, calling my name. My mother shooed me inside, and I went to my bedroom, where I couldn't shake the vision of my beloved toy alone in the cold, dark truck.

I heard the engine start and fade into the distance.

After my tears waned to body jerks, my mother came into my bedroom.

"Sometimes, Jenny, you have to say goodbye to things even if you don't want to. It's a tough lesson I learned far too early in life."

It would be something my mother said to me often.

"You should take swim lessons," she offered as a consolation. I nodded, unable to understand the message she hoped to convey, convinced she could never understand the break in my heart with Ducky gone.

After the incident, I went to several swim lessons. My mother took a picture of me while the instructor held me in a back float. I wore a white, green, and blue one-piece with my pigtails floating parallel to my arms. She put the picture in a photo collage months later. Then, like a lot of activities when I was young, the lessons stopped.

"I am afraid you are like me, kid, afraid of swimming," my mother concluded.

My father seldom admitted to a fear of anything except snakes. As an engineer and a mariner, he spent his days managing large ships. Water was essential to his work. When I was younger, he bought a boat, and we spent our weekends cruising on Commencement Bay, surrounded by salty blue water, but never getting into it. Something about the chill of water that can cause hypothermia in minutes isn't inviting.

A few years after my incident in the pool, he had his own deadly experience while on a fishing trip in a remote part of Washington with a friend. The resort owners provided my father and his friend with their gear, including an unsinkable canoe. Starting on a cold, clear day, the men wore layers of clothing, fishing waders, and heavy boots. Hours later, as they drifted, a dense fog moved in. My father stood up to grab something from his pocket and fell. The boat flipped, and quickly, both men were submerged; the unsinkable canoe sank.

My father's friend, Bob, successfully removed his boots and announced he would swim to shore. My father wanted to as well, but unlike Bob, he couldn't get his boots off.

"Try to get someone to come for me," he said.

Bob made it back to land, exhausted and suffering from hypothermia. As he pulled himself onto the shore, people rushed him inside and into a steaming bath. "My friend is still out there," he told them.

My father treaded water as long as he could. Despite his efforts to stay afloat, he came to the realization he couldn't hold on much longer. As his clothes became heavier, they pulled at him like an anchor. He resolved it was time to let go.

When the threat of a storm rolled in, the woman who ran the hotel had worried about the two men fishing. She'd sent her husband and son out to look for them. As the fog became dense, the men had nearly given up when they saw something bobbing in the water.

"Is that someone over there?" the son asked. They motored over to the spot of color among the mass of gray.

What they saw was my father, barely hanging on. His teeth chattered so loud he couldn't speak. They could not pull him entirely into the boat, so the son held onto him as they raced back to the resort, half his body dragging in the frigid lake.

When my father returned home from his trip, my mother greeted him at the top of the stairs like she did every day. He wore one of his few outfits, khakis and a maroon and tan striped shirt, the same outfit he would wear when his mother passed away. Watching him from the kitchen table, he seemed like his usual self, neatly dressed and carrying a small bag in his hands. When my mother put her arms around him, he didn't offer his obligatory kiss; he collapsed in her arms and cried.

It was the first time I saw my father needing my mother emotionally.

"What's the matter?" my mother asked with alarm in her voice.

"I didn't think I was coming home," he said.

My father told the story of his near drowning only once, then never wanted to discuss it again.

Days later, as we got into her car to run errands, my mother paused and looked at me. "It takes a lot to scare your father, Jenny, but he was scared coming back from the fishing trip," she was near tears. "We're lucky we didn't lose him. I'm not sure what we would do."

I could see it then, my mother not only loved but admired my father. In that moment, I understood my mother and I had something in common; for both of us, then, my father was our hero.

CHAPTER FOUR

BANDAGES

Anna, 1949

Once Mommy brought home the babies, our house was full of people coming over to help. Family and friends came through our front door as if it were revolving. Being surrounded by others doesn't ensure you aren't lonely. In fact, it can intensify the feeling. The sound of conversations all around you. The daily intrusion of others in your space. The sense of feeling stranded even when people are milling around. At times, there were so many people crammed in our small house, it was hard to breathe.

Mommy spent several weeks in the hospital after the twins were born. All three of us kids begged to visit her and the new babies, but they wouldn't let us.

"No children allowed," Grandmom Eva, Mommy's mom—and my sister's namesake—said every time we asked. We heard one boy came out delicate, and we needed to stay away. We continued to plead, promising not to hold them until one day Grandmom screamed at us. Her Polish accent made it nearly impossible to understand her words, but her tone of voice made us stop.

After what seemed an eternity, Mommy came home. Tired and frail, she walked through the door, holding one of the twin boys. Daddy stood behind her holding the other. A collective sigh went through the house. Our parents were home. I secretly hoped this meant some of the people taking care of us during the day would leave.

The little boys brought excitement and joy to all of us. I loved caring for them, holding them gently, and singing songs to them. Even Eve, who had rarely smiled since we heard the news about the babies, grew happy again when the little boys were around. They were little episodes of giggles and moments of joy. But Mommy never returned to the way she was before. She no longer fluttered around our home caring for us. She spent her days resting and recovering from having the babies. I ached for her to be herself again, but something had changed in Mommy. Eve knew, and soon she would tell me, but not until the truth broke something inside her.

The first nine months with the twins were a blur of activity. I enjoyed the smell of baby powder and lotion. Even the scent of a dirty diaper made me feel alive because I knew it meant we were living—abundant life filled our little house. The twin boys kept Daddy, Eve, and me busy. It gave me great joy that others needed my help.

We were quickly leaving our childhood behind in a race to be grown up and helpful. Without saying it, Eve and I were motivated by the same thing. If we could fill Mommy's place in the house, life would seem normal again. The people helping would leave, and we could just be a family. As much as I wanted to be closer to Mommy, it seemed as if they—the people in our house—were trying to keep us away from her. She spent most of her time in her bedroom "resting," they said in a whisper.

John had big eyes and giggled often. Jim, the smaller of the two, sat so quiet you sometimes forgot he was there. The twins were with us most of the time, except when they were carried away by adults and up the stairs to Mommy. Even though she came home, there was a separation between us.

One evening, after putting Howard in his pajamas, a new chore that filled me with pride, I came downstairs and found Eve motionless on the sofa. Her gaze frozen, she refused to look in my direction. She was always aloof with me, and at times she frightened me. I never knew what her reactions were going to be, so I existed in her presence without saying much.

Yet, after sensing something was wrong for some time, I burst out, "Why is Daddy sleeping on the sofa at night, Eve?"

She rolled her eyes, reminding me I was a nuisance to her. Never once looking in my direction, she walked out of the room, leaving me alone in my discomfort, my question still hanging in the air.

My eyes became blurry with tears. I didn't want anyone to find me crying, especially Daddy. I worked hard for him to see me as a big girl. Frozen in my mix of pain and confusion, I looked at my bright pink slippers.

Usually, the sight of them made me feel happy, but not this time. Wishing for somewhere to go, I longed for a room that was mine.

I sought refuge in the bathroom until I could make the tears stop, but I bumped into Eve again. She sat on the stairs where Mommy used to sit when tired. In Eve's small hands was a roll of white fabric. Looking up, I noticed her face appeared pale, and her eyes were rimmed in red. Eve, too, was crying. Despite my trepidation after my mistake just minutes before, I found the courage to ask her why she was upset. She only cried harder, and guilt surged through my veins as I continued to feel like I could never do right around her.

Her body quivered while she gasped for air. I said nothing but sat down and put my arm around her. She didn't pull away but leaned into me.

"She's dying. She's dying, and there is nothing we can do about it. Look, Anna. Look at what I'm holding. There's a giant hole in her chest, and she's dying."

Eve's hands clutched a roll of white gauze. I had seen the fabric before, wrapped around Howard's knee after he crashed down on the sidewalk, leaving blood seeping from a tear in his skin. The sight of blood caused my knees to quiver.

Looking down at Eve's hands, I saw blood on the white fabric. I didn't feel afraid of what I saw this time. Curiosity swallowed any fear.

"A hole in her chest? What do you mean? How can Mommy have a hole in her chest? Did it happen when the babies came?"

Eve snorted. She took the gauze in her hand and wiped the moisture falling from her nose. Witnessing her cry, I felt close to Eve, less afraid of her.

"Anna, she has cancer. They tried to cut it out of her, but they couldn't. Daddy said it is everywhere."

I didn't know what cancer was, but a part of me didn't want to ask. I could feel my insides twisting in discomfort at yet another revelation I couldn't understand the way Eve could.

"Eve," Mommy called faintly from upstairs. We both jumped, worried our talking and crying woke her. Eve sat up straight, as if at attention. I waited for her to walk up the stairs on her own, shutting me out like she usually did. Instead, she stood up and gave her nose another wipe with a piece of fabric.

"You know now. Come with me." We walked carefully up the stairs and heard Daddy snoring in the room the twins shared with Howard. Sometime later in the night, Daddy would head downstairs to sleep on the sofa.

Eve pushed the door open, and I stood in the frame of the narrow door. The room was dark except for a small lamp on the side of the bed. There was a glass of water sitting next to the Bible on the nightstand. The room was warm, but Mommy lay covered in blankets. Eve walked over, lifted the shade, and raised the window a crack. Cold air rushed in and broke up the heaviness of the room. Noises from the outside crept in.

Mommy's head moved from Eve to me, and she smiled. Her hand patted the bed next to her.

"Such a big girl now, aren't you? This is hard on all of you, isn't it?" Her voice sounded different. Her voice was soft, like a bird's chirp, but now speaking seemed to be an effort.

I wondered what she thought was hard. Taking care of my brothers? Living in Eve's shadow? Seeing her like this? There were so many things I wanted to ask, but all I could do was nod.

We lay down on either side of her, letting our heads take a small portion of the pillow, "There, that feels lovely," she said, and within moments her breathing turned heavy as she fell asleep.

I listened to her chest rise and fall. As I lay close to her, I feared hurting her. My mind created a horrific image of what her chest looked like underneath the covers. I kept my eyes open until I could think of something else. Eve whispered good night over the slow rhythm of Mommy's breathing.

The next morning, I awoke to the sound of Daddy rising. His heavy footsteps headed to the bathroom, followed by sounds of a flushing toilet and tooth brushing. Then the door creaked open as his head peeked into the room. I kept my eyes closed, not wanting him to disrupt this moment with Mommy. I longed to feel her skin against mine.

I heard Daddy sigh as he went downstairs to breakfast. Opening my eyes, I noticed the wilted flowers on Mommy's dresser. They reminded me of her lying in bed. Frail, ready to break. I nestled close to her warm body, still trying to grasp everything Eve had told me the night before. What was cancer? Could I see it on Mommy? Was Mommy going to fall asleep one day and never wake up again? My questions swirled in the stale air and escaped through the crack of the window onto the dark streets of morning.

I could hear the twins moving in their cribs. Then the bed moved as Eve jumped up and motioned for me to follow her. I kissed Mommy's cheek and quickly followed my big sister. Looking back, I saw Mommy resting in her bed next to the two indentations where Eve and I spent the night with her.

The memory of ruffled sheets would stay with me for the remainder of my life. For the rest of my mornings, I would straighten and stiffen my sheets to erase any lines. Not only because the housemothers would flip quarters on the beds to ensure they were made tight enough, but because wrinkled sheets reminded me of seeing Mommy there, alone.

After Eve's revelation, I began to see the changes. Mommy moved a little less each day. Eventually, Daddy carried her down the stairs and positioned her on the sofa where she would sit for days covered in blankets and buried in sweaters to keep her body warm. We children would wait until she felt comfortable, and then carefully nestle close to her. Even after Eve told me Mommy was dying, I still didn't grasp what would happen, not just to Mommy, but to all of us.

CHAPTER FIVE

GINGER

Jennifer, 1986

Coming home after school, I entered a house where the air was quiet except for the sound of classical radio playing and the pitter-patter of my dog Ginger's paws prancing as she greeted me at the top of the stairs. As the only child living in the house, Ginger was my companion and furry sibling. She followed me during the day and slept on my bed at night.

Dropping my school bag, I fell to the ground, and she would too, offering me her belly to rub. After our greeting, we made our way to the kitchen where I would open every cabinet and the fridge to find something to fill the hole in my belly. Ginger's nails clicked on the linoleum as she anticipated my moves, hoping I would feed her a morsel of something. I always did.

Ginger was a yellow Lab with a face like a seal. My parents adopted her from the pound when they lived in Pennsylvania. They often told the story of the day they rescued her. Walking up the concrete aisle, observing the dogs in their kennels, my father liked the way Ginger sat motionless in the corner. Her head down, only her sad brown eyes lifted in his direction.

Summoning my mother, he pointed his finger to the sullen dog in the corner. "That's the one," he said, pleased to have found such a calm dog among the others' frantic yapping and yelping. They filled out the paperwork and made it official. Twenty minutes later, the same dog came out choking herself against her leash, panting and hysterical, her tongue hanging out of her mouth like a piece of raw bacon.

"No way in hell that's the same dog," my father said, refusing the end of the leash handed to him.

"Rich, it's the same dog. She's just nervous," my mother replied. It took her several minutes to convince him to let the agitated animal in the car. Soon, Ginger spent her nights curled up on my father's lap, even though she weighed seventy pounds. She slept with him often, my father's arms wrapped around her in an intimate snuggle.

I always enjoyed hearing the story told, not only because it reminded me of the dichotomy of my parents, but it also showed my father could accept beings in their imperfect form. As a young girl eager to be the light in my father's eye and often feeling like a failure in that regard, Ginger was a source of hope that his compassion would reveal itself at times. I too longed to snuggle with him on his bed.

My mother cooked Ginger a warm breakfast every morning that began with boiling a kettle of water that whistled with steam before being removed from the stove. She mixed dry and wet food with the hot water and put it in a bowl on Ginger's place mat on the floor. After inhaling her meal within a matter of seconds, I would open the sliding glass door—the one my father smoked cigarettes out of—so Ginger could take her morning cruise around our neighborhood and leave piles of poop in our neighbors' yards.

The routines of my home revolved around Ginger and the sound of my mom going about her day. If she finished her housework early, I would find her playing the piano. On some days, as I walked up our dead-end street, I could hear the sound of my mother's playing soaring in the air for all of the neighbors to hear. On rare occasions, I would catch her still cleaning the house, clearly behind her self-imposed schedule. Most days, the windows and doors would be open even if it was cold outside. In freezing weather, she would be dressed in a winter jacket and gloves, putting the final touches on her house's daily cleaning. Hearing me come up the stairs, she would stop the vacuum with a jolt and turn to me. "How was your day? Grab a snack in the kitchen." Before I could respond, the vacuum would be roaring again.

Sometimes I would find her in the bathroom she and I shared with curlers in her hair and the small, brown Vidal Sassoon blow dryer running on high. Startled by my presence, she would let out a yelp while continuing to move her hand over her curlers.

"Jesus, you scared me. I'll be done soon," she said with a quick smile while shooing me away.

After completing her hair and makeup, she would greet me in the kitchen where I sat at my familiar spot at the table, eating a processed snack typically orange in color. Doritos with melted Tillamook cheddar cheese was a favorite.

"Did you have a good day?"

"Yeah," I would say.

"Have something to eat, and let's make sure you practice piano before your father comes home."

After slowly eating my snack, I would gather my sheet music from the bench covered in white pleather, sit down at the piano, and play. As I touched the notes, inevitably my mother would shuffle from wherever she flittered in the house to stand at my side and give direction.

"No, not like that," she would interrupt and place her red painted nails on the piano—several octaves above—to show me how the notes should play. At the sight of her fingers moving on the keys, my spine stiffened. I let out a sigh, hinting for her to retreat, but she continued. Eventually, she disappeared to another part of the house.

Something was perplexing about my mother and her piano. Her relationship with the inanimate object seemed secretive and mysterious, causing a sensation within me where I would walk away from it entirely.

Why did my mother seem possessive around the piano as if it were something she controlled? And why did I feel I had to go through her to play it?

My mother's beloved possession, her grand piano, was a gift from my father on her fortieth birthday. The black, shiny, six-foot Yamaha sat perched in the corner of our living room like a sculpture. It replaced the used upright piano hidden in our basement.

Before it arrived, the store gave her a true-to-size cutout of the piano's shape to move about the room before deciding where it should go. She spent days shuffling furniture around and repositioning the cutout at various angles before finally settling on a corner in our living room where it appeared like a beacon.

The piano's arrival was treated like the announcement of a newborn. She took pictures and printed multiple copies. She wrote cards and inserted photos to send to friends who lived thousands of miles away. Recipients included her sister in Lake Tahoe and her brother John in Reno. Her other brothers, Howard and Jim, lived nearby and were invited to see it in person.

Something about her gift symbolized my mother arriving somewhere or achieving something. She invited her few friends over to see it. On several occasions, I observed her walking into the living room and pausing to look at it, only to smile and turn around without touching it. There existed an eeriness in her relationship with it, a mysterious connection I found puzzling.

At the piano my mother was the most expressive. Around others, she could be quiet and submissive, though looser with a glass of wine or two. At gatherings, long after dinner and guests had settled into their buzzes, my mother would be asked to play the piano that waited for her in the corner.

"Oh, dear, not now. I've had too much to drink," she would say. After a game of cat and mouse that I sensed she enjoyed, my mother would relent. Then, as her hands moved furiously across the keys the room fell silent until she finished.

"How beautiful," guests shouted after the applause. "Where did you ever learn to play so well?"

"The Home I grew up in," she would say with a hint of coldness in her voice.

When my mother referred to her childhood, she looked into the distance at something only she could see. There were vignettes from her childhood that lived in our world. I would overhear her talk about losing her parents, living with the siblings she loved, and alluring moments in a place called "the Home." As a young girl, I didn't know what questions to ask, so I just listened and observed changes in her demeanor as she spoke of a place that reminded me of the story *Annie*.

"What an incredible story you have. How tragic and sad. You should write a book," inevitably someone would say.

"Maybe one day I will," she replied.

Whenever these exchanges happened, and they were frequent, I would watch as my mother gave a forced smile and lingered in silence. She said nothing more and, after a few awkward breaths, would get up and walk into another room to complete a task she manufactured for herself.

In my final year of middle school, tumors began taking over Ginger's body. Lumps the size of tennis balls were protruding from her yellow and white fur. The hair on her nose grew gray.

"Jenny, Ginger is getting sick," my mother mentioned to me. "It'll be time to put her down soon."

"Look at her; she's fine and happy. She isn't going anywhere," I said.

"She needs to go before she suffers."

I didn't see the hardship; I only saw the dog I loved growing older and every part of my being wanted her to stay. Who would I have other than my neighborhood friends once she was gone?

As the months passed, I was confused by my mother's conviction about letting Ginger go. She was heartbroken, it was clear, but she was marching Ginger toward death at what felt like an accelerated pace. I wanted my father's support to make my mother stop, but he was oddly absent. Why isn't he involved, I asked myself repeatedly. He loved Ginger. He cuddled her on the floor, played tug-of-war sock with her at night, and could be found nestled with her while he slept, an intimacy I rarely—if ever—witnessed between my parents.

The morning my mother chose to let her go, I dressed in my favorite outfit—a blue V-neck sweater with a white turtleneck, pale jeans, and gold hoop earrings. I hugged and kissed Ginger, burying my face in her fur, as my mother warmed her meal. I watched as she put two tranquilizers on the counter and squashed them with a fork. She mixed the white powder into Ginger's meal, "to calm her down," before the vet would come to our house an hour later.

Despite my resistance, I realized I couldn't stop my friend from leaving our world. My mother had convinced herself, and was intent on persuading me, that her leaving was the only option. Slowly the fight to change her mind turned into a heavy ache in my heart.

I sat at the kitchen table crying as Ginger went to her bowl to eat her last meal. When she finished, I got up to let her out the sliding glass door like I always did.

Ten minutes later, seated in my chair and barely eating my breakfast, I noticed a neighbor boy walking by our house and turning back to look at something in front of our four-foot rock wall. He glanced at something I couldn't see. He kept glancing down and then looking back up at our house before eventually making his way to the bus stop.

"Jen, it's time for you to go before you miss the bus."

I walked down our stairs, my mind in a sad cloud. I didn't say anything to my mother as I left.

Carefully walking down our steep and slick driveway, I came to the bottom and turned to find Ginger lying on our street, near our wall, panting and confused.

"Ginger, *no*! Oh, *no*!" I cried as I dropped my backpack and raced to her. She laid on the pavement, unable to move, dizzy from the medicine my mother had snuck into her morning meal. Her deep brown eyes looked up at me while her pink tongue hung from the side of her mouth. I saw the familiar smile on her face. Scooping her up, I held under her belly and slowly walked up our steep driveway to the garage.

"It's okay, Ginger, you can do it." She was panting heavily in my arms, barely able to move her legs.

My mother came downstairs and stood at the garage door. "Bring her to the rec room," she said, her body twitching as she spoke.

I couldn't look in my mother's direction as disappointment and pain rose in my throat. A ping of anger raced through my veins but was drenched by the ache wrapping my heart as I held my dog up and inched her along.

I carried her through our dark, narrow hallway. I noticed a white sheet spread out on the floor, like a makeshift hospital. The starkness of the sheet and what it meant grabbed my heart and squeezed it until I lost my breath.

I helped Ginger lie down. I got on the floor with her and rested my whole body against hers like I had done a thousand times before when we shared my twin bed, or when I came home from school.

My mother stood over me, fluttering in different directions but saying nothing. She left the room, and I heard her footsteps go upstairs.

"Ginger, I love you so much. I don't want you to go," I held her in my arms as her panting slowed. I imagined the room was spinning for her, so I pet her body gently. My hand ran over several of the tumors covering her belly. I found her paw which smelled of popcorn and held it gently. Her chocolate nails that clicked on our linoleum floor every morning in the kitchen were silent. We were one in the moment, the two of us, as we had always been.

As I heard my mother's feet move in a furious pattern on the floor above, my mind swirled like Ginger's.

No, not now. This is terrible. Look at my sweet dog lying here in a panic. My friend, my companion, Ginger. She deserves better. Cancel it, Mom. Where is Dad? It wouldn't be like this if he were here.

Nothing came out but tears and gasps for breath. I could feel her heart racing, just like mine.

"It's okay, baby girl, I'm here."

Please let these words help her.

I promised I wouldn't leave her. Lying in our mutual state of panic, I decided I wouldn't let my mother near her. We would lie together on the cold floor, and she would take a nap while the drugs moved through her body. Minutes later, my mother appeared in the doorway with her large purse over her shoulder and car keys in her hand.

"Jenny, let me take you to school. You don't want to be here for this," my mother said. I hyperventilated into Ginger's fur. I clenched her tighter and she panted.

"You need to go to school."

I didn't move or say a word.

"The vet is on his way," she said.

I could tell my mother's mission was too far gone. She was determined to let Ginger go, and I could not persuade her otherwise. I wanted to stay with Ginger forever, but something pulled me away.

I kissed Ginger one final time, letting my lips kiss her fur, and my nose take in her scent. With weak legs I stood, looking back, and I saw her eyes move in my direction. She could no longer lift her head, but her gentle gaze fixed on mine one last time. She was slowly going somewhere else, and I couldn't save her.

I cried the entire way to school. A part of me wanted to ask my mother why her death was happening in such a way. Nothing about it seemed right. Ginger lying in the street on her final walk. The white sheet on the floor in my basement, and the strange way my mother behaved. But something told me to give up, to not resist, like Ginger.

My sweet friend, my sibling, my bed warmer, my companion was leaving my world, and she sat alone on our brown shag carpet on a makeshift hospital bed alone in my basement before she did. The pain lived in my heart, stomach, and head. A swirling mix of emotions, so visceral, I nearly choked on the tears flooding out of me.

Ten minutes later, my mother pulled in the school parking lot, and I exited in a hurry. I arrived at class late. The eyes of other students turned toward me, and I broke down in tears. Friends asked me what was wrong, and I told them my dog died. I didn't want to share with them the horrific process happening in my house.

Getting off the bus after school, I made the slow walk up our dead-end street, hoping to see Ginger at the top of the stairs waiting to greet me. As I opened the door, I paused, but she never came. I heard the sound of my mother playing *Moonlight Sonata* as I had many times before. Only this time, she didn't stop when she heard me climb the stairs and look in her direction. She finished the piece before coming to hug me. When she did, I felt her thin frame holding me tightly while tears slipped from her eyes.

"I buried her in the yard and planted a tree; would you like to see it?"

I followed my mom down our hallway, through their bedroom sliding door, and up our small dirt hill that once held my tree house. At the edge of our property wet earth was surrounded by a circle of rocks; a small thirsty tree stood in the middle. We stood in silence and my skin tightened in frustration. After a few moments I retreated inside and refused to visit that part of our yard for years.

CHAPTER SIX

FIVE TINY ROSES

Anna, 1949

Once Mommy returned with the babies, Daddy started staying home from work. At night after the dinner dishes were cleared and washed, we could overhear him having long conversations with Mommy's family downstairs. In bed, my eyes open and fixed on the dark ceiling, I heard their voices rising. I thought it was strange how they talked about Mommy as if she wasn't there anymore when she slept in the room next to me.

One evening after dinner, they sat us kids down and told us to pack our suitcases. They explained that Aunt Mildred, Daddy's sister, and Grandmom Eva, Mommy's mom, were going to take us to their homes for a little while.

"Aren't we all going to be together?" Eve asked. Daddy's head stared at his feet as it shook, "No." Howard and I would go to Aunt Mildred's, and Eve would go to Grandmom's with the twins, which made her shoulders straighten and rise at attention.

Howard and I said our goodbyes and piled into Aunt Mildred's car. Pulling up to her house, it resembled ours, but a different color. As the door swung open, we were greeted by Uncle John sitting in an old worn chair. He had lost his right arm below the elbow in a factory accident. The sight of his stump caused me to shudder and stare at the same time. We heard he no longer worked and collected government checks because of his injury. He spent most of his days sitting in a recliner in the living room, smoking cigarettes with his left hand and listening to the radio. He mumbled to himself and occasionally shouted when he didn't like what he heard coming from the speaker. Given Aunt Mildred's sweetness, it was a wonder she married him.

"John, the children are here," Aunt Mildred announced, a hand resting on each of our shoulders.

"Sounds like your mother is sick and that father of yours can't keep all of you together." He put a cigarette in his mouth, and a puff of smoke surrounded his face.

"There are two rules here: stay quiet and keep out of my way."

At the sound of his growl, I reached and squeezed Howard's hand. Aunt Mildred scooted us toward the kitchen. "Let's get something warm in your bellies."

Our initial stay with Aunt and Uncle began our time seeking comfort with people and in places we found uncomfortable, even terrifying. We were relieved when Uncle John started to spend most of his days at the local bar down the street. He returned swerving through the front door, sat down for dinner, slurped up his entire meal, and finally retreated to his room and fell asleep. I would sigh with relief when he marched upstairs. Even Aunt Mildred's face softened when she heard the sound of him snoring.

I cherished the hot chocolate with whipped cream Aunt Mildred made for us at night. The taste of orange juice and a warm breakfast seemed to calm the uneasiness in my belly. After eating, I loved visiting the chickens she kept in a small cage in the backyard. They chirped and clucked as I opened the small door and filled their bowls.

The little things helped me forget I was away from my parents. Away from Eve and the twins. Away from my bed.

At night, Aunt Mildred tucked me into bed on the sofa. The large, scratchy wool blankets she laid over me reminded me of Daddy covering me up in the mornings before he went to work. With Aunt Mildred's goodnight kiss, I smelled the womanly scent of her perfume, and I felt my heart flutter.

Several days later, Aunt Mildred announced, "We're going to visit your home today." I put on one of my two outfits and helped Howard. On a cold winter day, the kind with clear blue skies, naked trees, and air that created smoke when you breathed, I dressed us in layers, putting a hat on Howard that he quickly pulled off to play with.

On the drive, Aunt Mildred remained quiet except for the occasional blow of her nose into a handkerchief. As our car pulled up to our house, I grabbed the handle to open the door while she was still parking.

"Slow down," she said, as we skipped up the stairs.

Barging through the front door, we found Daddy sitting stoically in his chair. He opened his arms and hugged us tightly. I missed his smell and let my face bury into his shoulder, sitting there for what felt like an eternity.

The front door opened, and there in the doorway stood Eve. She held baby Jim, and Grandmom Eva stood behind her holding John. Grandmom's face was the color of a gray sky. I jumped up and hugged Eve, the little boy between us.

Daddy called for all of us to sit with him. We piled on him like puppies, and he remained silent for several minutes. He placed his hands over his eyes and through tears, I heard him say, "Mommy is gone."

"Whur'd she go?" Howard asked his hat twisting in his hands.

"To heaven," Daddy said. Then an unrecognizable noise escaped him causing my skin to cover in goosebumps.

Eve buried her face in Daddy's shoulder while I stared at the empty sofa across the room, hoping if I looked hard enough, Mommy would appear before us.

We were home for a short time before we were asked to go. As we left the house, Daddy sat in his chair with his face buried in his hands. Once we got to the car, Aunt Mildred sat in the driver's seat, keys in her hand, and cried. Howard and I stared at her as she repeated, "It will all work out. Really, it will be okay. I promise, kids."

Two days later Aunt Mildred asked us to get dressed again.

"Anna, please wear this pretty dress. Then help your brother in his suspenders," she said quietly, almost in a whisper. "I'll help you." We dressed in silence then, walked down her narrow stairs to her car where Uncle John waited, his hand out the window and a cigarette smoking between his fingers.

Our house was full of family and strangers. Despite being cold outside, a large fan blew air in the stuffy room. A dark brown box lined with pink satin sat in the corner near the window. Getting closer, I noticed Mommy in it, completely still.

"Why is Mommy in the box?" I asked out loud to the crowd of adults towering over me.

There was no answer. Someone gave me a gentle pat on the back as I heard them sob quietly.

Howard grabbed a ball, and we began playing in the house. An old woman I didn't recognize opened the door, guided us to the fresh air, and told us to go outside. Neighborhood children joined us on the street, and we played. We yelled. We forgot about what waited for us indoors until Aunt Mildred stood at the top of the stairs and called us inside, the sound of her voice stopping our feet abruptly.

"It's time to say goodbye to your mommy now," she declared. A white handkerchief hid half her face, and she blew her nose into it hard making a honking noise. The sound made me want to laugh, but the look on the faces of the people in the room stopped me. Aunt Mildred placed her hand on my shoulder and nudged me closer to the casket.

I peered closer, Mommy's face just inches from me. Her eyes were closed, and she looked peaceful. I let my hand touch the pink satin surrounding her. The color of the fabric reminded me of my slippers—the ones I would occasionally look at to make myself happy. She was wearing a black dress. Tucked in her hands were five tiny red roses.

I wanted to lie next to her like I did on her bed those many weeks ago.

I could feel Daddy's presence next to me. His voice spoke softly in my ear, "Those roses are one for each of you, Anna. She is taking each of you with her."

"Where is she going? Is Mommy ever coming back, Daddy?"

I could feel the tears filling my eyes until they spilled over. I turned to Daddy and hugged him for a long time, my emotions taking over my body. The sound coming from me reminded me of the noises Daddy made a few days earlier when he told us she left for heaven.

I knew I didn't want to see Mommy in her box anymore. I wiped my face on Daddy's jacket and refused to look in the direction of the large wooden mass. Someone came to say something to Daddy, and I let go of him and raced outside to where the other children were playing. Several minutes later, men hoisted the box with Mommy in it on their shoulders and out our front door. Everyone froze and watched as they rolled it into the back of a long black car. They drove away as the adults stood on the street in silence, tissues in their hands. Daddy got in another car, and they followed the severe-looking car with Mommy in it. We stood motionless on the street as they disappeared off into the distance.

I have two distinct memories from that day. It wasn't just seeing Mommy there, in her final form, holding a rose for each of us. I would always be tormented by the idea, right after my last look at Mommy, I went back to playing ball with my brother Howard as if nothing had changed.

When Mommy left us, the world shifted to a place I would eventually call "the presence of others." Those people—family, friends, and strangers— became our caretakers. A slow progression that eventually led me to a twin bed in a crowded room at an orphanage.

Neighbors and family members came over with arms full of food, and large casserole dishes were placed in the oven, filling the house with the smell of normalcy. After feeding us, the guests would pack up their belongings, hug Daddy, and whisper a few words to him before the door closed softly behind them. Each day, our rooms filled with the chatter of voices, and the noisy needs of the twins mixed in the air. They were still so little, just babies. Babies who lost their mommy before they could ever know who she was or what she looked like. They were starting to walk and demand attention from whomever entered the room.

"How sad for these boys," I heard people say. I wondered why it was especially sad for them. Wasn't it painful for all of us?

Mommy's family hung around a lot more after she passed away. They scared us with their thick accents and the way they yelled at Daddy when they were talking to him.

Mommy's two older brothers were big with crooked teeth, broad shoulders, and hands so scarred and worn from working, it looked like they were broken. Their fingers and nails were stained black, which made me stiffen whenever they came near me.

For reasons we would never understand, Mommy's family was angry with Daddy. I can remember them all sitting around the kitchen table yelling at him in broken English. Mommy's father, Grandpa Frank, raised his finger and shook it at Daddy as if waving a stick. His face red, the veins on his neck bulging. Daddy sat at the table, shoulders forward, head down. I wanted to go sit on his lap to comfort him, but something told me not to.

The tension in the house made me miss Mommy even more. She would have quieted everyone down, making her family seem less scary. Grandmom sat still without saying a word. I wanted her to speak up like Mommy would have, but she didn't. Tears filled her eyes and slowly ran down her cheeks.

I ran upstairs and found Eve sitting at the edge of our bedroom doorway, hoping to catch the words as they floated up the stairs. She shushed me as I walked into the room and flopped down on my bed. She obsessed over the adults' conversations and kept her ear aimed towards the stairway.

"They're talking about Daddy. They're talking about him going back to work," she whispered my way. "It sounds like we're staying here. And Grandmom is going to take care of us."

Soon, we were living our days with Grandmom by our side while Daddy went off to work. Howard and I walked with her to drop Eve off at school every day. I wanted to follow my sister the way a little duckling follows its mother. I imagined her grabbing my hand and pulling me through the large metal doors of the school, so I could get a taste of her big girl life.

We continued this routine for a few months. Eventually, the trees changed. Little blossoms would soon bloom and give us shade just in time before the sweltering, humid summer heat arrived. As the temperature outside continued to rise, Grandmom wilted under the demands of five young children. Each morning, she looked more tired than the last even though Eve and I were helping with cooking, cleaning, and the twins. At the end of every day, she waited on the edge of the sofa with her purse next to her. As soon as Daddy's hand touched the door, she would rise from her seat and make her way to him. A look of guilt blanketed his face.

Nightly, we brought a book for Daddy to read. I loved feeling his voice move through his body and vibrate against mine, like a cat purring.

It didn't take Eve long to offer her opinion about the situation, as she often did.

"I don't think Grandmom wants to be here anymore, Daddy. She's frustrated with us and yells a lot."

"It's been hard on all of us," Daddy said. He paused from reading. "We need to stay together...somehow."

"Daddy, you aren't sick, are you?" I asked, his words stoking fear in me.

"No, no, sweet girl. I need to work even though I would prefer to be home with you. This means someone needs to help. Maybe not Grandmom."

"Who else can take care of us?" Eve's voice quivered.

"I don't know, girls, because it costs money, and we have very little." His face held a mixture of pain and confusion. Then he paused and looked out into the distance as if he saw something we couldn't see. "I've been going to church to pray, like Mommy did. I've been praying to God to find us a solution to our problem."

"Is God mad at us, Daddy? Is that why he took Mommy?" I asked.

"Snooky, he's not mad at us. He will help us, I promise." This was the first time we heard Daddy talk about God the way Mommy spoke of him.

Mommy had gone to church on her own every Sunday until she became sick, church being the only time she left the house without us.

Despite his assurances, I could feel Daddy's fear. I sensed perhaps the worst part was not Mommy dying, but that we might lose Daddy too.

CHAPTER SEVEN

SOMETHING THAT WAS MINE

Jennifer, 1986

For a long time, I refused to go into our backyard, where my beloved yellow-haired companion slept. Losing Ginger was met with a lingering silence all too familiar in my house. I wanted someone, anyone, to stop what they were doing and sit down and console the ache living in my heart, but we continued to march forward.

Descending our stairs to the basement, where we entered the garage, we walked by photo collages littering our dark basement walls. There were several pictures of Ginger and me together. One of them taken at the photo studio in Kmart. My dog and I posed together like siblings, my arm wrapped around her. My pale hand is grabbing the ripple of skin below her collar. Ginger is sitting tall, smiling at the camera. We look happy to be together.

Other pictures surrounded the image of Ginger and me. The parties. The trips. Dad's family. My mother with my aunt and uncles. Pictures of me as a baby. Photos of my sisters. Sometimes, we would stop and talk about the images, laughing or commenting on the moment captured. Something elusive lived in the images as if they were capturing moments in time so infrequent; if the photos didn't live on the walls, we might forget my sisters, aunt, uncle, and family living thousands of miles away.

High in a dark corner lived a black-and-white photo of a woman with three children on her lap. None appear to be looking at the camera, and the young children seem too restless to sit still. The woman has a broad smile, and her eyes gaze lovingly at the children. They are sitting on the front steps of a narrow house, a white-framed front door behind them.

"Who's that, Mommy?"

"That's my mother. It's the only picture I have of us together. And it's your Aunt Eve and Uncle Howard before Mommy got sick."

She would pause and seemed lost in the memory.

"Never forget how lucky you are to have a mother, Jenny," she said and we left for whatever errand was scheduled for the day, the forward motion of our lives barely stopping.

As I stumbled into my teenage years, I sensed an ache growing within me. A desire for something that was mine. A longing for a sense of self and accomplishment. I had a gang of friends who seemed to live in different existences than me. They had siblings, dinner with their parents, and sports. While my friendships enriched me, I wanted more.

The stillness of my home and the consistency of my routine became perpetual. Walking through the door daily, I would find my mother cleaning the house like she always did or teaching a piano lesson to a local kid. Often, I was greeted by the sound of the wrong note being struck repeatedly. Making my way up our stairs, I would roll my eyes and offer a faint and irritated "hello" to the student and my mother as I escaped to my parent's bedroom to watch television.

My first true battle with my mother—and my pursuit of independence—was fought over the piano. After several years of lessons under my mother's guidance, I started a campaign to make her quit as my teacher.

"Well, if you aren't going to listen to me, you can take from anyone else," she yelled in frustration and stomped away—raising her hands in surrender.

Something about my mother's relationship with the piano created a wedge between the instrument and me. The piano being hers as if it were not only a possession but an obsession.

Music was inside me; learning came naturally and made sense. Music served as a companion in the solitary moments in my room. Songs as a form of comfort began with a record player, and a Muppets album eventually led to cassette tapes of Duran Duran, Michael Jackson, Wham!, and

Madonna's *Like a Virgin*. If my mother heard Madonna's voice, she would cringe and take the cassette from the player.

"Virgin? This is horrible. You could only imagine what the place I grew up in would have done if they heard this music," she would say.

It didn't matter if she didn't like Madonna or Michael Jackson; I wanted music I felt, which spoke to me.

I took up the violin but found the position of my chin shoved against my shoulder and pushing on wood confining, the whine of the strings uninspiring. My father complained it sounded like "a cat dying" whenever I practiced.

In sixth grade, when I entered junior high, I chose the clarinet. It was then I felt something waken inside me. A sense of freedom and wonder at using my ability to read music and apply it to an instrument my mother knew nothing about. She could no longer come from wherever she lingered in the house and say, "No, not like that. Like this."

By seventh grade, I found myself battling a boy for first chair. The thrill of performing swirled in my veins for the first time. This new feeling—the taste of confidence—was something I chose to keep secret. I was concerned if I told anyone about my newfound determination, it would certainly be the end of it. Until this time, whenever thrown in the mix of competition, whether dodgeball, running track, uneven bars, or four-square, I wilted and retreated before I really tried.

I could sense a powerful feeling rising in me, an unfamiliar surge of determination masking a sort of shyness I often felt when it came to being on stage. During band, seated in the front row next to my rival and near the band teacher, I competed—and at times, I was victorious. The crowded band room shrunk to being just the three of us, a type of focus I rarely enjoyed until then.

After school one day, I found a formal letter addressed to me sitting on the kitchen counter. The return address said "The Tacoma Youth Symphony." Ripping it open, I scanned the page and realized this type of invitation was unlike anything I'd received before.

Shouting from the kitchen, I said "Mom, I've been asked to try out for the Youth Symphony." Coming from another part of the house, my mother took the letter from my hands and held it up as she read. She didn't appear happy; her face appeared confused by the invitation.

"You have to try out?" she asked, unable to camouflage her true feelings.

"I'll talk to your father about this tonight," she said, handing the letter back to me and hurrying off to her next task.

She left it on the counter for me to take back. In celebration, I tacked the letter to my bedroom wall above the light switch. It appeared next to my posters and collages of glossy pages ripped from fashion magazines.

Several nights later, in my room, while practicing the clarinet, my mother knocked and then opened my door, her feet avoiding my bright pink carpet. I stopped playing, the instrument resting in my hands like a rifle.

"I spoke with your father, and I called the Youth Symphony. If you make it through tryouts, it's a big commitment, and I would have to drive you to Tacoma at night in the dark. We aren't sure this is something you should take on. You know, lots of kids probably got this letter."

The paper with its exciting invitation glowed on the wall next to her; the black logo on the official letterhead nearly jumped off the page at me. I looked from my mother to the letter, unsure of what to say.

For minutes, I stood in silence as I stared at the music sheets crowding the music stand in front of me. Lost in the moment, I remembered years before during the 1984 Olympics when a local girl, Rosalyn Sumner, won a bronze medal in ice skating. As a ten-year-old I became obsessed with Rosalyn's triumph after watching it on TV.

Excited about the prospects of being an Olympic champion, I'd taken my mother's ice skates from our storage room in the basement and attempted double axles on the carpet of our rec room. My mother often said she was never very good at ice skating because of her "thin ankles." After a few successful turns, I went upstairs and cornered my mother.

"I want to ice skate. Maybe go to the Olympics."

Startled at my request, she insisted on a family meeting in my parent's room once my father returned home from work. Hours later, my mother sat on the edge of their bed as he stood at his dresser, undoing his watch and changing into his "I'm home" clothes.

"Rich, Jenny wants to take up ice skating," she said, a hint of stress and confusion in her voice and a strange, crooked smirk. I stood uncomfortably at the entrance of their room.

"So, you want to ice skate, huh? Go to the Olympics?" my father asked.

"I just want to try it to see if I like it."

"Do you want to drink raw eggs and wake up at five in the morning?" he asked with a chuckle and looking towards my mother.

Making a face and looking down, I said, "No."

"Then you don't have what it takes to be in the Olympics. Looks like we solved that problem."

She sighed with relief as I left the room. My skating career ended before my blades touched the ice. Six months later, during the Summer Olympics, Mary Lou Retton won gold in the gymnastics all-around, and I turned my athletic fixation on her. My mother eventually agreed to gymnastic lessons only when she learned I would go with a friend. "It's so important to have friends, Jenny."

My mother stood before me, her eyes concerned as in times before when I wanted to try something new.

I looked at the black instrument in my hands and the music in front of me, wondering if I was good enough to be part of the symphony. I was the clarinet second chair, still battling the same boy for the first chair, but what did that mean? Like my mother said, there were probably a lot of kids invited. It didn't mean I was special.

"Okay. I don't have to try out for the symphony," I replied, wishing her away from my room with my words.

Her back straightened, and she smiled. "Let's just stick to gymnastics with Christina. It's good to do things with your friends, don't forget," she said.

"But, Mom, I'm not very good at gymnastics. I really should be in ballet." After some time in the sport, it was clear I belonged in ballet or dance; tumbling intimated me.

"Well, you certainly have the finish down," she smiled, referring to my ability to raise my hands in triumph after a routine. She closed my door behind her.

I knew I had pleased them, which provided some satisfaction as the discomfort of heartbreak tightened my throat. I put down the clarinet and got ready for bed while my parents retreated to their seats at the table and drank their nightcaps. I left the invitation on my wall for a few days before throwing it in the trash. Eventually, I stopped bringing my instrument home to practice, leaving the clarinet in my locker where the reed would remain dry.

Despite all the changes in my life, there remained one constant. At home, our piano sat perched in our living room, showcasing the gateway to my mother's emotional release. In a quiet sort of rebellion, I ignored its presence.

"You should take piano lessons again. You have such a nice touch," she encouraged me randomly.

Noticing the shining black wood instrument glistening in the room, I would walk over and stare at it as if we were in a standoff. Resting in the corner, next to the music, was a framed black-and-white photo of my mother seated at a piano wearing shorts. She sits with perfect posture while her teacher stands over her, holding a clipboard. The woman has black-rimmed glasses and is taking notes on my mother's performance.

Occasionally, while staring at the photo, I would guide my finger over the glass to see if I could feel my mother's presence. Observing her as she was then, only a few years older than me at the time, the only emotion I could extract from the image of her was sadness. Unbearable, inescapable sadness.

CHAPTER EIGHT

LEAVING DADDY

Anna, 1950

Mommy died several months before, and the shadow of her hemline still appeared in my imagination. Sometimes, I saw her in our kitchen, tending to a meal. I would focus my eyes in the room, wishing her to be there, but she never came.

After she passed, we started attending the Baptist church every Sunday as a family. When still with us, Mommy would attend while Daddy read the Sunday newspaper in his chair in the front room. The radio would be on, and the soft crackle of voices would mix with the rustle of the paper as he turned the page.

With her gone and having spent our days cramped in our house, at the end of the week, Daddy's baritone voice would bellow up the stairs for us girls to get dressed and tend to the boys; we wore our best dresses and outfitted the boys in their pants and suspenders.

After a lot of commotion and occasional tears, we loaded ourselves into the car and sat on the slippery leather seats that reminded me of a playground slide. As the engine roar bellowed through narrow streets, we became quiet as we took in the scenery along the way.

In church, we sat together in a row—I spent much of the time looking to my left and right surveying my family. A grand black piano stood near the pulpit, and a short, gray-haired woman played as the choir sang. I sat entranced by the melodies and harmonies escaping the magnificent black frame. How a single person could create such beauty from nothing—just a board with keys perched on three skinny legs—seemed like magic.

Listening to the sermons and gospels, I began to sense the divide in life. As much as everyone wanted to go to heaven, the threat of hell lurked around the corner, hiding in the shadows.

After the service, Pastor Harting and his wife stood near the wooden doors of the church, shaking people's hands as they left. As we approached, I would reach for Daddy's hand; certain Eve already clutched the other one. Clenching his fingers tightly, my arm would overheat while we waited our turn to escape to fresh air. Eventually, standing in front of the couple, I would focus on the round of skin escaping Mrs. Harting's tight leather shoes. They typically spoke only to Daddy while glancing at all of us waiting impatiently by his side.

Settling into our new life with one parent, Daddy hired a babysitter named Joyce. As she walked through our front door, I noticed Daddy's shoulders soften as he picked up his lunchbox and jacket then kissed us goodbye.

Joyce was in her early twenties and wore black-rimmed glasses that sat on the tip of her nose. I liked her red lipstick and the way the curls in her hair stood at attention. Greeting Daddy, she smiled and tossed her head from side to side as her voice became a whisper. After he left for work, her smile stiffened and attention moved to the twins while occasionally raising her voice to tell Eve, Howard, and me to play outside.

While I liked a woman's presence, Eve barely looked in her direction. At first, Joyce demanded Eve answer when she spoke, but she soon realized the force that was my sister. Even at age ten, Eve could overwhelm someone twice her age.

Daddy, tired after a day's work, seemed relieved to be coming home to dinner on the table. As we settled into this new rhythm, the lines on his face lessened, and he even laughed a few times.

One morning, we were startled awake by Daddy's voice rising.

"My money! My money is missing." We rushed to his room to find him tossing clothes from his dresser onto his bed just as the front door opened as I heard Joyce's heels click in the kitchen.

Eve stood next to Daddy like a soldier at attention. "You should ask the sitter. She cleans your room every day." Eve's eyes darted down the stairs in Joyce's direction as if to tell her, *Don't think you can fool me!*

Daddy left for work as if nothing had happened. When he returned home, he ordered us all upstairs as he pulled out a chair from the kitchen table and motioned for her to sit. The legs made a screeching noise against the floor, raising the hair on my arms.

Through our thin walls, I heard Daddy's voice rise. Then Joyce's voice became loud, too. A door opened and slammed. I expected Eve to run downstairs and ask Daddy what happened, but she sat frozen still.

"Eve, what happened? Why are they fighting?"

"Oh, hush," she said as if she already knew what transpired and what it would mean for us.

Daddy didn't go to work the next day or the next.

The following Sunday, he parked in front of the small white church as people filtered up the steps. Taking the key out of the ignition, he turned to all of us. I noticed the skin on his face sagged like melted wax. My lips began to tremble.

"Children, I need you to pray for our family," he said.

Eve reached over and touched my skirt as if to comfort me. I didn't wait to get to the church to pray; I bowed my head and began sending my thoughts to God.

Please let us be okay. Please help our Daddy.

We listened to Pastor Harting deliver his sermon while his hands held a Bible. His devoted wife sat directly in front of him, hanging onto his every word. As he became excited over a verse, his voice rose. His other hand went to push his thick, black-rimmed glasses up higher on his nose. Occasionally, spit launched from his mouth, making me want to laugh.

These moments helped me to forget the chill and ache in my bones. Even though it was warm outside, the air conditioner blared, keeping the room bitter cold, so we stayed awake. The discomfort of frigid bones and tired eyes would always be something I associated with God.

After the service, we walked up to Mr. and Mrs. Harting. Daddy spoke to them in a calm voice, and I could hear the pastor say he prayed for us as he put his hand on Daddy's shoulder. I noticed our father's eyes filled to the brim with water. Mrs. Harting leaned down to our level and said how beautiful Eve looked, and she liked my dress. Something about the Hartings made me feel like they knew us too well. I wanted space between us; Daddy's leg was a start.

After church, Daddy treated us to ice cream at our favorite diner. We sat in a booth engrossed by scoops of melted cream. The twins were fastened in high chairs at the end of the table with chocolate streaming down their faces. Daddy's voice emerged from the clatter and noise of the people around us.

"Kids, I love all of you very much. I want you to know our family is the most important thing in my life." He cleared his throat. "There's going to be a change for a little while. The church is going to help us."

"The Hartings?" Eve asked.

"Yes, Eve, they are part of it. They run a home for children whose parents are having hard times. It's a beautiful place. Grandmom and the rest of our family can't help the way we need them. We can't have other bad things happening."

"Like the lady stealing your money?" Eve asked.

The table fell silent as the twins wiggled in their seats as the sugar hit. Daddy nodded.

"Let's finish our ice cream, kids. Any change we make will be a temporary solution, I promise you."

"When?" Eve asked.

"After church the following Sunday, but it's temporary. It's important to keep all of you together. The most important thing is to have you together."

"Daddy, isn't it important we have you?" Eve asked.

His head bowed, and he left his spoon in his dish. I watched as the white scoop turned to liquid and then looked at Daddy; it appeared to me both were melting.

Life continued, except on Sunday, by the front door were little suitcases filled with our clothes—five of them together—before Daddy loaded them into his car's expansive trunk. As the hood slammed, I jumped. Daddy's large frame sank into the driver's seat, causing the automobile to squeak as he put his hands on the wheel.

"Ready for church and a new adventure?"

Eve and I stared straight ahead, unable to take our eyes off the road before us.

Once the service ended, Daddy drove through neighborhoods lined with tiny houses that eventually became tall buildings. We drove through the city of Philadelphia where metal structures reached for the sky. Men dressed in Sunday suits and women in fancy dresses hurried along the streets. Daddy drove slowly, stopping early at each light before it turned red.

The skyscrapers slipped away, and trees replaced the buildings. Row houses like ours appeared. I saw a mother sitting on her porch swing, holding her baby, and I remembered Mommy. My stomach churned at the thought she was no longer with us. I closed my eyes to see her in the darkness for a moment before I let light in again.

Beside us was a stone fence snaking along the road. Brick buildings appeared through the blur of trees. Daddy slowed the car, and we stopped at a large metal gate between two stone posts. Sweat was forming on my forehead, and I turned to look at Eve to see if hers looked the same. Her eyes met mine briefly, and she placed her hand on top of mine and gave it a gentle squeeze.

There was a plaque on the post to our right, but I couldn't read what it said. I leaned over to Eve, "What does the sign say?"

She let her eyes focus on it momentarily and turned the color of a strawberry. "It says 'Baptist Orphanage.'"

"What does that mean?" I whispered.

"Shush," she said, keeping her eyes fixed ahead of her.

Daddy rolled down his window, and a man in dark pants and a white shirt with a clipboard approached. "Mr. Rangnow, we're expecting you. Pastor and Mrs. Harting are at the house up the drive to your right. It's the small brick house with yellow trim. If you get to the building with the statue of a bear by the door, that's the infirmary, and you've gone too far."

Infirmary, what a scary word.

Covering the area were brick buildings resembling miniature schools surrounded by tall, full trees and a large swimming pool.

"Pool!" Howard yelled from the back seat.

Ahead, standing on the sidewalk looking in our direction, were Mr. and Mrs. Harting, their faces a mix of authority and enthusiasm. The car jolted to a stop, and Daddy's right hand jerked the handle to park. He lumbered out of the car and went over to the Hartings; their hands shaking his. He motioned for us to follow him, and we slowly stopped in the frame of the large car door. Daddy's hand motioned for us to come closer.

I followed Eve as she marched toward them, her back stiff and tall. Moving her shoulders toward me, she created a space for me next her. I walked closer as my legs shook, and my eyes squinted in the sun. Mrs. Harting placed her hands our on shoulders while Daddy gathered the boys from the backseat.

"Let me show you to your rooms, girls." I smelled coffee and mints on her breath. She bent over and grabbed the suitcases Daddy placed on the sidewalk.

Meandering down a narrow concrete path, we came to a house reminding me of a giant dollhouse. The home had a wraparound porch, and ivy was growing up the walls. The wooden stairs creaked as we approached the large door, which swung open to reveal a woman standing there.

"You must be Eve and Anna. I'm Phyllis, the housemother."

Peering in the house, I glimpsed a young girl, maybe six years old, sitting in the living room. She wore glasses and held a book in her hand. Her head turned and glanced toward me and then quickly turned away.

Phyllis smiled warmly in my direction and took my suitcase in her hand. "I'll put this on your bed."

My heart raced so fast I thought I might pass out. I glanced over at Eve. Her eyes darted from place to place as she turned and gave me a weak smile.

As if anticipating our nervousness, Mrs. Harting started talking as we walked. "That, girls, over there, is the pool. It is open during the weekends. Once schoolwork and chores are done, you can use the jungle gym and swing set. Right next to it, that building with yellow trim is the gymnasium. Eve, your home is over there, Rohrman Cottage."

Following Mrs. Harting's pointed finger, I saw a three-story brick building with wood-paned windows and a small white porch surrounding the front door. I thought how beautiful the building was and a pang of jealousy grabbed my stomach.

"Mrs. Harting, are our beds apart?" I asked.

"Anna, Rohrman Cottage is for girls ten and older," she said swiftly as her heels clicked on the sidewalk. Her voice lacked softness, which caused me to twist my hands together.

Rohrman Cottage reminded me of a giant estate, the type of home we could only dream of, and as the door opened, I marveled at its grandeur.

A chandelier hung above the staircase and entryway. The halls were quiet except for the noise from a nearby kitchen where the smell of food escaped and made my belly growl.

Leading us down a hallway, Mrs. Harting stopped at a tall wooden door with a beautiful bronze knob. We entered a room with peach-colored wallpaper.

"Why are there so many beds?" Eve asked.

"We share rooms, Eve. Over here, this is your bed, next to the window." In the corner I noticed a small twin bed with dark brown wood. I watched as Mrs. Harting placed Eve's things on top. The room was grand with long fabric curtains and a few mirrors. I noticed a stuffed teddy bear on one bed.

"Our cook made a special meal for us to all have together before your father leaves. You'll have a chance to get comfortable and get to know us better."

To hear the words Daddy was leaving emptied any wholeness lingering inside of me since Mommy died.

We followed Mrs. Harting outside the sun hitting our faces. Looking over the expansive campus for Daddy, I wanted to run into his arms and tell him about all the strange buildings and rooms we'd seen and how I so very much wanted to get out of there. To leave with him, Eve, and the boys.

We spotted him in the distance and let out his name in unison.

"Can we run to him?" I asked.

Mrs. Harting nodded, and our feet left the ground before our ears received her voice.

He pulled us in his arms for his familiar bear hug, his body a tree with extensive branches.

The Harting's home smelled of warm meat and a well-used fireplace. Eve and I sat beside Daddy in the living room while the boys played with a bin of toys Mrs. Harting dispersed on the floor. After a few awkward minutes, we sat down for dinner, served by a woman named Florence. Our forks and knives clanked in a room otherwise silent until our plates were carried away and comments were made about how little we'd eaten.

Eventually, Daddy's voice rose over the stillness.

"Kids, I'll be leaving now. Remember, this isn't forever. This is temporary while I get things settled. You stay here with the Hartings now," he said.

Kneeling down, we clung to him like puppies while the twins stayed with the toys on the floor, unaware of what was transpiring. He gently nudged us from his embrace while he stood up. Taking his hat from Mr. Harting as a signal to leave, we watched the two men walk out the door as dusk settled. I felt the small, plump hand of Mrs. Harting on my back as we stared. She quickly shut the door.

Noticing the curtains were open, I rushed over to watch the men outside, and Eve followed. We were transfixed as if watching a TV. They shook hands and hugged, alerting me to an intimacy between them we had not witnessed before.

As the driver's door closed, Daddy's break lights turned on, and slowly, the car pulled away down the driveway, and the gates shut behind him.

CHAPTER NINE

COMING AND GOING

Jennifer, 1989

High school marked the change of everything.

Months before entering my freshman year, my father announced he semi-retired from his shipping company, which was the reason we moved from Philadelphia to Tacoma, Washington when I was four. The ships he loved—*the other sisters*, we called them—had worn him out. For over a decade, he lost sleep, fretted, and nearly stressed himself to death worrying about the vessels as they made a weekly, dangerous voyage from the Port of Tacoma to Anchorage, Alaska, and back. His demanding career as the head of operations was the reason why I wanted to be his secretary in second grade: "To be closer to him."

Suddenly, the man I wanted more time with as a young girl spent time at home more often. The often distant and overworked man I looked up to was suddenly changed.

Each morning, after fighting my naturally curly hair and putting on clothes laid out the night before, I raced up the stairs from my new bedroom in the basement to grab something to eat before my friend picked me up in his loud, angry-looking Impala.

Walking into the kitchen, I found my father doing a crossword puzzle at our small circular table. Wearing his familiar maroon bathrobe purchased from Kmart and given as a Christmas gift from my mother, he peered at me over the "cheaters" he bought at the drugstore, dozens of pairs scattered throughout the house.

"Good morning," he said with a voice hoarse from years of smoking.

"Morning," I said quickly, unsure how to engage with him and his frequent presence. To me, then, my father appeared as a force. A stern personality with a rough edge. Someone who said a great deal by saying very little.

"I made corn muffins; have one," he said as he looked back to his paper and wrote an answer with his mechanical pencil.

I smiled and took one of the yellow muffins. It was hard as a rock. Just as my teeth were recovering, I heard the roar of my friend's car coming up our dead-end street and felt relief.

"He drives too fast," my father said, looking out the window and glaring down the driveway where my friend's car rumbled. My friend Jeff always looked up through the windshield to smile and wave in my father's direction, a Camel cigarette dangling from the corner of his mouth. I wondered if my father was jealous of him in some way.

"Maybe it just sounds fast," I said and raced to the front door as my father let out a *humph* in the direction of my back.

As I left for high school, my mother got ready for her part-time job at a veterinary clinic. Before my father semi-retired, my mother began working as a receptionist again. "I worked my entire life until I had you," she would say. It left me wondering if I should feel guilty.

Her familiar Vidal Sassoon blow dryer ran on high; she yelled for me to have a good day before making their bed, getting dressed, and putting the finishing touches on her makeup. It took her an hour to get ready, no matter where she was going—a process that drove my father mad, especially when she sat down to paint her nails as he waited in the kitchen. In protest, he would retreat to the garage, back the car onto the driveway, and wait for her while the engine ran.

I was perplexed by my mother's desire to work more now that my father stayed home.

Didn't they want to spend more time together? Travel?

Perhaps she wasn't interested in difficult-to-chew baked goods or my father inspecting and instructing her on the housework she'd managed for over a decade on her own, in silence.

Left alone to meander throughout the day, my father would spend his time golfing and playing cards with friends, returning home around dinnertime to pour a cocktail and stand on our deck, taking in our view of Commencement Bay as my mother cooked. After a decade of cutting down hundreds of trees on our street, we had a near-panoramic view except for a lone fir tree—my father's nemesis—positioned in the middle of our view.

Occasionally, one of his ships sailed by, and he retreated to the phone to see how "she" did on her voyage. Although retired, his obsession with the ships never wavered.

Besides work, my mother's obsession was reconnecting with her son she'd found years prior. After my brother returned home from his first visit, I summoned the courage to ask my mother what happened. Seated in the kitchen doing homework, while she was putting away groceries, she began relaying something about her son. A familiar look of excitement and warmth appeared on her face, like someone talking about a crush.

"Mom, how did you have a son and give him away? What about the father?" I asked, curious how losing a child happens.

She danced between the stove and the sink as if there were hot coals under her feet.

"I think you have all the information you need for now. You are too young to understand it all. It's really an adult discussion for later," she said.

She was shutting me out of her world and her relationship with her son. I always felt close to my mother, but something changed. I didn't know what to believe about her past—or about mine. It felt like the truth drifted out the windows my mother left open every day to air out the stale smell of Marlboros.

Were there other secrets not yet revealed?

Despite the confusion I felt around my mother's story, there was a lot of revelry and celebration with my new brother in the picture. We settled into our new family dynamic, including my sisters, with enthusiasm and love. My family loved to laugh and have fun. We went on trips together. Photos were taken, printed, and framed, and albums were made.

Then, things became quiet. Eerily quiet.

On a crisp April day when I walked up our gravel street to our house, gazing upon it, I realized my life was going to change.

A similar feeling emerged years before when my grandmother passed away. She, along with my Uncle Frank, stayed with us before she was to move into a nursing home. Rheumatoid arthritis ravaged her body, causing her limbs and fingers to twist as if broken. That day, when I glanced toward my house, I sensed something was terribly wrong. When I found my father lying down on his bed, crying, he would embrace me and whisper, "She's gone."

In my childlike memory, it would be the first moment I acknowledged my father expressing sorrow. The second was the time he returned home after nearly dying on a fishing trip. The third would be that cool spring day that marked the change of everything.

I entered our home to find my mother distributing laundry throughout the house. Moments later we were all seated in the living room where my father announced he no longer wanted to be a part of our family. Then, the most unnatural thing transpired. For some reason, instead of leaving, he stayed. He continued living with us but started a new life while he did.

Shortly after declaring his desire to exit, he began taking long trips alone with "friends" and looking for "investments." He returned from a several week-long trip to Australia and—when asked to share his experience—left two black Kodak envelopes full of pictures for us to peruse. Stacks of glossy photos were resting on the kitchen counter for my mother and me to flip through.

I sat at our kitchen table and slowly went through the images. There he was golfing, there he was bowling, there he was in the swimming pool smiling for the camera. I looked at the picture and felt the pang of recognition in my gut. Before me was an image of my father, arms folded on the side of the pool, his left hand without a wedding ring. The look on his face showed happiness and joy, an expression I hadn't seen him wear for some time. The look he gave the camera said it all. The trip he'd claimed included a male friend wasn't real. There wasn't a man on the other side of the lens; there was a woman—someone he loved.

"Look, Mom, he doesn't even have his ring on," I said, disgusted; repulsed my father could be so brazen, pissed off my mother hadn't accepted the truth and kicked him out of our house.

"He takes it off when he swims, I think," she replied.

"Mom, he's with someone else. Can't you see it? Jesus Christ, wake up. He doesn't want to be here. Let him go. He said it himself."

The words escaping my mouth felt foreign; they felt adult but emerged fluidly and with assurance.

What the hell is happening to me?

My mother paused and sat down; the shiny photos spread out before us. After a few minutes of staring intently at nothing in particular, she spoke. "I see what you mean. These trips, everything lately, have been too much. I'll talk to your father about it."

She proceeded to walk down the hallway to their room, where she phoned him at the golf course, summoning him home. Later in the evening, they argued in the kitchen after I went to bed. Their muffled voices carried through the walls, down the stairs, to my bedroom, which was cold and musty.

Life carried on. My mother continued to cook, clean, and busy herself with errands while working as a receptionist. I would come home from school to an empty house. My father was somewhere in the distance while my mother helped people make appointments for their beloved pets.

I remained home among the quiet creaks of a family transformed and held prisoner by truth. My father admitted the dark reality of his desires but denied himself the pleasure of honoring them completely. My mother found the child she lost but soon would learn her husband wanted to leave. My parents were consumed in their own emotional battles.

My mother dug in and fought with everything she had to keep her sense of normalcy with my father and me in the house. My father denied himself the freedom of agency but still did everything in his power to live the life of a man on his own.

Me, I became invisible not only to them but to myself. I was already standing on what felt like shaky ground, and now, the truth was out. Love was absent from my home. Gone was the family a child wishes for—open, loving, and connected adults lifting their child up. I was meant to retreat to my basement bedroom and live as before. Quietly and out of the way. I was to be seen and not heard, a line my parents would relay frequently throughout my childhood.

At fifteen, I realized my job was to remain silent, so the two adults upstairs could face their demons.

On occasion, when family came over for special events, they breathed life into the sad, muted routines we were living. On the outside, everything remained the same after my mother confronted my father about the pictures from his trip.

One Christmas, seated in the dining room, we were surrounded by my sisters and brother. I remained grateful for their presence and the sense of normalcy they brought with them. My father took his place at the head of the table. The lights were dim and classical music played through our oversized speakers. Tall candles were lit and flickered in the darkness. The adults were well into several drinks.

This became one of those rare occasions where a few glasses of wine got my mother to open up.

"Our mommy died, and then things got bad. Daddy tried to keep us, but the babysitter stole his lunch money or something along those lines." When she spoke of this part of her life, a room would always stand still to observe her remembrance.

I noticed my father's jaw clench.

"I'll never forget the moment when he dropped us off at the orphanage. I was so confused. Why is this happening? Where is he going? Why is he leaving us here? I just wanted my daddy. We had lost Mommy, and I just wanted Daddy."

As my mother lifted her hand to her face and closed her eyes tightly, she appeared broken, unable to control her emotions. Then she began to cry, reliving the experience as if it were just happening.

"My God, woman, that happened forty-some years ago. You have to move past it," my father shouted, cutting the silence taking over the room and throwing his napkin on the table.

"Easy for you to say; you don't know what that kind of pain feels like," my mother said, scowling.

My father's head bowed, and his lips remained tight.

This would be the first time I heard my mother speak to him in such a way. In me was a mixture of pride and fear, unsure how such a shift would unfold between them. Especially since I knew the truth that their relationship was over even though I didn't know how to express it to others.

I wanted to tell my sisters what was transpiring in my home, but I didn't know how to explain the events unfolding. How could I get them to understand my existence since it was so foreign from their childhoods? We were a fractured family in that way. My brother was getting to know his mother and new siblings. My sisters were spending time with their beloved father, who had moved away years before.

I was on an emotional island.

Yet there existed something more terrifying than the passion in my mother's response to my father's agitation. Her tears created a feeling of dread. In the flicker of yellow flames, I began to fear the woman leading me through the trauma of her broken marriage was nothing but a young girl herself.

CHAPTER TEN

WAITING TO GO HOME

Anna, 1952

It had been two years since Daddy dropped us off at the orphanage with the promise, one day, we would return home with him. The angles and doorways became so familiar I could navigate them with my eyes closed. Living with so many girls under one roof felt noisy and cramped. Someone was always waiting to use the bathroom, ruining any chance of privacy. My possessions were minimal: a bed and a closet with a few dresses.

If you were late for mealtimes, food disappeared before you could fill your plate. I went from living in a small house with my four siblings to cohabitating with twenty girls I knew little about except that there were painful reasons why we were there. What brought us to the Home remained private. A strict rule among the children was to not to dwell on our sad stories.

"You must forget what happened to you before you came here. There is only onward," Mrs. Harting would remind us.

My brothers, sister, and I were different because our daddy would get us on visiting day when only a handful of children whose parents had permission would take them off campus.

Not all visits were joyful like ours. Mary Ronald's mother showed up in a short dress with a cigarette in her hand. We all gaped at how much of her body she revealed. The male driver never got out to introduce himself; he just sat listening to loud music. Mrs. Harting chased them off the property before they could see Mary, who peed her bed for months straight after hearing her mother came, and she missed her.

Betty and Judy Maybree were Eve's and my best friends. Because we were close, they sometimes talked about their mom and how she promised to get them one day, just like our daddy. Weeks would pass, and there were no postcards or calls made mentioning a visit. Then, one morning on a visiting day, Mrs. Harting alerted the girls to get dressed. As we waited for Daddy to pick us up, Betty and Judy dressed in their best clothes and sat patiently on the Hartings' step.

"She's coming today," they said with broad, happy smiles as we passed by on our way to Daddy's car.

Later, when we returned, Betty and Judy sat in the same spot, their eyes swollen as if stung by bees, still waiting. Later, Betty would tell me her mother came, but she could barely stand. She drove her car onto the Harting's lawn, and they refused to turn the children over to her. The girls pleaded and wailed, but Mrs. Harting sent them inside. Mrs. Maybree yelled, with little effect. One of Betty and Judy's final memories of their mother was her fist raised in defiance out her car window as her vehicle swerved away, and the brake lights flashed.

When a new child arrived, we only heard their name and age. Not a single mention of their family or where they were from. Eventually, we would all come to understand how deplorable some of the children's experiences were. Children raped by family members, drug-addicted parents who lost their children in court, and so many more horrible stories of children who needed to be saved.

The routines created for us by the Home were our great distraction. They helped us to forget why we were there. We thrived under the consistency of each day. We woke up at the same time every morning to the housemother's footsteps coming down the hall and opening bedroom doors. "Up, girls. Time to get up." Chores were done when you returned from school, followed by near-daily piano lessons. We were quiet and in bed by eight every night and attended Overbrook Church on Wednesday nights and twice on Sundays. By the end of the second sermon on Sunday, my body ached from sitting on the hard, wooden bench. Although I didn't agree with God's choices, I reveled in the hymns and the music to calm my heart and mind.

Since the days were predictable, the only way to judge the passing of time was through the seasons reflected in the maple trees that decorated the property. They stood like giants outside our windows, alerting us to the time of year. Each time I observed our view transforming with the weather, I wondered if it was the season Daddy would bring us home.

God, is he ready for us now?

Howard and I enrolled in school as soon as Daddy left us. I dreaded the ride on the bus and walking through the door to class most days. Unlike my sister Eve, who was popular with students and teachers, I stood shy and skittish. It didn't help the teacher called our names on the first day of school and asked us for our address. As she called my name, my hands began to sweat and kneed the top of my thighs.

"Anna Irma Rangnow?"

"Present."

"Speak up, dear," the teacher said, as her pencil tapped on the clip-board she held.

"Your address?"

My heart sank at the realization I would have to reveal where I lived in front of a classroom of strangers.

"Fifty-eighth and Thomas," I whispered. The teacher paused, looked at me, and nodded. The children's heads turned in my direction, their eyes transfixed on me with a look of shock.

Such attention from the outside world fueled my shyness and helped me fulfill the role of "one of those children." I kept to myself, giving off the air that, yes, I had a story, just not one I wanted to share.

After school, we returned to the Home immediately, even if someone invited us to their house. In all my years there, only once did I have permission to visit a friend's home after considerable effort to get approval.

As would be the pattern for the rest of our lives, Eve seemed untouched by the experience. She did not give the appearance of someone broken; quite the opposite, she was near perfection. The way she carried herself in the outside world showed me and everyone else that she was unaffected. Her beauty became her shield. Her effervescence made teachers and students gravitate toward her. She was the star of almost every play, on several committees, and active in sports. Seeing her on stage dressed in a pink gown with a crown and star-studded wand, I envied her radiance and bravery.

If only I could be more like my sister.

∾

Just as children from different places surrounded us, we were being raised and supported by a community of people who volunteered their time and money. As much as we didn't ask for these people to be in our lives, we needed them. The auxiliary board consisted of the churchgoers and volunteers who helped support the Home and the children in it.

We nicknamed the auxiliary ladies based on what they did for us. Before school started, we were taken by our "clothing lady" to go shopping at Wanamaker's, Gimbel's, and Thom McAn's shoe store.

My "clothing lady" was a wealthy woman, Mrs. Hollowell, from the Main Line in Philadelphia, where rich and powerful people lived. She wore a diamond ring and a mink scarf, with the animal's face draped over her shoulder. I had seen her wearing both of them at church. They were missing the day we took the bus downtown to shop for my school clothes. This made me happy as I loathed seeing the poor little creature draped across her shoulder with his dead face staring back at me.

I leaned away to ensure our bodies didn't touch. I gazed out the window silently, planning to speak to her only if she said something. In her hand was a little piece of paper she read intently. I could see the clothes I needed listed in cursive, floating on the blue lines on the page.

"Okay, Anna, you need a dress, socks, and shoes. I think we are missing something here," she paused, running her slender finger down the list.

"Indeed, we are missing something. You need undies."

A few passenger heads turned in our direction as the sound of *undies* echoed throughout the bus. My head dropped so no one could see my face, my head like a wilted flower.

Please, God, take me anywhere but here.

In the horror of my embarrassment, I thought of my mother. If she were alive, would we ride the bus together to buy school clothes? She wouldn't shout "undies" would she? Biting my lip and refusing to shed a tear in front of a stranger, I would remind myself we still had Daddy.

This is temporary.

After a few hours of shopping together, we held two large bags full of clothes, everything I would need for the entire school year. As the "clothing lady" dropped me off on the porch of Rohrman Cottage, she gave me a pat on my back.

"Be a good girl, Anna. I'll see you next fall."

At dinner that night, I thought about Mrs. Hollowell as I pushed soggy mashed potatoes around my plate. I wondered what she ate for supper. Were her husband and children at the table with her? Did she talk about me with her family? Did she tell them everything she bought for me that day? Was it the nice thing she did to improve her status in front of God?

As I wrote my note to her the next day, I could not find a way to be grateful to her, even as I wrote the words, "Thank you."

During the rhythm of our routines, I saved my inner feelings for my time with Daddy. Once every month, Daddy would pick us up after school on a Friday.

When the weather allowed, he loved to take us to the amusement park because the boys liked it best, and my sister, Eve, wasn't afraid of anything. Terrified of rides, I would stay with Daddy as they all rode the roller coaster time and time again.

"Don't you want to take a ride, Snorky?" the sound of Daddy saying my nickname caused the hair on my arm to rise.

"No, Daddy, I'm fine right here." And I was. I couldn't imagine a place I would rather be than sitting next to him, licking away at my giant lollipop with rainbow swirls. I nestled as close to him as I could.

"Daddy, do you think we'll be home soon?"

A long sigh came from deep within him. "I do, Snorky. I'm working hard to save enough money to have all of you living with me. And do you remember what I told you the last time we were together?"

Obsessed with the lollipop, I couldn't remember anything but my last lick.

"Remember what I told you about my friend Mary? We have been spending time together. One day, we hope to marry."

"Will she be like our mommy? I'd like to have a mommy again."

"She will live at our home and be something like a mommy to you kids, but she certainly won't take the place of your mother. No one will."

"I'm just tired of the orphanage and want to come home. The girls there are all so loud, and some are really dirty and don't have manners. This new girl, May, doesn't know how to use the bathroom. She pees in the corner of the room. But, oh boy, did Mrs. Harting set her straight."

"It will be over soon, Snorky, I promise." He leaned over and kissed my head.

Our life at the Home was a symphony of orchestrated distractions intended to lift us up, and they often were precisely what we needed to keep going. Despite my longing for Daddy, there were incredibly joyous times in the orphanage. The holidays were my favorite time of year. The glittering decorations, the fires in the fireplace, and the stacks of gifts donated by families were all part of a magical time at the Home.

On our second Christmas, Eve and I were in charge of putting a garland around the wooden banister at Rohrman. Living room furniture was pushed aside to make room for a giant Christmas tree so tall we needed a ladder to put decorations on the top. Some girls spent hours stringing together popcorn for garland.

When Christmas morning came, everyone woke up early. We put on our best outfits and bounded downstairs to the dining room, where we inhaled our breakfasts, cleaned our plates, and sat back down at attention.

Once we were seated, Mrs. Harting spoke. "Girls, Christmas is an important holiday as it marks the birth of Jesus Christ. Please bow your heads in prayer." Our collective heads dropped so quickly it made a sound. "Thank you, Lord, for all you do for us, for the generosity you bestow on us, and for those wonderful people who donated these gifts to our children. Amen."

"Amen!" we shouted.

This cued us to walk to the main hall. The tall wooden doors to the living room were closed to hide what was behind them. Mrs. Harting stood guard as if holding back a tidal wave. Slowly, she revealed the dark wooden room with the fireplace burning and our presents stacked high. When we heard her say "Go," we ran to find our pile with our name in front. It was chaos as children yelled to one another, "Yours is here. Where's mine?" Once we all saw the stack, we ripped open the packages: Tinkertoys, pick-up sticks, jacks, Lincoln Logs, Lego, dolls, and some things we couldn't even identify. For this brief moment, our life was abundant; we were cared for and held mementos of love.

Inevitably, a new child who didn't have a stack of toys sat alone, looking scared and sad. We quickly rushed over to them and shared our gifts without hesitation. We had all been there before, lost in the shock of where we lived; we were a family that way.

After our Christmas celebration, I felt confident it would be our last. Eve agreed we would go home soon despite her dislike of Daddy's new girlfriend.

I grew impatient and began asking Eve if she knew when. "Daddy told me it was soon. Do you know how soon?" I pleaded, only to get a familiar hush from Eve.

"Stop asking, you're making it worse. Soon."

My head dropped in shame. "I just want to go home. That's all."

"Sis, don't forget, we're the lucky ones. We know we're leaving. The others—they don't get to."

On a freezing day in January, we went to Sunday Mass and came home to the stillness of Rohrman Cottage. The rooms were frigid. Large swirls of freezing air would creep in under the doors. The old buildings were drafty, and many of us slept in our beds fully clothed during the winter.

Eve and I were reading by the large fireplace, trying to stay warm. In little moments like this, curled up like a cat, I had a rare feeling of comfort in the large, expansive space.

Mrs. Harting walked in and called our names, asking us to follow her to the office. She turned swiftly and waited by the main door as we wrapped ourselves in our jackets and scarves. We'd been trained not to ask questions when she beckoned us. I glanced at Eve, wondering if she understood what was happening, and she shook her head no.

Daddy! I bet it's Daddy getting us! It's our Christmas present.

We walked the frozen path to the main building and into Mr. Harting's office. I noticed my brothers sitting on the worn leather sofa. I ran to the boys, excited to see them. "Jim, John, Howard...what are you doing here?"

Eve stood motionless in the doorway, her face frozen like the ground outside. "Come in, Eve; please sit in the chair right here."

Eve walked to a seat and plunged into it; her arms crossed against her puffy coat. The boys were chatting loudly and wrestling with one another against the slippery leather.

"Boys, cease," Mrs. Harting said. They obeyed.

"Anna, why don't you sit down over here next to Eve, please?"

Mr. Harting sat at his desk; a large painting of the Overbrook Church behind him. Pictures of his family—his wife, son Daniel, and daughter Maria—filled the table behind his desk. His children lived on the campus in the Harting's home but lived a very different existence from ours. Neither wanted much to do with the kids who lived at the Home; they made that clear by sticking to themselves and ignoring us in the school hallways.

Pastor Harting's desk was spotless except for a Bible positioned on a leather blotter and the pen he rolled slowly under his fingers.

His eyes went to each of us slowly and methodically. He looked at Mrs. Harting, who stood beside him, and she nodded. He opened his mouth, but no words came. He took a deep breath. Then, with his voice cracking, he said, "Children, I have very bad news for you."

Again, he looked to Mrs. Harting, whose eyes filled with tears. "You know terrible things happen we cannot explain. When these things occur," he coughed to clear his throat, "we have to look to God to find peace."

I could hear the boys rustling, their jackets making a swish-sounding noise. I listened to the arm of a clock tick at each second.

"My children, something terrible has happened to your father."

"Is he dead?" Eve asked, her limbs crossed in defense.

A long pause.

From the other side of the desk, Mrs. Harting said, "Yes, your father died last night in a car accident. He was driving home and lost control and hit a patch of ice. He died instantly."

Silence.

"He's not coming back?" Howard asked. They both shook their heads.

In that brief moment, everything we hoped for vanished. Mrs. Harting moved from her place against the wall and hugged us girls tightly. Pastor Harting rose from his desk and sat with the boys, who remained motionless, too young to understand. A swell of inaudible tears and pain enveloped each of us. We folded like chairs, broken, no longer in use.

We stayed long enough for the air in the room to change permanently, its smell to become an enduring memory.

There were no more plans to make outside the stone wall surrounding us. The window pane between Daddy and us permanent.

He was gone, never to return.

CHAPTER ELEVEN

YOU ARE ON YOUR OWN

Jennifer, 1991

"Where did my sweet girl go?" my mom asked the universe as the three of us sat in the living room in our familiar spots. My father in his chosen chair, my mother and I seated next to each other on our long sofa.

"You were such a good baby. You were so quiet I would pinch you to make you cry."

At seventeen I broke curfew again. I came home from a high school party at midnight, not ten. The night before, I opened the front door only to be greeted by my mother standing at the top of the stairs, her satin nightgown and face wrinkled with worry. I could hear the TV playing in my parents' room, meaning my father was still awake on the verge of snoring.

"Do you see what time it is?" She stood next to our captain's clock fixed to the wall, which made a ticking sound as the hands moved. When it struck twelve, it would let out a thirty-second chime, almost like a church bell.

"Your father is furious."

"Sorry," I said with a slight smirk as the beer I drank hours before flowed through my veins.

I didn't like being in trouble, but I gained a weird satisfaction from making my parents mad. Several years had passed since my father said he wanted to leave and never did. Few words were spoken between the three of us during the day. I sought response—any sign my parents were engaged—even if they were yelling in frustration at my recent behavior. My days consisted of going to school and working at night. The moment I possessed my license, I got a hosting job at a busy and large restaurant. It was real work and, at my age, real money. Any schoolwork was barely completed and certainly not with passion or effort indicative of my intelligence. I snuck off campus at lunch with friends to smoke cigarettes. We attended high school keggers advertised with photocopied flyers distributed in the hallways during breaks between classes. On nights and weekends, we drove around our small village of a town aimlessly, randomly meeting in parking lots, friends' homes, or heavily wooded empty lots perfect for parties.

While I was evolving into a less likable version of myself, my parents rotated in a familiar pattern. They ate dinner together most nights, but not before consuming cocktails at a rapid pace, their drinks leaving wet rings on our fabric tablecloth. A small, six-inch, black and white portable TV was perched on the window sill kept my father company as he sipped vodka and barked at Alex Trebek on *Jeopardy*.

I looked up at my mother before descending to my bedroom, waiting for a sign she was done with me. I was.

"Have you been smoking that funny stuff?"

I laughed at her name for marijuana. My mother was funny, especially when she didn't intend to be. I dismissed her accusation with a "Nope" and sank to my basement lair, rolling my eyes as I went.

After shutting my door, I heard her footsteps as she marched to her side of their bed and the familiar sound of the mattress springs squeaked as she went horizontal. The muffled sound of their voices went on for a few minutes until I heard my father snoring.

The following day, I climbed the stairs to the kitchen, where I found my parents prepared for battle. They directed me to the living room, where our most serious talks occurred. After an awkward silence, they announced they wanted to take my car away for a month.

"If you can't get yourself home in time, you lose your car," my father said.

"I have a job, remember? I work until ten at night, and the restaurant is twenty minutes away. There's no bus. How do you expect me to get to and from work? Or should I quit?"

I had an overwhelming sense my parents didn't like me much.

Did I feel this way because of upsetting them, or was it because *I* didn't like me? I shed the skin of my younger self, the excellent student whose vices were limited to John Hughes movies and sneaking out with my girlfriends during slumber parties. In high school, I found rebellion was a knife I could use to feel, even if it brought unwanted attention. Suddenly, everything in our house revolved around me. I was the problem. I was broken. I was wayward. But deep down, I knew the truth. They were broken, too.

I kept waiting for us to have an honest conversation as a family. Instead, they moved on to a new reality after burying the truth and then expected me to pretend like it never occurred. There were no questions about how I was feeling or what impact their broken marriage was having on me. The solution: pretend like everything was fine. Front and center lived my conscious rebellion designed to make all of us feel the suffering no one spoke about.

I no longer recognized any of us. My father appeared angry, short, and bitter. My mother looked like a deer in headlights: timid, scared, and frozen. If I was a color, it would be red. We were changed, and my good memories from childhood evaporated. What existed between us were secrets, denial, tension, and hurt.

"You need to stop lying and breaking the rules. Mess with the bull, you get the horns, kid," my father growled at me across the room.

"What the hell do you care? You said you wanted to go years ago. Why are you still here?"

He leaped out of his chair like an angry lion. A wave of fear shot through me, but I stood my ground. Pointing his finger at me, his veins inflamed, "We love you, but we don't like you."

Gotcha. There, he did it. He finally said what I'd sensed for years. My parents don't like me.

Leaving the room, I heard the familiar sound of the garage door close, his car starting, and the hum of his engine as he drove away.

My mother sat still next to me. "Why do you do that?"

"Do what?"

"Make him mad? Why are you doing things to upset him? It doesn't help our situation."

Defeat lived in her voice as her eyes became glassy.

I began to feel sorry for my mother, for her life unraveling like an errant string. I was causing her pain, but I didn't know how to stop doing so as I witnessed her freeze in front of a man she should be furious with. So,

I swallowed her fury and made it my own. It became clear she was too kind to rustle with my father. Instead, she assumed the role of victim. I knew it because I saw it, but also because she told me she was, often reminding me how vulnerable she was her entire life.

Didn't she see what I saw? Observing my father in his chair, wearing his captain's hat, he resembled a drunken, angry sailor. I realized the woman next to me, my mother, was still the young girl in the candlelight all those years before.

"What I do doesn't matter, Mom. This situation is hopeless, and help left a long time ago."

Like my father, I got up and left the room.

On a shopping trip with a friend at our local mall, I started a war with myself in a dressing room. Attempting to pull on a pair of size ten pants, I couldn't get them over my wide, round hips. I needed a size twelve. The retail clerk tapped the door, "How are things fitting?"

Inside, I wanted to scream "terrible" and break down in tears, but I didn't want to upset the nice girl who was helping me, so I muttered, "I need the next size."

The fluorescent lights above me were ruthless and offered zero camouflage to my body's reality. My hips were wide, like a pear. "Birthing hips," my family told me as I was growing up. They didn't mean it as an insult, but a child's mind can do wicked things with words.

The top of my body was lean, a gift from my mother, but unlike her, my chest was flat. "Not sure what happened to you in that department," she would say. I could see my thighs and butt were lumpy with hints of cellulite. My "bubble butt," the other name my family used when referencing my body, was not like the images I saw in magazines. I didn't look like a young girl with smooth skin and toned legs. I looked like a middle-aged woman with no breasts.

The words *flawed* and *unlovable* were racing through my head as I tried on the larger size.

My razor-thin friend with me told me how great the pants looked, a compliment I refused. Seeing my body reflected in the mirror, I focused on each of my flaws. She was lying to me; I was convinced of it. Instead of embracing her kindness, I broke into a wrath. I became raw, unhinged, and inconsolable.

Unable to listen to my meltdown further, my friend demanded I drive her home.

Back home, in the privacy of my bathroom, I stood in front of my mirror, hoping to see something different than what I observed in the white light of the dressing room. My heart didn't lift or lighten; it remained angry.

How did I get here? How is this me?

Years before, in the swinging eighties, when adults did rowdy things in hot tubs, my father built a cedar sauna in our basement bathroom. We used it several times before it became the home of my mother's scale, and where she dried sweaters that stayed there for weeks. I opened the door, walked into the small, wood-smelling box, and felt the heaviness of my feet landing on the black platform of my mother's scale. The orange needle climbed to a weight I never thought imaginable.

Grabbing a blue eyeliner from my drawer, I turned and held the sauna door in my hands. With the pencil in my hand, on the edge of the door, I wrote a goal weight under the initials JG + MR written years before. It was a weight so inconceivable—like my old crush—yet it seemed to be my only hope. I closed the sauna to keep my wish secret from the outside world.

One day, if I am that weight, perhaps then I will be happy.

The pursuit of thinness would lead me to the most dangerous of places. Losing thirty pounds was a daunting task for a high school student who went to school, worked nights, and wasn't into sports. I cut things out of my diet, followed rules from my mother's diet books, like *Fit for Life*, and started denying myself food as much as possible. After a brief period of starvation, I would eat again, feel the pain of regret, and starve myself as punishment. It became a vicious cycle. Hunger became a companion, but perfection still eluded me.

One hot, perfect Pacific Northwest summer day, blue skies, green hills, and blue water surrounded us. We lived for these days after months of rain.

My friends and I descended on a house party where the parents were out of town. I'd eaten several strawberries for breakfast.

We had several drinks, and shortly afterward, I found myself behind the wheel of a friend's car: a gorgeous blue convertible '65 Mustang. While I was frequently the driver for my friends, I had never driven a car like the one in my hands. The alcohol I just consumed interfered with my good judgment or any decent driving skills. Turning a wide, well-known blind corner in my neighborhood, I made an egregious mistake. The steering wheel didn't have power steering, and I overturned the car. Hurrying to straighten the crooked automobile, I was steering straight in the other lane when the hood collided with an oncoming vehicle. Jumping out in panic—realizing what I had done—I checked on the other driver, who was scared and furious but uninjured.

As the police arrived, I apologized to my friend and quickly proclaimed the accident was my fault.

Then, the calm set in, followed by an unrelenting number of tears. No one was hurt, and I cried even more at this realization. I was lucky, but I was also in big trouble. There were red-and-blue flashing lights, confusion, and there was me in the back of a police car after failing a sobriety test. My friend who owned the car would come over, "It's okay, Jenny. This sucks, but we're okay." He also said he loved me; not a romantic gesture, but the love you have as friends who've known each other since kindergarten. A broken car doesn't break that connection.

As people cleaned up my mess, I sat alone in the police car, inconsolable.

The sun set, the lights continued to fill the sky, and I wondered how much time passed as I watched dozens of people stand around. I crashed at the apex of our community. It was more than the taste of shame living in me; if someone told me they could take me away forever, I would have gone with them.

The mother of one of my childhood friends approached me; she had known me since I was five.

"Sweetie, are you okay?" Her kind, round face was inches from mine as she touched my leg. I met her question with deep guttural sobs.

"Oh, honey, you're okay." I looked up, unable to say a word, and could see she was crying. I noticed the lights swirling in the trees behind her.

"Sweetie, you made a mistake, but you're okay. No one is hurt; everyone is alright. I want you to know I'm here for you. You can call me."

Hers was a face of an angel. A kind, forgiving angel who put her wings on me for a moment and mothered me when I needed it most.

Months later, I would see her at the local store and be overcome with emotion as we stopped to talk; her face mirrored my feelings. She hugged me hard. Once I collected myself, I thanked her for her kindness that night—an evening where my life fell apart in front of so many.

"Oh dear, I saw you sitting there alone for so long and knew I had to tell you I was there for you. It broke my heart to see you isolated. You needed someone. It could have been any of you kids it happened to. That night, it was you."

Growing up in a small village of a town, we were an army of children running around completely free. A wild tribe of cousins in a way, but that night, one mom stood out for understanding that at any point, my mistake could have been any of ours.

At the police station, the officers were kind and gentle with me. I wasn't their usual Friday night visitor.

"What did you drink today?"

"I took a few shots of whiskey."

"What have you eaten?"

"A few strawberries."

"That's all you ate today?"

"Yes."

Dressed in all white, they asked to see the bottom of my shoes. Not only were they curious about how such an accident could happen, they seemed to be trying to solve the riddle that was me.

Looking at the bottom of my shoes, they asked, "Did your feet slip on the pedals?"

"I had no idea how to drive the car. It was…just too much. I'd just gotten behind the wheel, it was stupid." The relentless tears emerged again.

Hours after the crash, I took a breathalyzer and was barely inebriated. They concluded I wasn't legally intoxicated at the time of the accident hours before since I had just consumed the alcohol before the crash. In my twisted teenage logic, I thought I planned my consumption well. Their collective assumption was right. Was I stupid? Yes. Belligerent, no.

"Young lady, you're not of age to drink, and certainly eating only fruit is a recipe for disaster. We need to call your parents."

I nodded; everything he said was true.

As one officer scolded me, another brought something from the vending machine.

"You can't call my parents. You definitely can't call my father," I said. "They'll kill me. Well, my father will kill me. We don't really talk, all of us."

"But you live together?"

"Yeah, my house is kind of a mess. I would rather stay the night here, thank you very much."

I could tell the officers didn't want me to spend the night in jail. They knew it wasn't a good place for a seventeen-year-old girl with a headband and purple belt with matching shoes. After debating with them for more than an hour, they promised to hang up if my father answered. Even though I knew he was asleep and snoring, likely incapable of answering the phone, I needed to know he wouldn't be the one hearing the deep voice of one of the officers sitting across from me. The olive-green phone sat on the table between us.

"My sister did something similar to this, and he told her never to call him if she was caught drinking and driving. So, when she was, she didn't call. She chose to spend a night in jail."

"Well, young lady, this is a jail in Tacoma, not a great place for you."

With the gentleness of teddy bears, the two officers convinced me they would only speak if my mother answered.

I watched in fear as they dialed my number.

"Hello?" I heard my mother's voice on the other end.

The soft-spoken officer explained I caused an accident, and everyone was fine, but I needed to be picked up at the police station. She was asking questions, clearly confused.

"Ma'am, your daughter doesn't want her father to hear this. I suggest coming as soon as possible."

After they hung up with her, they looked at me with a degree of softness.

"It sounds like things aren't good at home?"

"They've been bad a long time, sir. It's pretty ugly." I could have gone on for hours about the slow decline of my nuclear family: the lying, the cheating, the arguing, the ice-cold relationship, the anger, the accusations, and most of all, the abandonment. Sure, the walls of our house were still standing, and our roof was attached, but the joy left a long time ago.

In the room with mint and white walls, the air filled with phones ringing, sirens, and walkie-talkies blaring, I felt clear. There was alcohol in my body, but I didn't feel intoxicated. For the first time in a very long time, I felt heard. I experienced compassion while sitting in a sterile, cold place meant for people who do horrendous things. How was it after all the years of struggle, of being blamed for everything wrong in my home, I sat across from two men wearing police uniforms, and I felt like they were on my side? My shame threatened to ruin me completely, yet the kindness in their eyes, the softness of their voices, and the reassurance I was going to be okay gave me hope. There were people who cared about me in my worst moments; my brokenness did not mean I wasn't seen.

Thirty minutes later, my mother pulled into the narrow parking lot, and I came down the steps to her waiting car. The officer motioned for her to speak with him under a white-lit sign with black writing that read "Police Station."

Through the open window, I heard him say, "She's a good girl who found herself in trouble. We hope she learns her lesson and turns things around. It sounds like she's in a lot of pain. Everything okay at home? I have to ask."

My mother nodded, "Yes."

I knew my mother wouldn't like hearing such things from the man with a gun at his side. She often reminded me she didn't like airing our dirty laundry to others.

"Well, well...then officer, thank you."

On the drive home, she didn't speak a word. I could see the sadness on her face from the corner of my eye. She wasn't mad. She wasn't overly emotional. She appeared numb, like me.

"We won't tell your father about this," she said. "I'm not sure what it would do to our situation." For the remainder of the twenty-minute drive home, I cried, sometimes hysterically, and apologized for my mistake—for all my blunders.

Once we were home, my mother stopped me in the hallway before she retreated upstairs

"Good night. I'm tired. I have nothing to say." I watched her back slowly ascend the stairs I never wanted to climb again.

Walking into my bedroom, I found a piece of paper perched on my pillow. Written in immaculate cursive was a short note she had written before getting me.

> *Jennifer, know I love you and always will. Tonight is the final straw for me. I can no longer help you. I am here for you, always, but you are on your own.*
>
> *Love, Mom*

I read the note several times, and as I did, my endless wailing subsided. A calm pulsed through my skin as I reread her words until they were part of me, like a branding.

On your own.

My mother was telling me I was on my own as if it had just happened, as if she were just parting ways with me.

Sitting on my bed, I held the note and looked around my room. I sighed from a place deep within me, a depth I had yet to touch. It felt like such a sad and lonely spot, my bedroom, as if I was banished to live alone in the dank space because it was where I belonged. I was meant to be separate from them, the warring parents upstairs. But I wasn't; I stayed in the middle no matter where you put me. Basement bedroom, jail cell, open road in an out-of-control car—I was their mess.

Despite the horror of the hours before, the weight of pain and shame, I also felt relief.

In the darkness, a single lamp providing light, I heard a voice so clear I wondered if it was God.

Jennifer, you are on your own. And you have been for some time.

PART TWO

SEEKING AGENCY

CHAPTER TWELVE

CLOUDS

Anna, 1952

Someone once told me people who went to heaven rested on the big white, fluffy clouds. At the Home, I would spend hours looking at the sky, hoping to catch sight of Mommy and Daddy. "They are up there, looking down on me," as my head tilted towards the moon and where Daddy and Mommy now lived.

The Hartings told us Daddy passed away on a Sunday. Afterward, we went to their small house for dinner. "Children, you may stay home from school tomorrow," Mrs. Harting said between bites of buttery pasta. "Give yourselves a day to process the news."

"We have to go to school this week?" Eve asked.

Mrs. Harting nodded in her affirmative way. Listening to her chew, I thought about how alive she seemed. Unlike our parents, she sat before us, a living and breathing person. Her pale face showed dark circles caused by rising before the sun and going to bed well after midnight. How could she live and not Mommy and Daddy?

As I stared at the food resting in the bowl, my face felt swollen and my cheeks raw. I took my fork and stabbed at the circle of noodles until Mrs. Harting gave me a look telling me to stop. Then, as if remembering what happened to our Daddy, her mouth curled up in a smile with a look of compassion. After dinner, we sat by the fire in the living room while they read to us. We were walked to our beds well after bedtime, returning to our crowded bedrooms, making sure the tears we cried were quiet, so we didn't wake everyone else up. After a single day of reprieve we returned to school, placing one foot in front of the other as we went.

Lying in bed at night memories would emerge in a flood of emotions, my mind racing until I fell into fatigue and slumber. Despite my soul aching from losing my parents, underneath my sorrow was a type of resistance. A combination of grief and anger, a feeling the world owed me after taking so much away. In the dark alleyways of my dreams, I imagined love filled the empty spaces. I craved normalcy above all things, and it became a singular pursuit.

My dreams became an affirmation I would say to myself in the darkest of times.

I will have a family again. Someday, I will have what God took from me.

The Hartings loved us in their own way, and they became the stewards of our story, past and present. Under the shade of our new reality, they reminded us we were different from the others at the Home because of our story.

"Your father loved you children madly. After your poor mother passed, he was at a loss as to what to do. He came to our church to pray often, and one of our auxiliary ladies came upon him crying. 'What is bothering you, my son?' she asked, and he told her about all of you."

"It wasn't until your father trusted us enough to know we would keep you together he brought you here," she said. "We swore on the Bible we would never separate you, and we won't."

Mrs. Harting relayed the story until it was woven into the fabric of our existence.

"You must always remain together and take care of each other. Your father didn't want you going to your family, where you would have been separated. Your grandmother wanted to take the twins, but we knew that wasn't his wish."

Every time, Mrs. Harting concluded our conversation the same way: "Life and living are mysterious, wonderful, and ever-changing. You must be grateful for the grace of God."

As much as I loved hearing about our daddy, I resented her when she said things about loving God and accepting life's heartbreak. I found her depth of her wisdom frustrating. *What does she know about loss?* She had her family. Working with the children of the Home was her husband's calling from God. We were her occupation.

And there was God. No matter how many hours we spent in the church, I never forgave him for taking our parents from us. The combination of gratitude for being in a place that took care of us and my resentment for what we lost caused me always to have conflicting emotions about Mrs. Harting. I could never adjust to the fact she—and God—were all we had left.

Mrs. Harting demanded respect and maintained strict rules. Like God, she possessed firm opinions on how life should be lived, and we all obeyed her.

On occasion, I would catch her looking at me with sorrow on her face. Or did I notice pity? Observing her watching me, I returned her gaze. In these moments, I would drink her in; she wore dark shirts and skirts, and a large ring of keys hung from her wrist. They clinked as she marched around the Home, causing a chill to go up my back. It was as if the children's voices were calling from those keys.

In the stillness of my bed surrounded by other girls, I dreamed of leaving the Home and creating a life for myself. I perceived my life would begin once away from the other children. Days became something to count, night after night, with little time to dwell on my resentments. When I cried, it was alone in the bathroom, in the yard by a tree, or at night in bed. All of the children cried, but we did so in private; in our beds when we couldn't forget we were not at home. Where we came from, what we were missing and aching for were not things to be shared. The Home was where you started over, where you buried the past, and survived the present.

Endless activities kept us occupied: cleaning, cooking, piano lessons, ironing, and more. One of my favorite responsibilities was tending to the garden. Seasons marked the passing of time. Each falling leaf or budding flower indicated we were closer to being free. We were like tulip bulbs planted in the garden. Youthful sprouts covered in soil, waiting to emerge. Like the flowers planted, we dug deep holes inside ourselves and buried our memories.

Seeing my siblings and sharing a laugh shone light in my life. My brothers, kept on the opposite side of the property with the rest of the boys, were good-natured, cherub-faced pranksters. They had dark flowing hair and easy smiles. John laughed like Santa while Howard's smile tilted to the right as if there should be a feather sticking out of it. Jim, in all his sweetness, grinned with his lips sealed.

Eve and I saw them during church, events at the Home, and during school. The reunions between us felt affirming, as if I were staring in the mirror, validating I was still present, life still moving. Humor became a way for all of us to bring ease to the waiting we endured.

"If we don't laugh, we might as well be dead," my brothers would say. Jokes, pranks, and making light of our situation helped to dry the tears threatening to emerge. Humor became our connection and our salvation.

As an usher at church, Howard would put a giant cattail into his pocket, so it appeared like a tree branch sprouting from his robe. When he walked down the aisle, the branch swayed back and forth in front of his face. Mrs. Harting bristled as the entire congregation laughed. Howard was handsome, and all the girls gossiped about him. He met their attention with indifference and would for the rest of his life.

John stood tall and boisterous, commanding attention because of his size and deep belly laugh. Jim was quiet, the nicest and the sweetest of all of us. He saw only good in the world, and we worried about him the most.

The years at the Home were lived with a focus on the future, the time when, after graduating from high school, we would leave. What the children in the Home would do once they left captivated our imaginations and consumed our conversations while we were there. Some girls counted down the months as they approached high school graduation. Most children welcomed leaving, but there were a few who sat quietly, wild-eyed at the prospect of being on their own. Terrified to live in the world that had, in some way, already failed them. They were the girls with the darkest stories, the ones who saw too much at a young age. They were the girls who cried, kicked, and screamed as Mrs. Harting held them and told them they had to forget what had happened in the past. Those girls never forgot how treacherous the world—and the people in it—could be.

I neither flourished nor succumbed to my sorrow. I treaded. Holding my head above water daily whereas Eve seemed to float. She thrived in our world at the Home. As the years went by, I began to understand an incredible burden lifted from her once we moved there. She loved Mommy and missed Daddy, but she was free to be a child and not a caretaker, a role she would have a hard time letting go as she sought to mother her younger four siblings. She was the beautiful shining light of our family, and I would find my place in the shadow she cast.

At ten I moved in to Rohrman Cottage with Eve. We spent nearly every day playing the piano for ourselves and each other. Every child played the piano because Mrs. Harting felt it was a good discipline, and it kept our minds off other things. Some kids struggled, but my sister Eve and I welcomed the lessons and daily practice. Listening to Eve tickle the keys, I knew I could never match her beauty and grace. Yet, I wondered if I could play a song better than she could. The piano became a way for us to connect and compete in an unspoken sisterly rivalry.

I promised to emancipate myself from her shadow by finding a piece I could play better. Finding my voice in the white and black keys of the piano, I would play better and louder than all the other girls, including Eve. Playing the piano became the vehicle for overcoming my retreat into silence. As the years went by in a steady unison, my playing improved. It was when we were nearing our final years at the Home, that I decided I would master Rachmaninoff's "Prelude in C-Sharp Minor."

As I set my intention, I believed the melody represented liberation and somehow, I would no longer feel powerless. I would have something that was mine.

CHAPTER THIRTEEN

PIECES

Jennifer, 1992

At seventeen, I had broken my mother's heart, but just as important, I broke my own heart. Through a series of terrible decisions, I shared with the world every ounce of doubt, shame, and sorrow I carried in silence for years. I let my heartache spill onto the street as fenders collided, and the police arrived. I stood alone at the apex of bad decisions and regret. That night, my mother left me a note in her perfect cursive and perched it on my pillow. "I love you, but you are on your own." She wanted to be separated from me, from my actions. We were not different from each other in some ways. I wanted to be separate from myself as well. After the accident, my engagement with my parents diminished to nearly nothing. The veil of secrecy in our home became a cape we all wore. Hiding my mistake was a covert operation run by my mother and me. Her primary motherly duty: keeping me away from my father.

"If he found out about your accident, who knows what he would do. This doesn't help my marriage," she said.

I hated my father for hurting my mother and me. When in one another's presence, there were short "hellos" and grunts made in my direction. The man who rescued me from the pool by my pigtails was no longer present and had been replaced by a quiet, brooding man whose presence hurt me with a glance.

Searching for answers to fill the ache squeezing my chest, a solution for control came home with my mother one day when she returned from her hairdresser.

"Jenny, you should see Terry; she looks incredible. She's taking these pills and lost a ton of weight. She's selling them now, too." I watched her grab bottles from her purse and place them in the cabinet next to the salt and pepper, cinnamon, and decade-old Quik mix. My mother was a product of seventies fads like the grapefruit diet, starvation, and eating only wine and eggs; she, like many women of the time, fell victim to any movement promising thinness.

Something about seeing her place tickets to weight loss in our cabinet I found hopeful. I began taking two pills before breakfast. The appetite I once had was masked by a nervous surge of energy and a sense of fullness. I kept track of what I was eating on a sheet of printer paper next to the dice cup where my father kept his mechanical pens. As my appetite subsided, I found a confidence that remained elusive.

In pursuit of a new version of me, as pounds dropped, I limited myself to eight hundred calories a day. Eventually, the food I allowed into my body was minuscule: an apple, eight saltines, another apple, and maybe a baked potato with cottage cheese for dinner. The record of my success remained on the counter next to the microwave as a badge of honor.

Elation soon took over as my clothes loosened, and I shopped for smaller sizes. Before, seeing myself in a dressing room mirror ignited the worst kind of pain; my naked reflection in the fluorescent light would bring me to the darkest of places.

My new thinness caused me to experience a long-awaited satisfaction. But it also brought tremendous fatigue. Sitting in the wooden chairs at school caused my rear end to ache. Standing up, I became dizzy. Coming home from school, I would fall asleep on the beige carpet at the top of our stairs. I would wake up later to do my homework and get ready for my job as a food runner at a local restaurant. My coworkers began to notice my weight loss and complimented me on my resolve and new figure. Getting positive feedback from others was filling a void. I told the much older servers, for whom I ran food, about my pills and several of them bought some from Terry the hairdresser. I was making a difference not only for myself, but others.

Arriving home from my shift at ten o'clock—starving and exhausted—I would sit down at our kitchen table and eat an apple while I stared at pictures in a cookbook. As I turned each page, I salivated at the appearance of food but was satisfied with my discipline.

Within months I was close to the magical weight I wrote on the side of my sauna door nearly a year before.

"They're really working for you," my mother said and quickly restocked the shelf. I could feel her happiness for me, satisfaction knowing her daughter was thin and pleased with herself. I put her in a difficult position; my spirit was lighter as I was disappearing, and since my contentment was her goal, the situation appeared to be working.

On a warm day when the sun was shining, blue waves rippled in the bay, and my mother's wind chime tolled. I walked into our kitchen in jeans reflecting my dramatically reduced frame. I opened the fridge to contemplate eating something light. My parents were in their familiar spots in the kitchen; my mother was at the stove stirring a pot for their dinner, and my father was by the phone waiting for a call. He always seemed to be waiting for someone to free him from being with us.

"Rich, doesn't Jenny look great?" My mother beamed at my slender body.

The sound of their stilted dialogue made my stomach turn, not in hunger, but in frustration. I stared at the open fridge with its light on and fan running and wondered for a moment what my father could possibly say to my mother in response. I felt hope; maybe he would say I was beautiful.

Peering at me over his glasses resting on the tip of his nose, I felt his eyes on me. "She looks anorexic," he said.

I closed the refrigerator door quickly, the air sealing inside tightly.

I lost more than thirty pounds in several months. I was standing before my parents, five foot eight, 110 pounds. I knew it was an unhealthy number, but I didn't care. I liked how my collarbones jutted out, my stomach caved in, and my ribs showed. The hunger in my belly seemed to fill the empty ache in my heart.

This is how you deserve to feel.

My mother continued to stir, and my father turned his head away, lit a cigarette, and went outside.

I shouldn't have been surprised by their polarized views. My mother wanted me happy and thought I looked great. My father thought I looked sick. I left the hush in the kitchen and returned to my basement bedroom, shutting the door behind me. Nothing more was ever said about my vanishing frame as the three of us sought space in our separate areas of the house.

Eventually, coworkers, teachers, and friends would try and get me to stop losing weight. People noticed I turned a dangerous corner, and while I did my best to dismiss their concerns, I knew they were right.

Art classes during our senior year felt like a reward for surviving high school. The room was expansive, littered with art, materials, stained glass windows, and plants hanging around the room grasping for sun. Worn long tables were scattered throughout where my friends and I painted, drew, made mosaics, or fused glass together while rock-n-roll played on speakers. Walking down the long hallway to the entrance of the room you imagined you were in an eighties movie, Judd Nelson waiting at the door so you could go sneak a smoke. In fact, our school was in several Hollywood movies. I met River Phoenix in our stadium as he filmed, *I Love You to Death*. Later, our beloved art room was part of *Ten Things I Hate About You* with Heath Ledger. Why leading men in those movies met tragic deaths after filming in our high school always seemed like a type of haunting. Our school stood like Hogwarts on steroids, overlooking the Port of Tacoma and Commencement Bay.

Mr. Swanson, the art teacher, a kind, bespectacled man was missing his right hand and liked to float around the room, stopping to say, "Great, great work." Occasionally, he would put his handless arm on the table to demonstrate how to do something; our eyes would all connect in recognition. After taking attendance and checking in on our projects, he disappeared to somewhere unknown for the rest of class. One day, local celebrity and friend of Mr. Swanson, Dale Chihuly, came to the room to say hello. He was a world-famous glass blower with a patch on one eye. The moment was lost on us. The two left shortly after, and we assumed they were smoking a joint.

I gravitated toward stained glass. I liked the process of choosing a design, breaking it into parts on paper and laying it on glass, to then cut each section; I loved the exacting sound of the knife carving. When the shapes were cut, each section was sanded until the edges were smooth, and the pieces fit together like a puzzle to be soldered. The fragmented pieces turned into something beautiful. A work of art to frame and hang in a window for the light to shine through. One of my largest pieces my mother framed and hung in our living room window.

I created this from nothing.

During my senior year, I picked a single project for the entire semester. A beautiful, colorful peacock resembling a Tiffany design with hundreds of pieces. I asked Mr. Swanson what he thought about such an ambitious design.

"It's a big project. Beautiful. It'll take all semester. You can do it; you have the talent," he said in his mumbling, supportive voice.

The design stood two feet high by three feet wide. I hunted down large glass pieces for the bird's body and feathers. It took me months to cut every bit of glass and sand them down until one day, on my design board, were the makings of a peacock ready to fit together perfectly. I became restless with only two weeks left in school before we graduated. Rather than taking the time to ensure the puzzle worked, I jumbled the design into disparate chunks that no longer fit correctly. I stayed late after school trying to fix what I broke.

Alone in the art room, I stood over my broken and disparate peacock lying in front of me. I felt the thinness of my frame in my jeans. My waist cinched with a belt, and my pants hung off of me. I looked at my broken bird, and she reminded me of myself. I wanted to cry for her, for me. I ruined my stunning and ambitious project, just as I damaged myself in some ways.

Mr. Swanson found me on the verge of tears in the back of the room.

"It's okay, Jennifer. You tried it; it was a wonderful idea. A beautiful piece."

I heard his heavy breathing, and the sound of him murmuring something inaudible. His good hand patted me on the shoulder briefly. For a moment, I imagined his story, how he must have so many emotions around what happened to his arm. How the world was probably not kind to him and, in many ways, his art room was his safe place, like it was for me. He had a story, just not one I would ever know. I craved the art room during my final years of school because of the peace and freedom it gave me.

"Sometimes, it's the idea of the work that matters. The idea. The process. Whether you finish it or not."

It was the most Mr. Swanson said to me in my nearly year and a half of being his student. Overwhelmed by the wisdom he was bestowing on me, his words cut deep.

"Thank you, Mr. Swanson. I just don't..." my head fell as I felt the rush of blood to my face and the coolness of a tear running down my cheek.

"I'm sorry," I said as my voice quivered.

"You could've done it. You almost did it. I'm giving you an A because you wanted to do it and put in the effort. It just didn't work this time. That's art."

Standing in the art room, my graduation days ahead of me, I was having a soul-affirming conversation with my one-handed art teacher. The quiet, grumbly man said the most profound thing a teacher would say to me during my entire four years in attendance. My knees were weak at his kindness which wasn't required. Perhaps of all the adults in my life during this time, he saw me for me. Was that even possible?

Grabbing each piece of the slightly fused broken bird, I slowly put her in the trash, one fragment, then another. I wasn't only putting to rest the artwork that would never be, I was disposing parts of myself in a plastic bag a janitor would collect late in the night.

Then, the voice appeared. The one I heard months before when holding the note from my mother.

The voice was clear again, as if it were a long-lost friend.

Maybe, God.

Maybe.

There is happiness waiting for you somewhere else. You can't fix this, and you never could.

CHAPTER FOURTEEN

....

SUDDEN CHANGES

Anna, 1958

We were in the Home for almost ten years. Eve graduated from high school with honors and numerous accolades. In the yearbook, her senior photo, she looks over her shoulder, her hair perfectly curled, her eyes bright and happy.

The euphoria of graduating meant two things to the children of the Home: a diploma and freedom from the place we were raised. Without families to rely on, most girls went straight to boarding houses for young, unmarried women. Those boarding homes meant you could live outside the stone fence that kept us safe all those years—minus the curfew and nosy housemothers—but you were still living with strangers.

Eve decided to live with Aunt Mildred and Uncle John, Daddy's sister and her husband. "The thought of living in another house with strange girls would make me crazy, Anna. I just can't do it. No matter how wretched I remember Uncle John being, I want freedom from this life."

They lived nearest to us and helped many years ago when Mommy was dying. It wasn't the ideal place, but it was somewhere to be until she figured out what she wanted to do. Or better yet, got married.

I wanted a place to call my own, too. While I would miss my sister terribly, the only solace was getting my own room. Typically, your final year at the Home meant you would graduate to having a private room, a privilege bestowed on the oldest girls. At sixteen, I was given a room with a single bed, miniature closet, and a small table with a lamp. Stepping into the space for the first time, I placed my box of things on the tightened sheets and did a little dance.

A room of my own for the very first time.

Outside my window, a maple tree swayed, creating a perfect picture. The buds on the branches reminded me spring was coming. Soon school would be over, and Eve would leave. I watched the stems swing as if they were talking to me. Lying on my bed, without anyone around, felt glorious. The luxury of breathing the air of my own room, alone, filled me with a sense of independence I had yet to taste.

Within months, I watched Eve pack her suitcase with her few items. The Hartings loaded her things into their car and drove away with my sister as I stood at my window with relentless tears, grateful I didn't have someone in my room to witness my sorrow. To cry in privacy seemed such a luxury.

I sensed everyone in Rohrman Cottage grieving as their golden girl left.

Because our life in the Home followed a familiar pattern, little events became great distractions. Eve called me every Sunday night, feeding my curiosity about her life outside and how she tolerated living with Uncle John. Was he really as awful as I remembered him to be?

I listened to her excitement coming through the other end of the line, realizing her words gave me a glimpse into my life once free. Just another school year, and I could follow in her footsteps.

"There is just so much to do during the day now, Anna. It's really exciting. And a little nerve-wracking. Guess what? I'm going to be a Kelly Girl. Can you believe it? I'm going to have a job in an office and a paycheck."

"It sounds lovely, Eve. I'm so...so ready."

"Don't be too envious. I'm living with Uncle John. He really is a monster to our poor sweet aunt. How does she put up with him?"

"Well, Catholics don't divorce, even if they should," I said, and we both laughed.

"They're starting to charge me rent. Uncle John's idea, the moment I told them about the Kelly Girl job. Can you believe it? And remember the scholarship money I received for college? They made me give it to them, so they could buy a new toilet."

"No," I breathed heavily at the injustice but also at the realization I would never receive a scholarship.

A part of me wanted to say, "I'll be there soon to help you," but I couldn't envision how this was possible. I was sixteen. Saying I would be there to help wasn't in line with the rules of the Home. Also, I knew Eve could survive on her own. There existed something different about Eve; regardless of her circumstances and surroundings, she seemed unaffected by it all.

"Don't worry, Anna, it will come soon enough. I have to go. You won't believe what it's like once you're free from that place. It's everything and nothing they told us about."

We exchanged "I love yous," which carried me through the days until we spoke again. Yet, as the phone clicked, I felt a piece of me fall into the gaping hole in my chest.

By fall, my demeanor began to change, and Mrs. Harting took notice. For some reason, knowing Eve lived free in the world caused me to feel impatient and unsettled.

"Anna, you seem distracted these days, and your grades have fallen. Is this about Eve?"

Mrs. Harting looked at me, her lips slightly upturned. Now shorter than me, her curly salt and pepper hair perched on her head like a bird's nest. I narrowed my eyes in her direction. She could discipline me for such an expression of disrespect, but I didn't care. I wanted her to know how much I grew to resent her authority over me.

I watched her face take in my disdain.

"You don't know it now, but one day you will look back, and you will like what happened to you here. You'll appreciate it."

As she turned on her black heels and walked away, I said softly, but loud enough she could hear me, "No. No, I won't." Her steps paused momentarily, but she didn't turn around to scold me as I expected; she kept walking.

I thought, perhaps Mrs. Harting was finished with me, too.

I rushed to tell my best friend Betty about my act of defiance. Her door slightly ajar, meaning she was trying to hide. We were forbidden to close our doors completely, but I could always tell when Betty wished she could. The one thing keeping us separate from all the other girls in the house—

the calm girls, the crazy ones, the ones who didn't know how to take care of themselves—was a door we finally enjoyed.

It wasn't that long ago I'd been sleeping in one of the main rooms with six beds and six girls, creating a disconnected feeling, being lonely among others. Especially at night, when someone would inevitably cry. They would try to be quiet, but the darkness and pain would take over, and they would sob into their pillow. I would try to shut out the sound, but I knew what the tears meant. Someone was missing their mother. It didn't matter what kind of mother she had been: good, bad, broken, mean, abusive. We missed having one, and none of us was immune to shedding tears in the darkness when the feeling overwhelmed us.

I found Betty perched on her bed, holding a book. Her face lit up at the sight of me. Betty remained calm and methodical in everything she did. Her mother was a hopeless alcoholic who, it appeared after all these years, was never going to get her act together. Nothing her mother could do would allow Mrs. Harting to release her children to her, not even for a visit, causing Betty to hold a deep, searing hatred for Mrs. Harting for the rest of her life.

"I'm so tired of being here, Betty. Having to be home the same time every day, eating the same food, seeing the same girls day in and day out. It's Friday. We should be able to go to the Ridge and order sodas and ice cream. Instead, we have to be home by eight o'clock, stuck in this place."

"The curfew is all Mrs. Harting," Betty said. She nearly growled when saying the woman's name.

"I've been going to church three times a week since I was six! All to listen to the word of God. If there is a God, why did he put us in this situation?"

"We only have a year until we can be on our own."

"A year and a half if you go by the rules," I retorted.

She turned back to her book. She was an excellent student and pushed me to study when I didn't want to. I never felt smart like my sister, Eve, so why try too hard? School was something to get over with, like chores.

"Besides, what are you so eager to get to? Working? Living at your aunt's home? Or getting married? Frankly, the idea of marrying a man terrifies me. Can you imagine what *it* feels like?"

It was the thing none of us dared to talk about—sex. The fear of "sleeping with someone," as the housemothers called it. Intimacy with a man was one of the dangers in the world they warned us about frequently. Sex was seen as evil. If any girl from the Home were caught alone with a boy, she lost her privileges for a month.

As we aged, and they prepared us for the world, the housemothers and Mrs. Harting kept the conversations about intercourse brief. "*Relations* is for a husband and wife. You will ruin yourself if you do anything prior to marriage. When the time comes for you to make love, lie on your back and spread your legs. Let the man take control and try not to cry." Our fear of the act caused us to speak of it only in whispers to those we knew best.

"Your restlessness, it's because of Eve?" Betty asked, a tinge of pain in her voice.

My throat tightened. I didn't want to answer her question for fear it would undo me. The Home had long been an empty place for me, but with Eve gone, it felt desolate.

"Why does everything have to be about Eve?" I asked.

Betty's face fell.

I surmised Betty was okay with the Home, living there was better than the alternative of facing the world. Perhaps she liked the straight lines of the life where I began to feel claustrophobic; stuck, trapped until I graduated from high school. I had my own room now, but the walls were still closing in on me. The pressure was weighing down on my chest making it hard to breathe.

I felt myself starting to hyperventilate and moved to her open window. The warm air was being lifted by the trees, drifting into her room. I put my face near the opening and breathed in. The sun was beginning to set, and the sidewalk's yellow lights were illuminating. I lay on her bed next to her, and she moved to make enough room. I stared out the window for a long time, ignoring her suggestion I read a book to take my mind off things. I hoped to see something change in the familiar view—the open yard with play structures, the swaying trees, the familiar buildings clustered together—but it remained the same.

My thoughts were disrupted by the footsteps of our housemother, Ms. McKinley, coming our way as part of her nightly routine to check on the girls after dinner. Partly out of concern and interest in our day, but mostly to ensure we followed her endless list of rules, I could hear her talking to the girls in the next room and knew she was coming to us next. I closed my eyes and imagined her standing in the hallway, leaning on the doorway of the room next to us. I knew her path; I listened to it a thousand times. I smiled, remembering the evening years ago when she wanted all of us quiet, and we revolted. In frustration, she lined all of the girls up in the hallway outside our bedrooms in an attempt to call us to order. We lined up, but we were restless with giggles. We started banging our hands against the walls and yelling, "One, two, three, Ms. McKinley wants it quiet! One, two, three, Ms. McKinley wants it quiet!"

I chanted louder and louder until I could hear only my voice. It was the voice of defiance and revolt. "Ms. McKinley wants it *quiet!*"

As I closed my eyes in reverie, I loved the feeling of reckless abandon. She was yelling, "You *must* be quiet!" but I didn't stop.

I didn't see her coming toward me, but I felt her hand grasp my hair and bang my head against the wall as she yelled, "Quiet, *quiet!*"

When she grabbed me, the rest of the girls hushed, what remained was the sound of my head hitting the wall. I stopped chanting as my skull pounded. Her hand released my hair. I could feel her breath on my face. Warm and quick bursts of air. She straightened her skirt with her hands. I refused to cry. The girls' eyes were wide and stared at me in fear. She ordered everyone to their rooms for an early night.

My shame didn't come until the next visiting day when Daddy told me how disappointed he was in me. My heart broke with those words. I disappointed Daddy, and the regret would be a feeling I carried with me for the rest of my life.

Since my outburst, I always felt Ms. McKinley's presence. I knew the pace of her walk and the pitch of her voice as it grew nearer. Her head peeked through the gap in Betty's door.

"Girls, just checking on you and your day. I trust school went well?" We both looked her in the eyes—a requirement in the house. "Yes, ma'am," we said in unison.

"Betty, you will have tutoring duty tomorrow."

"Yes, ma'am, I'm looking forward to it. I love tutoring those young children." I always marveled at Betty's ability to please adults I knew she disliked. She reminded me of Eve in that way.

"Anna, you will have a piano lesson tomorrow morning at ten."

"Yes, ma'am."

A feeling of restlessness caused my heart to flutter and chest to rise and fall quickly. My mind raced for a reason to escape.

"Ms. McKinley, since it is Friday, and I don't have homework, is there any chance I could practice the piano in the chapel? I need to do the whole piece from memory tomorrow."

"I suppose, since it's Friday, Anna. Lights out at nine."

I thanked her and jumped from the bed while giving Betty a quick look. I rushed down the wooden stairs and grabbed my music book, ignoring any of the girls in the main rooms. Opening the large front door to the pathway, I saw the warm lights of the chapel.

Okay, God, if you are so helpful tell me how to get out of here. Not a year from now. Much sooner, please.

Often, when my mind turned frantic with overwhelming emotions, I would go to the empty chapel and practice on the grand piano. There was something empowering in being alone, surrounded by cement walls, and filling the quiet space with my music.

As I sat down to play, the voice in my head said, *I have this. At least the music is mine.*

I opened up Rachmaninoff's "Prelude in C-Sharp Minor" and tried not to look at the music perched before me. Years earlier, I decided this would be my victory piece, the one I would play better than Eve.

The music and the memories compounded in my head as I released everything onto the keys. Would I ever understand how this became our life? I continued to give myself to the melody until I couldn't ask myself those questions anymore. I closed my eyes and exhaled.

I played the piece without error. I accomplished the one thing I set out to do. I played "Prelude in C-Sharp Minor" to near perfection. All the anger, resentment, and tension raging inside me had escaped for a brief moment in time. Sweat dripped down my forehead despite the coolness of the church.

There it is: something that is mine.

"Beautiful, Anna." Mrs. Harting's voice carried from the back of the chapel.

Her keys made their familiar jingle as she came toward me. I wanted to tell her to silence her keys, but I had tested her enough lately.

I didn't notice anyone's presence in the room. The room was quiet and empty only fifteen minutes earlier when I made my way up the red-carpeted aisle to the grand piano, like a bride making her way to her future husband. The only noise came from the sounds of crickets chorusing in the night.

"You have mastered the piece. See what practicing gives you, Anna."

It was true. For four years, I practiced one piece. I stood up from the piano triumphantly. I accomplished something great. I moved from the shadow and into the light. I stared down at that majestic piano and its ivory and black keys. Its strings. The hammer keys ready to attack. The beautiful silhouette of an instrument feminine and mysterious.

Something shifted in me.

"I want to leave now." My words echoed in the canals of the walls.

"Leave the chapel, dear?"

"No, the orphanage. I want to leave."

Every bone in my body ached to live outside of the confining walls that had grown all too familiar. The piano let me scream it out, and Mrs. Harting witnessed my fury. Like the crescendo of the chords I'd just played, this was my moment to rise out of the music, to be a new version of myself.

"I've known something is bothering you. When you are seventeen in a few months, you are old enough to make decisions, my dear, even though I think it is too early. Where will you go?"

My eyes drifted down to my shoes. Could I break the pace of putting one foot in front of the other and run to the unknown? Was it possible?

"I'm going to live with Aunt Mildred—to be with Eve."

"You know it wasn't your father's wish. He didn't want you to live with them."

"He's been gone nearly ten years. His wishes seem useless now."

"You must remember I love you, and I always will."

She bowed her head. I knew she wanted to cry. I did, too, but I wouldn't let her see me do such a thing. My playing broke something timid inside me. I didn't need the Home, the church, the other girls. I needed to be with my sister.

"You will need to finish the school year, and then you may go for your senior year. I will make this special exception for you, but please don't tell the others yet. It's too much of a distraction. I hope it brings you peace, Anna."

Peace, what a strange word to say to me. Peace left my life a long time ago. My search was for hope. As much as I wanted to step out from behind Eve's shadow to cast my own light, I knew that to be free, I needed to follow her.

CHAPTER FIFTEEN

GRADUATING

Jennifer, 1992

Towards the end of my senior year, I found I was more comfortable. There was a routine to my life now, a focus. A good job, occasional exercise, a pristine room, and a renewed passion for school that had diminished for reasons it would take me decades to understand.

Despite my surge of new energy, my college prospects evaporated from what they once were; I had lost years and closed doors that were once open. With my sister Linda in town for a visit, she breathed life into our home for a few days, but I found myself sullen as I realized my school of choice, the University of Washington, wasn't an option. Despite getting straight As in my senior year, my other grades—from when I was disengaged and consumed with something else—weren't adequate.

The decision from my second choice, Washington State University, arrived shortly after. The envelope blended into the kitchen counter's white square tile with matching grout, except for the crimson and gray type on the front. I knew by the thinness it held a rejection. The sound of paper tearing was followed by my eyes reading *grades* and *essay*. I threw it on the counter, convinced of a terrible end, that I would have nowhere to escape. I did this to myself; I was responsible. My recovery took too long.

I retreated to my basement bathroom in shame and took a long shower, which, if my father were home, would drive him mad. He rarely turned the heat above sixty degrees, and water was treated like liquid gold. Yet, I found comfort in drawn-out showers at all hours of the day to rinse off work or a night out. Slicking my hair in a wet bun, I put on my favorite sweatshirt gifted to me by my brother when we first met from his alma mater Florida State University. I went to my parent's bedroom and lay down in front of the only television in an effort to be alone. The place on my father's side of the bed was a source of comfort and isolation for many years. As a young girl, it was the spot I would watch TV and eat dinner my mother prepared and brought to me on a dinner tray while my parents drank and talked until they were ready to eat at nine o'clock at night, sometimes ten.

I heard footsteps coming down our carpeted hallway and hoped my faraway look would send whoever it was away. My sister lay beside me with her head resting on my bent legs. Her touch was a foreign sensation.

"I'm so sorry, Jen." The room was silent for a long time as whatever show I wasn't watching played. Curious about where we were, my mother came into the room and smiled.

"Sisters, how sweet." She returned with her camera and took a picture of us before returning to her place in the kitchen.

Linda sat up and looked in my direction. "I know you're disappointed, Jen, but I read the letter. The school wants to hear from you about your experience in high school. They haven't said no; they just need to know what was difficult, why you had a few hard years."

Swallowing tears became something I was accustomed to, so I did.

"Lin, I can't stay here anymore. I just can't. It might kill me."

She nodded. She knew and didn't know at the same time.

I hadn't spoken the truth to her in such a way before, but the hollowness I was feeling gave me the sense that nothing—even the bitter reality—would matter. She sat up and rubbed my legs gently. I felt her kindness and began to cry.

My sister, who lived thousands of miles away for most of my life couldn't possibly understand my feelings. How could she comprehend the reality of living with my parents all those years? She lived on the opposite side of the country with her mother. My oldest sister, Beth, lived with us for a year when I was five years old, and she was seventeen. The moment she turned eighteen and graduated high school, Dad packed her things and moved her into an apartment. Neither of my sisters witnessed the slow decline of my parent's marriage and their personal unraveling.

"You have to try, Jen. Write the essay. Tell them about yourself. Tell them about your experience. Tell them you belong there. If it doesn't work, you can attend community college for two years. You can work and get your own apartment. It's not a bad route."

I idolized my sister Linda and always wanted to be like her—tiny, athletic, adventurous, and cute. Throughout my childhood, in moments of frustration, my mother often asked, "Why can't you be sweet like Linda?"

"I can see you want this. You deserve it. Come, let's get started on it," she said and reached for my hand. Pulling me from the bed, she walked me to the dining room table, where she put our word processor on the glass top.

"Just type; whatever you write will be enough."

Enough, what a funny and elusive word, I thought.

God, I love her; why hasn't she always been here? Would it have been this way if she lived with us?

Inserting the paper, I turned the feeder knob several times until the white space appeared ready for the intrusion of black ink. To the left sat the letter from the university with its list of questions. "Tell us about your high school experience. Can you explain why you had difficulty academically?" and so on. I pondered what they were asking for some time.

My mother floated by me and asked, "How's it going?"

I grunted, something I learned to do from my father.

Write about them. Write about all of it. Tell the university what happened to you the last four years. Tell them about your mistakes, all of your horrific mistakes. Own your story.

It would take me several hours to write four pages worth of answers to their three questions. At the end of the exercise, fatigue set in, an ache grabbed my heart, but most of all, I felt a release.

I folded the pages and put them in an envelope to send out the next day. Typing the appeals essay became my first hint that writing my story would be a path to healing. As the keyboard chattered, and my words filled a blank page, I realized brutal honesty—told to someone—created freedom.

Several weeks later, a thicker letter arrived in the mail from the university. Admissions thanked me for my honest reply and offered acceptance.

There were several steps before my emancipation. The last was an awkward dinner the night of my high school graduation with my mother, father, and sister Beth. Moments before, we took a stilted family photo in front of the restaurant, one of the last pictures taken of us together. I ordered a Caesar salad, no chicken, with the dressing on the side. The server delivered the adult's drinks of choice. A martini for my father that he sipped with his familiar grimace. A White Russian for Beth. For my mother, a glass of wine. Once she started drinking, the liquid caused her to open up with a litany of questions.

"Who were the kids on the stage for the entire ceremony?" my mom asked me.

"Those are the top twenty students. They had the best GPA all four years of high school," I explained.

"I see your friend Julie was up there and so was Erica. I was wondering why my daughter wasn't up there. Why weren't you in the top twenty?"

I looked at my mother with a sense of wonder. Where had she been the last four years? Did she see the miserable husband sitting next to her, sipping his drink in total isolation? Did she realize he was going to drive away, in a separate car, to a place that provided him refuge—away from us—as he did for years?

Didn't she see I had the body I wanted but did so at a cost to myself? My stomach hungry, I was unable to imagine eating a salad with dressing.

Hadn't she noticed the report card, my grades sliding downward with each passing semester?

Decades later, as my mother packed up her house to move to a retirement community, she gave me a box with school materials and old report cards. I flipped through my high school transcripts and began shouting in anger. In my mid forties and a mother myself, seeing what those grades showed—the AP student who suddenly fell off a cliff—enraged me to the point my husband came over to console me.

Where had my mother been when our family was sliding into despair? What reality was she holding on to?

I noticed the surrounding families seated around us celebrating. They seemed happy, proud of their graduate, unlike my small nucleus of a family appearing to be go through the motions of the meal with a sense of urgency and distraction. We weren't like them. Our table did not feel like a celebration; it felt like we were enduring, waiting to be set loose.

I let my mother's question hang in the air. The reasons for my struggles in high school was a long, winding explanation that began with, "My parents fell apart, and then I did, too." She returned to sipping her wine and devouring a large plate of seafood. My sister Beth made small talk, and her happiness for me was palpable. "I'm so excited for you, Jen. Going to college is going to change your life."

I knew she understood fleeing the place you are from. One of her greatest gifts was the one-way ticket her mother bought her from Pennsylvania to live with us in Tacoma. She had been there; she had done that.

My father cleared his plate and said his goodbyes. He had to go to the Port for a reason none of us believed, except perhaps my mother. I wondered if she believed he was being honest or chose to ignore the glaring signs. Belief is a powerful tool, even when misguided.

I couldn't comprehend the swirl of conflicted feelings for the man who quickly paid the bill and left. A distant man for years, consumed by something or someone else. Yet, I understood his darkness, his sorrow. I had it, too. We weren't different from one another, my father and I. We were consumed with how to escape the place we were living.

As I watched him exit the restaurant, I longed for him to hug me, to say he was pleased with my path: high school graduate, going on to college. Yet, it was his duty to be there; that's how he saw it. Our relationship ended with the turn of his body to the street and out the door.

"I don't want to be here anymore." Those words he uttered I would never forget. There was life before them, and life after.

Neither do I, Dad.

I looked to my mother and felt my love for her despite the fact she didn't see me sitting in front of her. The real me. The broken me. The poor-grades-in-high-school me. The starving-for-acceptance me. I hurt for her because I wondered if she knew what was happening—that my father and I were going to leave her.

As much as I wanted to save her, I knew I couldn't.

Two months later, I looked down at a parking lot seven stories beneath my dorm window, waiting to see her emerge. Eventually, I spotted her, keys in hand, burly white purse over her shoulder. She wore a yellow sleeveless shirt and white shorts. She almost always wore white and for some reason, in childhood, I often copied her. Minutes before she stood in my dorm room, nervously helping me unpack my boxes, coffee maker, and clothes. She watched me make my bed and hang items in my closet. She busied herself cleaning the desk and shelves until there wasn't much more to do.

The day was warm, and our small window was open to let the dry air drift in from the rolling hills of the Palouse.

"It's a nice view, Jenny," my mother said to break the silence.

I nodded, unsure of what to say. Observing my dorm, the pink bed-spread perfectly positioned with two pillows I made on my mother's sewing machine. I was excited about going to bed and waking up to a cup of coffee in my new world. On my desk sat a campus map I would use to understand where I was going among the tens of thousands of new faces. As I watched my mother trying to let me go, my bones were heavy.

"I'll go now. I need to say goodbye quickly. I love you."

Giving me a brief hug, I watched as she shuffled out of my room, her blonde hair flowing like wings.

I went to my narrow window sitting half open and sat on the ledge waiting to spot her. I noticed her shuffle across the parking lot, unlock her car and get in. My chest heaved as she reversed out of her spot and sped away. I could feel her pain, her total and complete heartache. I suspected my tears were terrifying my new roommate, who recently walked into the room. Her blue eyes were wide with concern. She probably assumed I was a mommy's girl who would cry into her pillow every night.

What I couldn't explain to my new friend, but soon would, was that I wasn't crying about the separation from my mother; I was crying *for* my mother. I knew she was going back to a house with a man who was going to leave her if he hadn't gone already. I knew it, but I also knew my mother still didn't understand what happened to her marriage.

My roommate walked over and gave me a hug, and I knew immediately I loved her. We would spend our days studying late into the night and sharing our stories. Having forgone the Greek system, we were at school to study hard and, in many ways, escape where we came from. Eventually, we put our desks facing one another, where heads down, we chartered a new path for ourselves.

CHAPTER SIXTEEN

BREAKING FREE
Anna, 1959

I left the orphanage at the end of May, weeks after my seventeenth birthday. Months passed since I sat in the empty chapel playing the piano and told Mrs. Harting it was time for me to leave. As if clinging to the only thing that could make me stay, she kept reminding me, "You won't graduate with your friends, Anna."

As much as I wanted to say, "I don't have many friends," I had detached from the efforts to make her see me and the root of my experience. In order to see my friend Marion from high school, I needed permission and only went to visit her home twice. Yet, the limited visits were a sort of relief since the pain of seeing Marion's family brought about conflicting emotions. When I stepped back on the grounds of the Home, relief washed over me.

My decision to leave the Home was the first time I'd felt the power of having a choice in the direction of my life. I didn't ask Eve or the boys what I should do. I just did it. The feeling of control was intoxicating.

Like other girls before me, I packed my boxes of belongings, mostly things bought for us by the auxiliary ladies. Betty sat on my bed, sad to see me packing.

"Anna, I am going to miss you terribly. You're my best friend," she said.

"Oh, Betty, I feel the same. I couldn't have survived all this without you," I said, leaning down and hugging her. Feeling the heat of her body, I realized how infrequently I was hugged or touched.

For the next few hours, we reminisced about people, funny situations, and gossiped about the many different types of girls in the Home. How strange and troubled some were, how we felt sorry for them. Betty reminded

SEEKING AGENCY

me how much she hated Mrs. Harting, and I listened as I usually did. As much as I wanted to distance myself from the woman who raised us, I never felt the seething pain of Mrs. Harting's presence as Betty did. The elder bothered me, but I didn't hate her. Perhaps because the Rangnow children knew the Hartings loved our father, and they loved us. Throughout our lives, they told us we were something special. They didn't see all the children and their complicated stories the same way they saw us.

"You must call and tell me what it's like outside. Call me on Sundays, as Eve called you."

"Of course I will. I can't believe ten years have gone by already. It's funny, I'm ready to leave this place, but I have no idea what to expect once I'm out in the world. Did they really prepare us for life outside? It scares me. We've been sheltered this whole time. We certainly experienced enough religion and rules forced on us, but is that everything? For heaven's sake, they told us to get a job, marry a good man, and we'll be fine. Seems simple, but is it?"

"What did Eve say?"

"Just it's exciting and different. That the orphanage is run like a convent."

Betty laughed, got up, and pushed my door until it was nearly closed. She looked at me with a wild expression, her hand reaching to tuck her hair behind her ears.

"Has Eve been dating? Has she been with men? You know, like *it*?" Betty asked, her face flushing at the reference to intimacy with men.

"Oh, jeez, Betty, I don't know. Gosh. I'm sure with her looks, the men are falling over her like always."

Betty nodded. We knew Eve wouldn't have difficulty finding a man to fall in love with her. Young boys were falling at her feet. Even young girls fawned over her.

"It scares me, Betty. The things the housemothers told us about sleeping with a man."

"Think about all the things they didn't tell us, Anna. All they told us about being with a man is to lie on our backs. There has to be more to it than that."

I shook my head, trying to shake the thought from my mind. I wanted freedom. I wanted to be packing my boxes and saying goodbye to the Home, forever, but a surge of terror raced through my veins. Before I could say what was on my mind, I heard Betty's voice say, "Thank goodness you have your sister."

Betty was right; I was escaping the Home and running into Eve's arms. The bond between us grew deeper over the years. If we were going to make it, all of us, we would need to lean on each other. It was something Daddy knew well before he left us.

The morning of my departure, I woke first. I watched the sun rise and color the air between the branches of the tree outside my window. My beloved room, I thought. Sitting on the edge of my bed, nerves took over any appetite I might have.

Heading downstairs to the kitchen, I quietly said goodbye to the housemothers. I noticed some were weeping. As the girls came down for breakfast, I hugged some and waved to others. The years condensed, and my memories relayed a movie at high speed. I looked around Rohrman Cottage one more time and smiled. The beautiful old building was like a friend who kept me safe. I loved her as I loved some of the housemothers.

Mr. and Mrs. Harting pulled up in front and loaded my suitcases into the car. I stepped in and shut the door, letting the clang of metal on metal reverberate through my body.

A decade passed, but Daddy dropping us off lived in my mind like it happened yesterday. As the car slowly pulled away, I watched as the buildings I grew to know so well passed by the car. There was steam escaping from the laundry building. The statue of the bear standing guard in front of the infirmary. The babies' cottage where Jim and John lived for the first few years. The gymnasium. The pool. All of it meant so much and yet nothing at all. I turned to watch as the metal gates closed behind the car—forever separating me from the plaque that read Baptist Orphanage.

Mrs. Harting attempted a conversation on the drive to Aunt Mildred's house. She asked about my enrollment in the vocational high school and how long we planned to stay with our aunt and uncle. I could sense her trying to fulfill her duties with me until the last minute. Didn't she realize her role ended? I was leaving her.

"Mrs. Harting, I enrolled in John Bartram High School. I'll take the bus there every day in the morning, and I have a job in the afternoon as part of the vocational program. My sister and aunt are there to help me if I need it. It's settled."

"I see it is, Anna." There was a touch of hurt in her voice. "I'm unhappy to see you go, but I'm happy for you."

Silence filled the car until we stopped on a street where cars were crowded in front of short, narrow houses. I spotted Aunt Mildred watering a pot on the front steps. I would live in a home with a front door and my family—my blood relatives—inside. I walked up the stairs into Aunt Mildred's embrace. After she hugged me for an eternity, she asked Mr. and Mrs. Harting to come in for coffee. We walked into her cramped living room, with a small sofa, coffee table, and a hutch with a TV; a departure from the beautiful and expansive Rohrman Cottage, but it didn't matter to me how small the room appeared.

Uncle John sat in his chair with a cigarette, the smoke hanging in the air. He didn't bother to get up and greet the Hartings. Eve came bounding down the stairs, her beauty causing the adults to pause their conversation. In the months since she was gone, I'd forgotten her beauty.

"Oh, Eve, how lovely to see you," the Hartings said, beaming.

Sensing the tension in the air, Eve grabbed my hand and took me upstairs to the bedroom we would share. Our window overlooked the small backyard covered in concrete and housed a chicken coop. Laundry was hanging from a wire strung from the sides of the fences and swung in the breeze.

Sitting on the edge of the bed, I looked at Eve. "Tell me everything. How has it been out in the world? Working?" I could hear my voice rising and trembling with excitement.

"I'll fill you in when we aren't here. I make sure to keep everything separate from Auntie and Uncle John. Something tells me to. Auntie is loving, but Uncle John can be a real you-know-what. Can you believe it, charging me rent?"

"Well, let's look at the bright side. We aren't at the Home anymore. Can you believe it? I'm here!"

"Don't get too excited. It's mixing one set of challenges with another. I don't want to burst your bubble, but none of it is easy. How on earth did you get them to agree to let you leave early?"

"I don't know. I just told Mrs. Harting I wanted to leave. It was rather easy, really."

"Well, good for you. Keep some of that strength for Uncle John. Now I know why Daddy didn't want us living with these people."

We heard our names called from downstairs. Mr. and Mrs. Harting were standing ready at the door. Clearly, the Hartings didn't have much to say to our aunt and uncle. There were stark differences between the two couples, a separation of manners, education, and religion. Aunt Mildred nervously asked us to say farewell as she wrung her hands. Mrs. Harting came close to me, only inches between our faces, and lowered her voice. "Anna, we have trusted you feel ready to be on your own. If you ever want or need to return, please call me."

Uncle John sat in his chair saying nothing. Smoking what seemed like an endless cigarette, he glared at the Hartings through a haze. "She won't be coming back to you. Your role in their lives is over now."

Mrs. Harting shot him a look I thought might kill the man on the spot. As eager as I was to say goodbye to her, I would miss her strength and fortitude. Her presence made me safe.

She turned to me with tears in her eyes. As she hugged me warmly, she said, "Remember, you are special, Anna." She said this to me so often I started to believe her. I needed to trust that if I waited long enough, I might know what she meant.

I patted her back casually in return. Pastor Harting followed with a handshake. In the ten years of knowing him, not once did he hug us except for the day Daddy died. He kept his affection to brief handshakes. His formality reminded me of all the sermons and talks he gave us girls about chastity, instilling in me a fear of men, even him.

I walked them to their car, and I watched as the people who raised me got in and closed their doors. Rolling her window down, Mrs. Harting waved her chubby hand in my direction. Watching them drive away and out of our lives, felt eerily similar to the sensation of watching the "clothing ladies" leave—appreciative of their gifts to us but ungrateful for the reminder they were in our lives because we lost everything. I felt the concrete beneath my feet as the wind lifted my hair. *Finally, I'm free of that place, of them, of the whole experience.* Every ounce of air escaped my body.

It would take me years to realize the influence the Hartings had on my life. The way we were raised would never leave us, even well after we left them. No matter how much distance I put between myself and the past, the words and lessons that were part of my daily routine at the Home would alter the course of my life forever.

CHAPTER SEVENTEEN

VOICE

Jennifer, 1996

When I was about twelve years old, on a rare occasion of togetherness, my father offered to teach me how to swing a golf club. The sport held his heart, and there were tipsy conversations of him wanting to turn semi-pro, yet that seemed more like an excuse to play often. On a hot summer afternoon, I wore blue nylon shorts and a neon striped shirt. He took me to the front lawn where he would demonstrate the art of a good swing. His first instruction was to move the golf club slowly, low to the ground, back and forth like the arm on our grandfather clock at the top of our stairs. He stood behind me coaching, and my mother, with her ever-present camera, captured a picture.

As I repeated this motion, I became restless to swing back like I saw the pros do on TV. Convinced if I performed as I had seen others do, my father would be impressed. I swung the club backward with gusto and heard a scream.

"God dammit." He was grabbing his elbow, withering in pain.

My father moved directly behind me moments before. As the iron came his way, he put his arm up to protect his face. My mother chased after him until he was in his car, driving to the hospital. At that moment, everything shifted in my attempt to be close to him.

Like most things in our house, there wasn't much conversation about his sore elbow, which thankfully, wasn't broken. I wondered if the silence was a way of letting me out of the embarrassment. It didn't help; the shame festered like cancer.

A few times, he mumbled, "You almost ruined my golf game."

Our time on the grass would linger in my heart and mind as I further retreated from attempting anything to please or impress my parents in some way.

Perhaps they were right; I was to be seen and not heard.

College provided freedom of a new kind. A chance to be someone different, to forge a new path. Walking the sidewalk up to the expansive Washington State campus, I felt lighter, as if doors a were opening to a new world. With each step on the bumpy concrete, lifted by the roots of the trees hovering above, I felt the history and stories of young adults figuring their lives out as they walked up The Hill. Seattle music blared from speakers teetering in open fraternity windows. The songs of Soundgarden, Pearl Jam, Alice in Chains, Screaming Trees, Nirvana, and Mother Love Bone assured me I found the right place. Their songs created the backdrop to our high school years and solace to my loneliness in my basement bedroom. As kids, we were convinced the music was written for us and our particular feelings, and we were right.

I entered each classroom with a nervous thrill. My focus during college was to do everything right. In high school, I sat in the back of class, slumped in my chair, quiet and often reading one of my mom's trashy books. Getting caught reading Jackie Collins's *The Bitch* by my science teacher wouldn't be forgotten, especially when he asked me to share my book with the class.

In college, I sat in the front of the classroom, took copious notes, and visited professors during their office hours. My curiosity and love of learning were no longer hampered by the quiet I thought others wanted from me. I always knew I was capable, but after years of hearing how I didn't measure up—I was loved but not liked—doing well became a climb from my own ashes. I was in pursuit of truths, both personal and literal.

I quickly chose an English major and excelled in my courses. Professors wanted to hear from me; they wanted to see my work. My rise was meteoric compared to the slow burn of the years before. Suddenly, my name appeared on the Dean's List. I made friends while studying long hours, and on a trip to see Green Day in a small bar in Spokane, WA, I met the boy who would be The First Love, and who would hold my heart for most of college. He was quick to laugh and loved having fun. His grades immediately improved once we started dating since studying was all I did.

Shortly after I left for college, once we went through the motions of the holidays, my father left my mother. We made valiant attempts to keep our relationship going; he visited me on my first Dad's Weekend. We attended a fraternity party and made his face up in KISS makeup. He checked out my dorm, met my roommate, and then drove home after twenty-four hours.

Our final Thanksgiving together as a family, the three of us seated in front of a small turkey and the traditional sides, I raised my wine glass towards my mother and said, "To us," leaving my father out of the toast. He threw the water from his glass on me.

The tension in the air, the one gripping our throats, exploded into yelling and explosiveness rendering us changed forever. My mother chased my father into the kitchen as he retreated for a smoke while I escaped downstairs into my bedroom until my neighbor came to get me. The house holding so much hurt, secrets, and regret fell. The angst was over; I released the valve.

Months later, my father moved into an apartment complex on a golf course called On the Green, where many newly separated fathers from our area found themselves. He possessed little furniture except a sofa, coffee pot, and a framed picture of a mallard previously hung on my bathroom wall. Walking around his small, beige-carpeted abode, I sensed he loved the simplicity of his new place. He sat on the sofa, but my discomfort kept me from relaxing enough to sit down. Looking out his sliding door onto a small patio with two chairs, I took in his view and realized how much his new space suited him. I stared out the sliding glass door to the fairway, a fountain spraying off in the distance.

"Nice view of the fountain," I said.

After a few stilted minutes, he offered, "Well, this is my home now. Don't be a stranger."

His comment turned my confusion to the ever-present rage always just beneath the surface, the monster that protected me all those years. My jaw clenched, and I tried to hold the anger back, but my skin was hot to the touch. I knew my emotions didn't serve me, and they threatened this fractured father-daughter moment we were barely having.

The disappointment was too big for me to control; my mother at home falling apart, and my father was happy to be in a small, cramped one-bedroom apartment.

The hair on my arms stood at attention. Turning to him, I couldn't stop what screamed from my heart.

"I don't know why you made us suffer all those years after you wanted to leave."

I saw his skin turn red and his body stiffen. I had bull's eyed his pain.

"I stayed for you," he grumbled.

"For me? You two loved putting me in the middle of your chaos. I know what you were up to all those years. It was so God damn obvious. You're a grown man; you could have saved us from that mess."

"You don't know the whole truth, young lady," he said, his head falling.

As much as I loathed this angry version of me, I couldn't let her go. I needed her.

"Well, this family loves half-truths and mysteries," I walked toward his cheap front door, ready to break loose. I wondered why I dressed up to see him.

"I was never your problem; you were your problem. But, with you two, it's all my fault. Always has been."

"No, it isn't your fault," he said to my back, and I heard sadness in his voice. For a moment, I wanted to pull back my furor to inquire about his pain, but I was without brakes, turning sideways like the car I crashed years before.

I slammed his front door and felt the walls rattle. As I screeched out of the cramped parking lot, I noticed his car under the carport and thought it ironic he lived without a garage.

I wouldn't speak to my father for nearly four years. He wouldn't call on my birthday, send holiday cards, or inquire about my progress. We were officially exiled from each other. I made sure of it, and so did he.

Two people entered my life and changed how I saw myself. The First Love taught me how to open up, and my favorite professor, Dr. Kay Westmoreland, taught me I had a gift. The niece of General Westmoreland, she stood under five feet, a southern belle who was intelligent, spirited, and impassioned. I took several classes from her in my junior and senior years. When she spoke about language, books, and writing, life started to make sense.

During my senior year, I wrote an opinion essay on Kate Chopin's *The Awakening*. On a warm spring day, as I entered my favorite classroom, Dr. Westmoreland asked me to visit with her in the hallway before class.

"You've done an exquisite job on your essay, Jennifer. Only a few times before have I given an A plus on a paper, and yours warrants it. Also, I've submitted it to a contest. I want to encourage you, after you graduate, to do something with your writing. You have a gift."

Her feedback stunned me. The paper was easy to write, almost too easy. The characters and the themes of feminism jumped off the page. I understood Edna's dilemma to find value in a society that relegated her to a specific role as a wife. Influenced by Mademoiselle Reisz, a gifted pianist, Edna desires the woman's independence because she is in love with another man, not her husband. At the end of the book, Edna drowns herself in the Gulf of Mexico after her forbidden lover Robert leaves her for good, saying he loves her too much to shame her by being with a married woman. The drowning. The desire to disappear. The relegation to the role of wife my mother lived. The piano as a vehicle to finding your voice. The overwhelming feeling of having the loss of love take over any sense of goodness in life—those experiences I understood. I realized my mother's story, where she came from, gave me a view into the world not usually seen by others. Much like Edna's in *The Awakening*, my mother's life had potential to be a good book, something to be examined and learned from.

I also began to wonder if separating myself from her experiences and living my life differently might save me.

The First Love and his family showed me love. They showed me how a family can be imperfect but stable. When they hosted a small party to celebrate the parents' twenty-fifth anniversary, I retreated to an upstairs bedroom and hid after witnessing a love that sustained for years.

I wanted to be good at relationships but constantly looked for land mines.

"Whatever you do, please don't cheat. I need to see something different than what I've known." It was a desperate plea to avoid a broken heart, but an appeal made to a college-age boy is like telling a dog not to chase a tennis ball.

For periods in our relationship, The First Love's ever-present ex-girlfriend seemed to appear randomly, her eyes locked on him as if I were invisible. She was smaller, thinner, bubblier—just less. I would sense the third summer of our relationship that the ex-girlfriend wasn't always his ex, even when we were together. They had reignited their flame. An easy transgression to catch, and when confronted, he crumbled in regret. We tried to make it work, but my respect had disintegrated. He was a young college boy with reckless boundaries. I hadn't made loving me easy on him. I was complex, fearful of love and intimacy. He did what a simple-minded young male does; he went for the fun—for the easy.

My mother loved The First Love and encouraged me to stay with him, "We all make mistakes, Jenny. Even the ones we love hurt us." Eventually, I ignored her suggestions seeing how holding on to my father turned out for her.

College had given me exactly what I needed to reset my life. I found something to call my own: my voice. I found my voice in writing, and I found it in letting The First Love go. One was good for me, one was not, but learning the difference was what mattered.

The harder lesson to absorb was that love hurt—I had always known it did—and relationships contained vast sinkholes of pain hidden beneath the surface. I decided to pursue the writing, not the love.

I would hear my father's voice for the first time in years on the day of my graduation. Gathered in my small, rowdy rural college town were my mother, brother, sisters, Beth's boyfriend, Aunt Eve, and Uncle Andy. In four years, so much changed for all of us. My mother lived in a new home three miles from the house I grew up in. She had gotten my childhood home in the divorce and then quickly fell in love with another three miles away. Knowing my father had wanted the house in their dissolution, she called to ask him if he wanted it back. At the sound of her voice, he hung up the phone. Two years later, he would buy the place from the couple my mother sold it to, inevitably buying the same house twice. He reclaimed his territory on his terms.

My brother integrated seamlessly as a sibling, a perfect, playful addition. My mother went to great lengths to bring him into her world. She organized trips for us, bought him a car, and included him in all corners of her life. I often wondered what his life was like with his adoptive household. Did they approve of his newfound relationship with us?

My sister Linda worked in Manhattan as an accountant, and my sister Beth found herself in a relationship with a kind and patient man. Many years sober after quitting drinking cold turkey one day, she said, "I didn't like myself when I drank." My aunt Eve lived near my mother in Washington State. They rekindled their relationship after not speaking for nearly nine years. Something happened when we visited her in Lake Tahoe almost a decade prior. Two sisters having martinis had a conversation, causing my aunt to cut my mother out of her life. Phone calls and letters went unanswered, so my mother eventually stopped trying. It wasn't until Eve heard my father left that she picked up the phone and called her sister.

"Mom, aren't you going to ask her what happened? Why she cut you out of her life after all this time?"

"I know my sister, and it's best left alone. I'll only upset her if I mention it. I would rather have her in my life than not."

I wondered why my mother refused to question the break in their sisterly relationship. Didn't she want to know and face the issue that broke them? Didn't Eve have something to say after nearly a decade-long silence? Watching my mother, I began to wonder why so much of her life seemed defined by abandonment.

My graduation from college was a vastly different feeling from leaving high school. Back then, I was running from something. After college, it felt like I was running toward something. My family was celebrating me; a sense of normalcy entered my life.

My small apartment was warmed with bodies and voices. The First Love and I hadn't been an item for more than a year, but he stopped by with this dog to give hugs and hellos to people who still adored him. The handheld phone in the living room rang.

"Hello?" I answered, unable to hear the voice on the other end. "Hello?" My family quieted down.

"Jennifer, it's your father." At the sound of his voice, all air left my body.

"Congratulations on your graduation," I heard him say on the other end of the line, and I began to sob. My sister Linda leaped from her place in the room and pushed me into the bathroom a few feet away, shutting the door behind me. I sat on the toilet seat, my legs nearly touching the wall across from me.

"Thank you," I said as I sucked in air, trying to gain composure.

"It's a big day. Congratulations." Hearing me struggle to speak, I could sense his discomfort. "I don't want to upset you. Let's talk when you're back home."

"Okay," I said and hung up without saying goodbye. Holding the receiver in my hand, I bent in half, realizing at some point, I might see my father again. Consumed by the richness of the day, I forgot he wasn't there. Life had become familiar without him. I had grown accustomed to the pain of his absence. I swallowed it, or it swallowed me. With the simple gesture of a phone call, I was meant to contact him when I returned home to Seattle. I realized I didn't know his phone number and someone had given him mine

My sister Linda entered the bathroom, and I fell into her arms. She was smaller than me, but I was reminded of her strength as I held her.

"Be proud of yourself, Jen. I know you don't think so, but Dad is proud of you. He loves you."

She wiped my tears, held my face in her hands, and smiled. I walked back into our living room and hugged my brother and sister as they saw the confusion etched on my face. As I smiled in relief the moment happened, I saw my mother sitting in a chair staring into a void. Observing her demeanor, I realized I disappointed her in some way. Or was the pain written on her face sorrow knowing she would never get a call from him again?

CHAPTER EIGHTEEN

WAITING FOR A HERO

Anna, 1960

Life in the Home was shaped with familiar, life-affirming patterns I sought to comfort and sustain me. My final year of high school in a vocational program allowed me to go to school in the morning and work in the afternoon. I never enjoyed school, so I appreciated the short burst of attendance the curriculum required. Earning money felt like a faster step toward independence.

Once Eve and I were home, we had dinner with Aunt Mildred and then retreated to our room to avoid the odd cadence of Auntie's marriage. Eve talked of her adventures in the office surrounded by exciting men and women while I tried to forget the monotonous work I performed at the library. I spent my nights writing letters to my brothers and a few friends in the Home. I shared my adventures with them as a way of giving them hope. My brothers sent brief notes sustaining our connection and affirming we would be reunited and living together again.

Howard had one more year after I graduated from high school. In his notes, he wrote of tricks he played on others and how he hoped to start a business as soon as he got out. He fretted over our little brother Jim and how we would care for him. Jim had remained sweet and naïve, and it became clear he would need our help throughout his life.

As Eve did, I called my brothers at their house every Sunday, even though catching them on the phone proved impossible. One lazy Sunday, eager to talk to them and avoid being downstairs with Uncle John, I dialed their house, and one of the boys there answered.

"Baptist Home. Who's calling?"

"Hi, Anna Rangnow. Calling for Howie, I mean Howard. Who's this?"

"It's Henry. Henry Tumble. Anna, how are you?" I immediately recalled Henry's handsome face. One of Howard's best friends, I had a bit of a crush on him the few times we spoken over the years even though we didn't entertain ideas of talking or flirting with boys as it remained the fastest way to get in trouble.

"Howard's out in the yard. You left the Home early; how is it out there? Where are you?"

He sounded genuinely curious about my life, and for a moment, I was speechless with no idea how to converse with a boy.

I spent so much time alone that suddenly I wanted to share my experiences. Once I started talking, I didn't stop for thirty minutes. Our conversation flowed naturally until I heard someone yelling at Henry that it was their turn.

"Anna, it's been nice talking with you. Do you mind if I send you a card?"

I gave him Aunt Mildred's address before he hung up.

I stared at the phone in shock over what had just transpired. The dial tone was buzzing back at me, but I couldn't move. Did I just have a conversation with a boy and enjoy it? I waited impatiently for Eve to return from visiting a friend, so I could tell her the news.

After several days, a postcard arrived. As I read his cursive, my insides did somersaults. The excitement I felt turned toward adoration, almost obsession, whenever I saw his familiar scribble.

I was surprised to learn he noticed my absence, and I had caught his eye over the years.

He understood where I came from; he knew the rules we lived by. Eventually, he wrote that he wanted to take me for ice cream.

"Eve, I think he wants a date. What do I do?"

"He likes you, Anna," Eve declared. "No boy writes letters like that if he doesn't like you. You should go and meet him."

"But Eve, is it proper to meet a boy alone?" All the rules from the Home swirled in my mind at a furious speed. My elation was quickly followed by a sense of foreboding.

"Just go, Anna," she said with a hint of irritation. "You can't put your head in the sand forever. I'll tell you, the things I hear at the office I'm working in are very different from what the housemothers told us. You wouldn't *believe* what some women do."

Eve worked as a prestigious Kelly Girl, or "Girl Friday" as they were called.

"Going for ice cream with him alone can't hurt, right?" I said, needing her approval more than anything.

"Just do it, Toots. Stop being afraid of your own shadow."

I wrote Henry back saying yes, after I graduated from high school the following week, I would love to meet for ice cream. As I licked the white envelope, I found pleasure in the strange taste of the glue. My hands shook as I sealed the letter and wrote, "Henry Tumble, 58th and Thomas, Philadelphia, PA," on the front of the envelope.

I wore a white cap and gown at graduation. At the conclusion of keyboarding class, I won a silver chain bracelet with a medallion that read, "Fastest Typist." As I walked across the stage to receive my diploma, the chain dangled from my wrist, reminding me it was the first award I received for doing something well.

As the teacher gave me my bracelet, she assured me my skills would be useful if I aspired to be a secretary one day. "An excellent choice for someone with your background," she said, fastening the chain around my narrow wrist.

Aunt Mildred, Uncle John, and Eve were the only ones who attended. Afterward, we went for dinner at the Five and Dime, a busy diner with a small convenience store. Sitting on the barstool next to Eve, I pondered what life would be like after high school.

"Why don't you sign up for Kelly Girl, Anna?" Eve asked.

Was I Kelly Girl material?

The big offices, smartly dressed men, and ambitious women seemed intimidating.

Uncle John's nasal voice traveled down two barstools to me. "Well, Anna, welcome to the real world. It'll be time to get a job like your sister. You'll need to pay rent soon."

Aunt Mildred's lumpy body spread over the stool like dough. She looked in my direction and smiled without saying a word. I wondered how she could be married to such a man, with his spindly body, missing lower arm, grimaces, and smoke-stained teeth. In his company for nine months, it was hard to find anything to like about him.

Eve nudged me with her elbow as if to say, "Welcome to the club."

I began to sweat with apprehension. I looked around the room for a distraction and noticed a sign on the mirror in front of us that said, "Help Wanted."

Taking a deep breath, I promised myself to return when my family, and especially Eve, wasn't around. Days later, I wore my best dress and told everyone I would be out looking for a job.

Walking into the Five and Dime, I noticed the help sign was no longer on the wall. My eyes darted around the store, trying to find where it could have moved. I thought about turning around. I spied an older gentleman with a round belly protruding over his belt. He wore a name tag that said Manager, and I thought he must enjoy the ice cream.

I found him talking, nearly yelling, at a young employee in a striped shirt and cap. "Excuse me," I said, trying to raise my voice to an audible level, "Does the diner still need help?" The manager wiped his hands on the towel hanging from his pocket, scooped up a piece of paper from the counter, and handed it to me.

"The job was filled, but we might need help soon because someone here doesn't know how to do his job." He tilted his head toward the young boy he raised his voice to moments before.

"Sit down and fill this out and give it back to me," he said, shoving the one-page application in my hands.

Minutes later, I handed him my completed form in my meticulous handwriting. "Here, sir," I said, a slight smile taking over.

Looking at the piece of form, his head jerked up suddenly. "It says here you lived in the Baptist Home on fifty-eighth and Thomas. How long were you there?"

"Ten years, sir."

His head dipped down again, and the look on his face changed. His grumpy exterior softened, and I could tell he was contemplating something.

"I know how to cook and clean. I'm a fast typist, too. I won the fastest typist at my high school," I lifted my wrist to show him my bracelet. "This is my award. It should make me quick at the register."

He sighed. "I don't have a position in this shop right now, but I have one in downtown Philly near Rittenhouse Square. Can you start Friday?"

I blurted out "Yes," so loudly that a few people in the shop turned their heads as my face flushed.

"One minute…Anna, it is? May I ask how you ended up in the orphanage?" I knew he was inquiring if my parents were troubled, which in some way might mean I was. At his question, I realized I never told anyone what happened to my parents. Their story lived at the grounds of the Home.

"My parents passed away. First, my mom. Then my father. He had to put all five of us in the Home after she died. He passed before he could take us home again."

His eyes searched my face as if looking for an answer I could never provide. "Well, I am sorry, young lady. Let's see what we can do about getting you on your way.

"Let me get you a uniform. You'll be working behind the counter, taking orders occasionally, stocking items in the back, and clearing dishes. Not a waitress yet, but maybe one day you could be a waitress if you're lucky."

Walking out the door to the busy sidewalk, uniform in hand, there was a bounce in my step. I had a job downtown as a clerk. The freedoms I had dreamed about all those years at the Home were mine. I was living in a house. I had a job. I was free.

On the first day of work, I rode the bus with Eve two hours before my shift to ensure I made it to the right place. Never by myself on a bus before, she let out her big sister laugh at my nervousness.

"Don't worry, Toots; I'll wait for you when your shift ends. See you at five-thirty right here." I watched her saunter away in her pencil skirt and heels.

The time with Eve on the bus—as the houses and city buildings moved by—filled me up in a new and overwhelming way. I observed faces and places that rushed past, creating a feeling of anxiousness. There was so much to see, so much to observe. For ten years, I witnessed the same things, heard the same voices, stared at every last crack in the walls of Griffith Cottage, then Rohrman Cottage. There was so much in front of me now that I could barely sleep at night.

Riding the number twenty bus from downtown Philadelphia to our home in the outer ridges of Manayunk took up to an hour in rush hour traffic. We either rode silently or caught up on our worlds and what was happening at work. Eve's experiences were full of glamour—masculine offices, dark wood desks, men dressed in fancy suits smoking while they read the newspaper. I came home covered in the sticky ice cream and chocolate sauce residue.

"Eve, do you ever wonder what Mommy and Daddy would say to us now?" The windows were open, the wind blowing our hair.

"I try not to think about them too much. I don't want to dwell on them being gone anymore. I know they would want us to stick together and find good partners. Mommy and Daddy loved each other, and I know they would have wanted us to have the same thing."

I wondered what she remembered of them that I didn't. She witnessed so much more of their lives. Looking at the one photo I had of them together, I could see their love was a testament and a beacon for what to seek in life. That was something I'd chosen to believe a long time ago—that our parents' marriage was good, and they loved each other, just like the romantic love in movies.

"Has Henry been by to see you?" Eve asked, shaking me from my thoughts.

Henry hadn't fulfilled his promise to visit me after graduation. In a letter to me, he had written the rules had gotten tighter after a few boys snuck off the property and were caught drinking. As I read his letter, his frustration spilling out in the ink, I could see Mrs. Harting as if she were standing before me. I wondered if I would ever escape her grasp on my life.

"Not yet. He says Mrs. Harting wouldn't let him leave. Imagine that!"

Eve let out a grunt. "You know, Toots, eventually we won't think about her as much. Especially once the boys are gone."

The worry of establishing ourselves remained a constant topic of conversation. How were we going to root ourselves into a life? I always felt finding a man would happen more quickly for Eve. She was surrounded by successful men who adored her. She didn't need to say it; I knew it. Most people revered her. Almost nightly, she came home with stories of men flirting with her, leaving notes on her desk, or asking her to dinner. Even married men were chasing her. She refused them all.

"I'm just not ready," she would say to me, and I knew it was only a matter of time.

On an ice-cold December day, as Eve got on the bus at 5th and Jones, she glanced at me urgently. Her cheeks flushed from being outside in the freezing weather, she rushed to sit beside me. Watching her come down the aisle, I was struck again by her beauty. Many people mistook her for Grace Kelly, and for a brief moment, you would see people's faces ponder what Grace would be doing on a dirty, crowded bus in Philadelphia.

I removed my bag from the seat I held for her, and Eve's body drifted down beside mine. Her gloved hand touched my leg. She leaned in to whisper in my ear.

"I told you about the attorney I work for, Preston Wilks, didn't I?"

"Eve, have you been drinking? Your breath smells like Uncle John's."

She rolled her eyes, "Yes, one drink. Let me get to the story. Preston has been taking me to lunch on Fridays, and I've thought nothing of it. I'm his secretary, and it seemed like a reasonable thing for us to do. We talk about his firm, where I went to school, and...oh, dear." She blew the hair off her forehead. "He asks me about the Home. I cringe whenever I talk about that place, but he seems genuinely interested. He asks me endless questions about who I am, our family, what I want out of life. At first, he frightened me, but now I'm starting to enjoy these conversations with him. He's so intelligent. I can't help looking up to him."

A wave of envy and jealousy pressed over me like a blanket. "Is Preston married?"

"Anna, heavens no. I would never get together with a married man." She shook her curls as if shaking something annoying out of them.

"Today he called me into his office. I brought my notebook and pen, prepared to take down a letter. And oh…." She let out a heavy breath. "Instead, he asked about Mr. and Mrs. Harting and how we got along with them."

"Both of us? How does he know about me?"

"Yes, you. He knows most everything about our story. He said he wanted to meet Mrs. Harting. I nearly broke out in tears. Why would he want to see the orphanage, of all places?"

Eve always had a way of cutting reality so thin it made it hard to breathe. I looked at the condensation forming on the glass. We were running away from that place, not planning to return to it. The idea of showing someone, especially someone of Preston's stature, our broken past made me sick to my stomach. Could it be that finding an eligible man meant we had to reveal our broken childhood? The thought terrified me. A reason I liked the idea of romance with Henry: his familiarity with the Home. If we found ourselves together, I didn't have to explain myself or my upbringing. It felt safer than what Eve shared with excitement.

"Anna, you know what he said today? He said he wants to *mold* me."

"I think that means he loves you."

Her beautiful green eyes grew wide, and she smiled.

"There's more. He wants us to leave Aunt Mildred and Uncle John's."

"Us?" *How did this become "us?"*

I never met this man, and now he bothered himself with including me, too. I was utterly confused and a little excited but afraid simultaneously. I felt as if our life, our bus ride, suddenly turned into a movie I watched on the TV screen.

"He mentioned there's a house for women, the Coles House in downtown Philadelphia, where unmarried women stay. They call it a boarding home. A place where we wouldn't be living under Aunt and Uncle's influence. Jesus, Anna, half our money goes to them as it is. And let's not forget Daddy didn't want us growing up with any of our family. There's a reason."

"Sounds like another orphanage to me, Eve. I thought we agreed a place with others isn't what we want." Terror washed over me as I could see how the story would unfold. We would arrive at the boarding home, and then suddenly, Eve would leave to enjoy marital bliss. I would be left alone, surrounded by strangers. It sounded all too familiar.

"Anna, we pay to live in Auntie's tiny house and share one room. We need our own life. Preston called the Coles House, and there's room for both of us. We would have our own rooms. And he would pay for it."

"A stranger would pay for us?"

"Not a stranger—Preston! We need to move there if we want any chance of making it in the world. Auntie and Uncle are a dead end."

I could tell these were not her words but Preston's.

"Would I owe Preston something after such a gesture?" I thought about all the people who had supported us throughout our childhood and realized perhaps it was the world paying us back for everything taken from us. A familiar sense of being owed something rose from my gut.

"What do we say to Aunt Mildred?"

"We can't tell her until the last minute. They would never let us leave."

And just like that, we created a new plan with Mr. Preston Wilks as the executor of our escape. I had yet to meet the man changing the course of our destiny. For two weeks, we secretly stuffed clothes and belongings into plastic bags we carried to work, bringing only a few items each day. As our things piled up at our respective workplaces, we were closer to escaping a muted fate within the hopeless row houses of Manayunk. Like two baby birds fledging, we were quietly leaping from the familiar to the unknown.

CHAPTER NINETEEN

HOME

Jennifer, 1998

As a young girl growing up with my parents, I often found it hard to know how to be perceived as good. What were the things I had to do? I was told to remain elusive in the presence of adults. Being clean and well-dressed were important. Great grades a necessity and came easily until the entry of my waywardness in high school. Was picking weeds—something I fought to do—the thing that would make me whole? Was it practicing piano? Many times in my life I wanted to ask my parents, "What does it take to be considered a good kid?" but I never did.

After college I quickly landed an excellent job and a year later got a sizable promotion and pay increase working for IBM. Since I was young, I enjoyed hard work, a gift from my father, even though my second position began at five a.m. My passion for writing hadn't diminished, and I set the goal of earning my MFA in creative writing. Dr. Westmoreland's words remained with me even as I sought to be a professional with cheap Bebe suits and a paycheck. Writing was a calling and a source of relief. I found freedom in the written word. I would scribble words and ideas on sheets of paper, on pages in books, and on the back of receipts. Once at work, I wrote a scene for a future novel in the blank pages at the back of the *Celestine Prophecy*, a book I would later lend to my mother to read.

"Jen, I saw what you wrote in the book you lent me. It was beautiful. You really can write."

At the same time slowly, very slowly, I began to exercise. I came to the realization I divorced my body long ago. But I needed her, and she needed me to love her. The only way I could eat without gaining weight after years of starvation was to move. So, I began to exercise and sweat, one painful walk or run after the other. Trotting around Green Lake, I sensed people could tell I was an imposter; embarrassed by my inexperience, I felt shame as I passed them.

Visiting my mother's house one weekend, I went on a short run around her neighborhood. Twenty minutes later, I entered her front door, where she greeted me. She always stopped her task to say hello the minute I entered. Since living alone, I could tell someone coming in the house thrilled her— as if it was a surprise—and how much it meant to have a visitor. I could taste her loneliness in those moments, and it broke my heart.

"Oh, Jen, your face is so red."

"I just ran, Mom. It's hot out."

"But it's *so* red…you know some people are allergic to exercise; I think you might be."

I looked at her with curiosity. How did she adopt such whimsy so quickly? It was part of her charm but also a riddle.

Thankfully, I ignored her medical observation and continued with my pursuit of health.

With a new promotion to editorial assistant at my company, I set a goal of obtaining my MFA from the school I wanted to attend for undergrad, the University of Washington. I fell short in the past, but I had come to accept the reasons why and knew they were no longer a part of me as a student. While studying for my English major, I tapped into my confidence and a belief in my capabilities.

In my weekly planner, I wrote down the office hours for the creative writing department and left work early to investigate my next step. I organized everything in a leather portfolio: letters of recommendation and clippings. Walking the intersecting brick path in the Quad, cherry trees in bloom, the buildings created the feeling of an Ivy League school.

This is where I want to be. I want more of this.

The campus map led me to the department.

Entering the office, I found a woman sitting at her desk. She had curly, unruly hair like mine and wore a long, flowery dress coupled with a pair of Birkenstocks. She turned my way with a forced smile, giving me an up-and-down look while she did. Immediately I regretted my business attire. She stayed seated when I introduced myself, then motioned for me to take the empty chair across from her.

"I'm here to inquire about the MFA program," I said, my voice going an octave higher as I did.

Unexpected nerves appeared, and with the brisk walk across campus, I began to feel my body temperature rise. I sat on a cushioned pleather chair, and suddenly, the cheap fabric of my pants felt like a scuba suit.

"Tell me, why do you want an MFA in creative writing?" she asked.

"I've always loved writing and was an English major at Washington State. I want to continue my studies. My professor, Dr. Westmoreland, encouraged me to continue writing in undergrad...her letter of recommendation is included. And, well, you will see some of my writing here."

I handed her my portfolio, which contained several published clippings from my internship in the WSU Communications department my senior year, a gift from Dr. Westmoreland. The day she gave me my assignment, she handed me the envelope and, in her raspy Southern drawl, said, "This the best internship we have. You've earned it."

I watched as she flipped through my pages, barely stopping to read my articles and papers.

"Do you write every day? Have you been published recently?"

Beads of sweat were forming on my forehead. I inhaled and exhaled slowly trying to cool down. The less-than-impressed teacher closed my portfolio and handed it to me.

"I'm an editorial assistant. So, I'm doing some writing just not as much creative as I would like."

"Where do you work?"

"I work for IBM in Bellevue." I wiped the condensation near my hairline.

The enthusiasm I held as I walked into her small office door moments before became a pit of nervousness dripping from my pores. I was letting her change the subject, and I didn't know how to stop it. Any confidence quickly flew out the barely cracked window providing little relief to her stuffy room.

"You know, there is a program through the School of Engineering, which seems like a good fit for someone like you; it's technical writing and editing."

I wanted to ask what "someone like you" meant but decided against it. Something in her nonverbal hinting told me she had ample dislike for someone like me. Perhaps she could tell I held disdain for Birkenstocks. I looked at her flower dress and realized we couldn't be more different in our appearances. Muttering where I could find the other department, she swiveled in her chair and turned her back to me.

I couldn't understand what just happened; how did my good intentions go so awry?

I took my time walking to the School of Engineering, trying to understand why the previous interaction ended so quickly and with zero enthusiasm for me entering her program.

Approaching the counter, a woman smiled in my direction.

"Hi, I was just at the creative writing department regarding the master's program and, well, they thought I should come here. I'm an English major, and I now work for IBM as an editorial assistant…I'm interested in getting my master's."

After a few minutes of explaining who I was and my background, the woman said, "We would be thrilled to have someone with your background," and proceeded to grab pamphlets about their new Technical Writing and Editing program.

At her suggestion, I signed up for Continuing Education courses at night to earn credits before applying for the fall program and to get references from professors. I worked during the day and attended classes in the evening. Some afternoons, I was so tired I slept in my car before school.

Months later, as I entered the lobby of my apartment and grabbed my mail, an envelope from the School of Engineering at the University of Washington arrived. So much transpired since I applied for college, and so much within me evolved. Sitting at my small kitchen table in my beloved 1920s studio apartment, I opened the letter and saw I was accepted, my hands trembling with excitement.

I kept my application quiet and told only a few people for fear I wouldn't make it. I called my college friend and coworker, Ann, whom I walked with a few times a week in my slow pursuit of health. Our walks were consumed with talk about the next stage of life.

Holding my several-pound cell phone, I dialed her number. "I got in, Ann! Can you believe it?"

Her reaction was consistent, like her friendship, "I sure can. You did it!"

Telling my mother that I got into graduate school didn't go as well as I hoped. Driving to her place thirty minutes away, I planned to ask for financial help, knowing that leaving my job to attend school would change what I could afford. My studio apartment, car, and living expenses were funded by my work.

"Mom, I got into grad school at UW and want to know if you can help me."

Her reaction wasn't of excitement but concern.

"You should ask your father for financial help now you two are talking," my mother bristled as she mentioned him. Post-divorce, she began emphasizing the "er" in the word *father* as if it were a weapon.

"Mom, we're barely talking, but yes, we are repairing our relationship...slowly."

I watched as her body stiffened, and her eyes widened. She appeared angry as if I shouldn't find a way to be in his life again. "Well, ask him for help. I'm on my own now."

What should have been a happy moment, one of celebration, was met with a familiar tension in my mother's voice when my father's name was mentioned. The divorce was final, but her feelings of betrayal remained.

"Jesus, Mom, why can't you ever say you're proud of me? I got into graduate school at a great school. The one I always wanted to attend. I have a great job, so why isn't this good news?"

"Well, I don't see why you need more schooling. You do have a good job."

What followed between us became a screaming match of epic proportions, but not one rooted in managing finances and how to pay for school. At the root of my mother's anger was that I had forgiven my father and let him back in my life.

"After what he did to me," she screamed. This would become a narrative that lived for decades; my father was the one who was at fault. He abandoned my mother, and me, but as the years went on, a much more complicated version would emerge.

I would receive an email from her the next day apologizing for our fight but not her thoughts on the perceived betrayal relating to my father. "I guess I never said I was proud of you enough because, frankly, it wasn't something I heard when growing up. I am proud of you, always have been."

The crumbs on her trail were becoming mine to follow.

A week later, I sat in my father's garage, which resembled an operating room. The walls were stark white, the floor a shiny grey epoxy. Open shelves hosted perfectly positioned items such as cleaning supplies and tools; the fluorescent lights let off a synthetic glare. He sat in a camping chair, a Marlboro Light clenched in his lips. I sat across from him in his girlfriend's matching seat.

"Dad, remember how you told us girls you would pay for school as long as we want to attend?"

He nodded.

"I got into graduate school at UW. The school I always wanted to go to; I finally got in for my master's. It's for Technical Writing and Editing, a growing major. You…" I felt nervousness stammer in my voice. "Well, I would love some help finically if you could. It will be impossible to keep my current job while going to school."

The light of his cigarette glowed and the tobacco crackled.

"Good for you. I would love to help, but I already have. Since we didn't talk for a handful of years, I gave your mother money for school when we divorced. You could go to school for a very long time. I've pretty much lost everything once we split and need to rebuild again. I'm back at TOTE."

Knowing he returned to a job which nearly cost him his life—in the form of a heart attack in his late thirties—caused me to pause.

His words rang in my ears; I reached for a Marlboro from his half-full pack, lit it, took a giant inhale, and released the smoke into the air.

I saved my tears for the drive back to Seattle. No matter what I did—or hoped to achieve—I would never be good in their eyes. My exciting news lived wrapped in a sadness I couldn't contain. For different reasons, my parents weren't excited for me.

There arose a heaviness in my gut as I realized pursuing a master's in Seattle might not be the best thing for me; perhaps the thing I needed to plan for was a getaway.

The following day, I ran stairs to the top of Queen Anne. Standing in Kerry Park so breathless it felt like my heart would explode, I looked toward the city and saw the Space Needle statuesque and flirty amongst the buildings; Mountain Rainier etched in the sky behind. Despite loving my studio apartment, my neighborhood, and the view in front of me, I could taste my future belonged somewhere else.

Keep running.

That same month, I would fly to San Francisco to spend the weekend with my college roommate, the one I loved instantly. Life crystallized on a beautiful summer day as the plane descended to SFO. There was the dark blue bay mixed with turquoise water, the bridges, the headlands, and a city that seemed to roll over hills like a ribbon of white and pastels.

This is it. This is what you have been waiting for.

Before returning to Seattle, I rented a 300-square-foot studio in the same building as my roommate. On the ground floor, a storefront with red velvet curtains and a pink sign surrounded by lights read, "Paris Massage." Despite the raunchiness of the entryway, the decision to live downtown in an unfamiliar city seemed like the most luxurious thing I'd ever done.

I returned home, quit my job, sold my car, and took out a small loan for living expenses until I found a job. Two weeks later I was in a U-Haul with my mom riding shotgun. As I left Seattle, Mt. Rainer in my view, I knew I would miss the people and place I came from, but I also knew it wasn't where I belonged anymore. There were enough signs.

When I arrived in my tiny apartment, I owned a queen bed and sofa, which faced my small bay window. Eventually when on a visit my father said, "If you tripped through the door, you fell out the window." The bathroom became filled to the ceiling with empty boxes I eventually carried down to dumpsters in the basement.

"I did do cities before; remember, I lived in Philadelphia and worked at the bank before I met your dad." My mother frequently reminded me of her adventurous years before she became a housewife.

"Are you sure you want to do this, Jen?"

There were so many things I wanted to say in response, but I knew better than to try to get her to understand.

A few days later, I put her in a cab and sent her on her way. Then, I was alone in my studio searching Craigslist and the wanted ads for jobs. My days were filled walking miles exploring my new city. Nob Hill stole my heart. I found refuge in Grace Cathedral where I walked the labyrinth before strolling the coolness of the church and finding a corner to pray. I wasn't religious by nature, but for some reason, her walls embraced me. The stillness, the dusty smell of wood and glass and concrete, offered me a form of comfort unfamiliar in my life. The air held peace and tranquility, a location where my internal voice was welcomed.

I scheduled and conducted endless interviews, often not realizing how far I needed to walk and failing to give myself enough time to cool down before my meeting. I was getting job offers and for the first time in my life, I felt I was in control of it.

I quickly realized San Francisco was a land of opportunity, and life just began.

On the other side of the country, my sister Linda went through a midlife crisis. Six years older than me, she worked in Manhattan as an assistant vice president at Chase Bank. As a CPA she paid her dues as an up-and-coming consultant at Price Waterhouse the years before, often spending nights sleeping under her desk. After buying a co-op with her boyfriend on the Upper East Side, she quit her job, moved to Yellowstone to wait tables, and spent her off days hiking the wilderness, the opposite of the concrete jungle she called home.

I was meant to be her last visitor that summer before she returned to New York, her boyfriend, and their apartment, but my sudden move to San Francisco changed plans.

"Lin, I would love to come see you, but I moved to San Francisco. I don't have a job or a car. I'm totally broke."

"Oh, I love San Francisco. I'll come visit you before I drive back to New York."

Linda never shied away from getting in her car to drive across the country. Growing up I was the only kid with siblings who lived thousands of miles away. One summer night, my friends and I slept on our porch and watched the shooting stars until we fell asleep. The next morning, as the sun was rising, we heard car doors slam and saw my sister and her friend walking up our driveway.

My father greeted her with, "Jesus Christ, you're here two days early. How damn fast did you drive?"

My sister was mysterious and the epitome of cool. Especially when she bought us wine coolers in high school.

It seemed fitting she would show up in angel-like fashion as she did in my childhood. Navigating the chaotic city, she pulled up in front of my building with a car full of camping gear and plans to stay for the weekend. On the pile of things was a stuffed teddy bear she brought for me.

"I'm going to have a hard time giving Bear up; I fell in love with him during the drive. He's the perfect stuffed animal," she said handing me the toy. "I got him in Yellowstone."

We spent two days driving around the city discovering new areas. Parking in the Sunset District one afternoon, a truck slammed her open car door, and it had to be towed to a shop for repair.

"Adam isn't going to like this delay. He's ready for me to come back," she said.

She hesitated calling him, so I poured her a glass of cheap wine and waited. Eventually, she took my phone to the bathroom and came out thirty minutes later, looking defeated. Noticing her brows pinched together I asked, "Did it go well?"

Rarely a smoker, she reached for a Capri—my social smoking cigarette of choice then—and inhaled awkwardly. "As well as it could go."

There existed an awkward silence as the roar of engines and horns rose from the streets, my hand hanging out the window to let the smoke escape.

"Do you love Adam?"

A billow of smoke followed my question.

"Of course. Yes, why?"

"Cuz if you loved him, I don't think you would be here with me. You've been away from New York for months now, and instead of coming home, you came here. I don't think you love him."

Here I was, someone void of experiencing healthy relationships, telling my sister she didn't love her boyfriend. A bold and crass move for her little sister. Perhaps it was my purview into relationships where love diminished that helped me to see her struggle. I could see the mixture of confusion and hope on her face. Should she stay? Should she go? She had taken a break from the things she thought were bringing her down, lived among nature, and found her peace, yet she still had questions. I witnessed the expression from others before, struggling with the role of duty above following their own heart.

My sister never left San Francisco. Instead, she moved in with me, and we shared my queen bed. The teddy bear she bought for me perched between our two pillows. As twenty-four and thirty-year-old sisters, it was the first time we lived together for more than a few weeks.

CHAPTER TWENTY

THE ESCAPE

Anna, 1961

Leaving Aunt Mildred's was a well-planned secret managed by Preston. I sat listening intently as Eve related in a whisper, breathless and with excitement, her conversations with Preston. After learning Eve's story, Preston decided we must surprise Aunt Mildred and Uncle John with our departure. Preston concluded Uncle John wanted us in their home as long as possible. Eve and I were paying rent, which meant we were a paycheck Uncle John could take down the street to the bar to drink away. Something in me ached at the thought this was our reality, the notion we were being used.

"But Aunt Mildred loves us, Eve."

"She does, but as Preston says, we have no future with them. We need to get out of there and have our own life. A life on our own terms."

The morning we announced our departure reminded me of the moment I told Mrs. Harting I wanted to leave the Home. Pride and fear tingled my skin as the minute hand on the clock ticked by. As we packed the few belongings remaining in our room after sneaking our items out the weeks before, we smiled at each other, proud of ourselves for keeping the secret.

"When is he coming again?" I asked Eve several times as we shifted from one place to another.

"Hush, Sis. Just act normal, please!"

Aunt Mildred cooked breakfast downstairs, the familiar smell of eggs and coffee in the air. I heard the melody of the chickens clucking in the backyard and realized they were the one thing—other than Aunt Mildred—I would miss about the house. My stomach rumbled, and nausea sunk in as I thought about hurting our sweet aunt. Eve watched as my emotions danced around the room.

"Anna, don't you dare cry now. We need to do this," Eve said.

"I know, it's just…never mind."

"Just remember, all we have is each other. We need to stick together."

"Yes, I just hate hurting people. We've been hurt so much; why do it to others?"

Eve paused and looked at me for a long time. I didn't recall her ever looking at me this way. It was a look of love and sadness.

"You know something, Anna? Avoiding hurt left our lives a long time ago. Maybe it's time we stop hurting ourselves and start doing something with our lives, whatever it is."

As the clock indicated nine a.m., we went downstairs. We found Aunt Mildred wiping down the kitchen counter, listening to one of her favorite radio shows. She was mumbling something to herself. Taking a seat at the table, I recalled how many events in my life centered around sitting down and hearing my fate. I was nineteen years old, and for the first time, we were the ones telling someone what was going to happen to us.

"We are moving to the Coles House today, Aunt Mildred," Eve's voice came out firm. Aunt Mildred took the towel she used to wipe the counter and sat down. "The Coles House, dear? What on earth is that?"

"It's a boarding home. A place for us to live while we work and get our lives together."

Aunt Mildred's shoulders slumped, and her hands went to her head. "I'm sorry, dear. What are you saying? This is all too sudden. Who said this was the right thing for you?"

"It's right for us. Mr. Wilks, my boss, has arranged for our rooms there. He has also arranged for Howard to enter the Navy when he leaves the Home in a few months."

Aunt Mildred started to cry.

"I can't…I can't let you do this. You need to be with your family. I am your father's sister, and you should be with me. You were ripped from us years ago. You can't be again."

"Ripped from you?" Eve's voice began to tremble. "We were thrown in a Home when Mommy died, and Daddy couldn't care for us. None of you wanted us."

"We did; we did," Aunt Mildred matched Eve's passion. "It's just…they wouldn't give you to us."

"No! You wanted to separate us. It was Daddy's wish we stay together. We have no hope here." I stared at my sister in awe of her bravery and composure.

I heard Uncle John rustling in the other room. Through the narrow doorway, I saw his stump rest on the arm of his chair as he clumsily rose to make his way toward us.

"What the hell is going on here? How you dare raise your voice to your aunt." Uncle John never showed much regard for Aunt Mildred's feelings, so his defending her was a surprise.

"John, please keep your voice down. The girls are just telling me about some plans they are considering."

"What plans? How can these unmarried, wayward girls have plans?" he shouted. "These…these *nobody* girls have no future without our help."

His words stung. Over the months, I sensed his true feelings about our presence. He rarely said our names and growled at us as we walked in and out of the house. When he did speak to us, it was to tell us to do something or to berate us for not cleaning up properly.

"We're moving to a young women's boarding home," I said out loud, alarming myself with the sound of my voice in such an uneasy moment.

The tension broke with the sound of the doorbell. Peering through the white curtains, I could see a long, black town car parked in front of the house. The black exterior and shiny chrome weren't the type of car you would find in the neighborhood. I watched as a couple passing by turned their heads to observe the mysterious automobile.

As Uncle John stood tall in the doorway, trying to intimidate us, I looked out the window in awe. The hero we'd been raised to seek and find in our lives had arrived. The man was here for Eve, but he was taking me, too. He looked like someone from a movie.

Eve brushed past Uncle John and opened the front door.

"Preston," she said. Her voice soft and ladylike.

I fell out of my chair trying to get a view of him from the kitchen.

Through the front door walked an older man dressed in a suit. His hair dark with flecks of silver. He was handsome and had a confident grin. Holding Eve's hand, he looked at her for what seemed like an eternity.

Then, his eyes did a quick tour around the room, taking everything in. His facial expression didn't change. He turned to Uncle John, who moved a few steps closer and quickly put his stump to his side and cleared his throat. Aunt Mildred stood up from the table, fluffing her unruly hair.

"You must be Mr. Jones." Preston's tailored sleeve reached in the direction of Uncle John.

Realizing he was reaching for the wrong arm, he switched hands. Uncle John awkwardly moved his other hand to meet Preston's.

"And you, you must be Aunt Mildred. I'm Mr. Preston Wilks. Eva works for me and has for some time. A lovely young woman she is."

He turned to me, and I lost my breath. If power had a look, it looked like him.

"And you must be Anna," he took my right hand, letting his other hand cup it entirely. I realized I had never been touched by such a distinguished man. I quickly dropped my arm holding his.

I listened as the three adults made small talk. Preston was charming, and I could see why Eve fell for him. His presence was captivating if not intimidating. After a few minutes of awkward conversation, Uncle John asked, "Why are you here?"

"I'm taking Eve and Anna to the Coles House in Philadelphia. A home for young, single, working women. It is safe and next to Eve's office. Anna will have a new job at a bank located nearby as well."

Eve had yet to tell me about a new job, but anything would be better than the Five and Dime. I hated the job and wouldn't protest. As the scene unfolded in the cramped living room, I felt as if I were watching a movie. In all my dreams when I was young, I never dreamed this.

Uncle John's voice rose in a fury, "You are *not* taking these girls out of this home. We are their family. This is my house."

Preston smiled and straightened the cuffs of his suit jacket. He remained silent.

Uncle John's face turned the color of a tomato with spit threatening to shoot out of the corners of his mouth. He reminded me of a dog barking at a passerby who was ignoring it. The more silent Preston was, the louder Uncle John became.

Finally, after several minutes of Uncle John's ranting, Preston spoke.

"Sir, I am Preston Wilks. I run a law firm in downtown Philadelphia. I'm getting all of the Rangnow children on a path to success, and the first step will be taking these girls with me today. Ladies, please grab your things and say your goodbyes."

Aunt Mildred fell into a chair and began crying hysterically.

"Should I expect you will want to marry Eve? Do you think you will marry her without my permission?" Aunt Mildred's voice sounded desperate.

"With all due respect, ma'am, yes, I plan on marrying Eve, and I will be asking the person who raised her for her hand. That is not you. Eve and Anna will no longer be living here and paying you rent. I will be covering their living costs. They will have their own lives now."

My ears were on fire—Eve was getting married. The one thing all of us girls were raised to want out of life was happening to her right before my eyes. I registered an overwhelming pang of joy and pain; joy being included in this adventure—and pain knowing nothing like this would have happened if it weren't for Eve.

After a few more minutes of arguing, Aunt Mildred and Uncle John were silenced by Preston's overwhelming confidence.

"Good day to you both," Preston said as he walked to the front door. Eve motioned to me, and we ran upstairs to retrieve the single bag holding the remainder of our belongings. As we ran down the stairs to escape, I stopped in shock at the scene unfolding.

"Girls, what about all of your things?" Aunt Mildred said, confused by how little was left to carry out the door.

"It's all gone, Auntie. We've been moving out for a few weeks now," Eve said.

The deception made Aunt Mildred wail even louder. She was crying so hard it made Uncle John, totally out of character, move to her side with concern.

We raced out the front door past Preston, who stood there like a guard overseeing our departure. Outside next to the town car, a man in a suit held the door open. Eve got in, and I followed. I looked to Eve, who sat poised but breathless.

"Eve, you've been in this car before?" I could think of nothing else to say.

"Yes, shhh, many times." I now understood Eve was hiding many things from me. The realization hurt as I recalled the times we sat in our room discussing nothing at all; she could have said something then. I closed my eyes and asked forgiveness for what we had just done to hurt our family.

Just follow her lead, as you always have, I thought. A moment later the door opened on the passenger side, and Preston got in next to the driver. He turned to Eve, gave her a loving smile, and then looked at me.

"Young ladies, you will never live in a place like that again. Your future is much brighter than this. I will see to it."

As the car slowly rolled away from the curb and down the street, I felt like an imposter, as if I didn't belong.

If Preston was going to marry Eve, what was going to happen to me?

It took several weeks for me to realize why Eve told me so little ahead of this moment. Why she instructed me to pack my bags and store things at work and only mentioned we were moving to the Coles House. With Preston at the helm, things were happening to her moment by moment as well. If she had told me about his shifting the course of our destiny with his presence—his command of all things and people—I wouldn't have believed her, and I wouldn't have kept it a secret.

As we rode in the black car smelling of leather and breath mints, I pondered what would come next; what was transpiring seemed full of hope and promise. But deep down, a familiar pang of uncertainty filled my belly with worry. Linking my life to Eve's would save me. The knight came for her and saved me along the way. A twisted type of hope, but the only one I knew.

The Coles House was a row house on 9th and Lincoln in downtown Philadelphia. The boarding home was founded by Mary Coles "to provide working women with a safe, comfortable home for a reasonable board… and to protect them from the various temptations of a large city." The tall brick row house was four stories high. There were three bedrooms on each floor and a single bathroom to share. On the lower level, the main floor, contained a kitchen, dining room, and living room with two bedrooms tucked in the back.

Eve and I moved into the bedrooms on the ground floor, typically saved for new arrivals. I wasn't eager to share my space with other single girls, but I enjoyed the options the bustling city of Philadelphia gave me. The community living at the Coles House felt different from the Home; we were free to leave the confine of the walls. We were among strangers again but working toward something: financial freedom and the hope of marriage.

After a few weeks in the Coles House, I would finish my job at the Five and Dime before starting to work at the Franklin Mint. The Mint, as people called it, was a popular and busy downtown bank requiring more professional attire. Preston provided me money to update my wardrobe, but for some reason, his gesture didn't feel like the "clothing ladies" from the Home because he was slowly becoming a member of our family. As his generosity spilled over, I couldn't help but ask Eve more about Preston.

"Is Preston wealthy, Eve?"

"It appears so. I haven't been to his penthouse yet, but he has one off Rittenhouse Square."

"Remind me, what's a penthouse?"

She giggled and explained to me he lived on the top floor of a building which meant his flat was one of the nicest in the building.

"I wonder what it's like to have a lot of money, to not worry about the next day," I asked. She shrugged her shoulders in response.

"I guess it feels a lot like having something we've never had, to make your own rules," she replied.

With Preston at the helm of our lives now, we were keeping our brothers informed of our transition into the real world. They listened intently as they realized there existed a plan for all of us. Henry and I remained pen pals after I moved. After months of waiting, he and Howard visited me at the Five and Dime on my last day of work. Seeing Henry walk through the door, I thought I knew him intimately, as we shared so many personal stories in our letters. He had sent me a school photo I kept in my wallet. At times, alone in my room, I would stare at the picture of his handsome face with its sly grin and big brown eyes. As he walked toward me, my heart raced so rapidly, I thought I might faint.

Seating themselves at my counter, Henry and Howard said they wanted free ice cream. "Come on, Toots," Howard said with his impish grin. "It's your last day; it's not like they're gonna fire you."

Howard was incredibly handsome, and even as his sister, it was tough to resist his charm. Girls swooned over him even though he mostly ignored the attention, which made them chase him even more.

Shaking with nerves, I decided to break the rules. I scooped up two servings of ice cream and handed it to them at no charge.

Between bites, Howard started talking about his upcoming move from the Home to the Navy, about which Preston insisted on telling Eve, "Howard can learn a great deal in the Navy. It's important to serve and see the world if he ever wants to succeed in business."

Howard reminded me of Daddy when sharing his ambitions. I could see a man who was hard-working and determined to find a way of making it in the world. It was how I remembered Daddy, purposeful and ambitious.

"When you talk like that it makes me miss Daddy," I said.

Howard looked down at the counter for a minute. "You know, Sis, I don't remember them. I know you and Eve do, but I don't. All I have are two small pictures of them. Not sure which is worse, to have no memory of them or to remember what they were like before losing them."

I often wondered the same thing. Was it better to have fleeting memories of our parents before they died? Or was it better to be like my brothers who didn't have a single memory of Mommy and Daddy? They were just people in photographs. They didn't remember their faces, their touch, or their tone of voice. I barely did, too.

The boys finished their free ice cream. I noticed Henry watching me as I cleaned up the counter. My body twitched in different directions from nerves. As the smell of the dirty rag clung to my hands, I became grateful I wouldn't have to serve people at the Five and Dime another day.

Howard got up to go to the restroom and gave Henry a knowing pat on his arm. "Anna," I jumped as Henry called out my name. "I'd like to take you out on a date later tonight. Are you free?"

I turned and stared in his direction, blinking.

"Do I hear a 'no'?" A flirtatious smile took over his face.

"Yes. No. I mean, yes, but not tonight."

I stood frozen like the barrels of ice cream in the freezer below me. I was thankful cool air made its way up to my face.

Howard came back, smiled, and kissed my cheek. He handed me twenty-five cents. Henry grabbed my hand and kissed it. "I'll call you for the date you promised."

Floating through the remaining two hours of my shift, I didn't remember saying goodbye to my co-workers when I left the job for good.

I burst through the emerald-green front door of the Coles House, giving a quick hello to two girls sitting in the living room, and rushed to Eve's open bedroom door. I found her standing in front of her mirror, dressed in an elegant evening gown. Suddenly, I remembered it was the night she was taking Preston to the Harting's house at the Home. "Eve, you look stunning. Are you nervous?"

"Of course. Can you believe it? Me, married? Such a relief in so many ways. But I can't get my hopes up. You never know what could happen."

"He wants to meet the Hartings; what else can it mean? Why else would he want to visit that awful place?"

The thought of Preston walking the grounds of the Home made me nervous for Eve and the prospect of marriage. What would he think? Perhaps he wanted to understand, like most lawyers, the facts of the case. I thought of Eve having dinner in a beautiful dress, with impeccable manners, waiting for her hand to be adorned with a ring. I could only imagine the relief that would bring.

The fairy tale was coming true for her. After she left, alone in my room to ponder the recent turn of events, I wondered if Henry was my fairy tale.

In the evening, nearly asleep, I heard the familiar jingle of the bell above the front door. Leaping from my bed, I let my head veer into the hallway and summoned Eve to my room. Her white dress and gloves glided down the hallway like an angel floating on a cloud. In the faint light I could see her radiant smile.

"Oh Anna, he asked for my hand." She leaned in and hugged me.

"How wonderful, Eve. Dare I ask, how is that place? Mrs. Harting?"

"Housemother Florence cooked the dinner and served us. She's still her sweet and timid self. Mr. Harting asked me to call him Dave now and took me out to look at the flowers we planted in the garden. Everything is so well-grown and beautiful now. When we returned to their house, Mrs. Harting and Preston were deep in conversation. They invited us to sit down. I was so nervous my knees were shaking. Mrs. Harting asked Preston, 'Why Eve'? Right in front of me. She is so bold at times, so pushy."

"Then he said, 'I never knew a girl like Eve existed. I love her and want to marry her.' He didn't take his eyes off Mrs. Harting."

"Did he give you a ring?"

She removed her white gloves. "No, no ring tonight. Preston told me to go to the jewelry store this week and buy one for myself. He said I should get a one-carat diamond."

"You're going to buy a ring by yourself? Without him?"

She threw her gloves on the bed with a mad thrust "Yes, he asked me to go get the ring by myself. To pick out what I want."

I could see a hint of pain on her face. I decided I wouldn't ask any more questions. It was Eve's moment to savor.

"I'll go with you to the store if you want." She smiled and nodded.

"You might not be the only one getting married soon!" She shot me a confused look.

"Henry came into the Five and Dime today for my last day of work, with Howard. They wanted free ice cream, of course. Then, Henry asked me on a date. We're going out next week. I need your help; I have no idea what to do."

"Oh, what a relief." A stab of regret hit my ribs knowing she'd been fretting over my future. "I hate the idea of you being here alone after I marry Preston. You're going to need to borrow one of my dresses and to do your hair. It's been rather frizzy lately."

I sensed our lives were moving in the right direction. Eve was about to be married, and I was going on a date with a man I admired. We were chasing hope in every corner of our lives.

CHAPTER TWENTY-ONE

THE WEDDING
Jennifer, 2001

L iving with my sister was like holding a mirror to my innermost emotions and seeing my reflection through different eyes. There were six years between us, but it was more than this reality. While we were both searching for the same thing, a place to call home, we were coming from opposing perspectives. We had lived contrasting childhoods, been raised by different mothers, and held differing views of our father. To her, he moved across the country with his new wife and young daughter when she was ten. She loved and admired him for his steadfastness. For me, the narrative seared into my brain during my teenage years was that the separateness in my family was my father's fault.

After a few weeks of playing with her little sister in our newly chosen city, Linda announced, "Okay, enough of just us hanging in the apartment. I want to meet people. Let's go out." My friend group lived for happy hours and dancing until the sun came up. My sister, at thirty and more level-headed than me, wanted something more substantial.

"After our interviews, we are going downtown to happy hour in the Financial District," she said.

Dressed in our suits, hers a shade of blue, mine the typical black, we grabbed bar stools at Harringtons and waited for the Friday rush. I called my rowdy friends to join since I was there for the fun, not the men.

Noting my sister missing, we found her huddled in a corner of the bar, talking to a guy wearing jeans with a threaded leather belt and glasses. "Who is your sister talking to?" my friend nudged me with his elbow as if I needed to rescue her.

I attempted to save my sister by walking over and giving the boy a proper up and down, "You okay, Lin?"

She nodded and gave me one of her big sister smiles. I didn't acknowledge the man standing beside her except to give my disapproving up and down glance and walk away.

"What was that?" he asked her after my stare down.

"That was my little sister. We have different taste in men."

The truth was a version of Linda's observation. It wasn't only we had different taste in men; it was something more complex. As much as I wanted to experience being in love and a healthy relationship, I didn't want the pain that came along with it.

Like all the years growing up, as sisters, we assimilated to one another quickly even though we were different. Eventually, Linda found a job in accounting, and I landed a technology sales role. After months of interviewing and several offers, I decided to pursue a career with a large upside—tech sales. It helped when a friend said, "Jen, there is no limit on what you can make; that is up to you."

After three months of sharing a queen bed in my cramped studio apartment, my sister and I moved into a newly remodeled two-bedroom flat. As the months went by, she fell in love with the boy from the bar, and she tuned into my emotional state. Throughout life, she had only seen me in spurts—short visits to the West Coast—but now, she had all of me.

In time, she formed an opinion centered around my fractured relationship with my father. After years of not speaking, he began to send me birthday and holiday cards again. An envelope would arrive with his neat engineering handwriting wishing me a "Happy Birthday" or a "Merry Christmas." To open a card and see his name caused my heart to flicker in a mix of fear and a hint of love. Excited to be hearing from my father again, I didn't know what it would mean for my life, if anything.

One evening, while sharing a bottle of wine, Linda spoke freely about her observations.

"I can see you're hurting from it all. Dad loves you, Jen. He is doing the best he can given the situation. He has always loved you."

I heard the word "situation" pausing my emotional wave for a moment. *Was my dad suffering something then, too?*

"Lin, he was awful to live with. Tormented."

"He stayed to be there for you. It takes two to make a marriage fail. It wasn't all on him."

Her words stung my ears. What did she know about my experience, I wondered. What did my sister know about what it was like then? No one asked me if I was okay when they knew my parents' marriage was failing. No one called to check in on me as a teenager when I started getting in trouble. In her frustration, my mother would tell me, "Your sisters think you have your head up your ass."

"You have no idea what it was like growing up in that home. Being with Dad—he was miserable. Just anger. Deep festering anger. He wouldn't leave. He wanted a new life, but then he refused to go. Letting his misery spill out everywhere. I fought with him, and my mother did nothing but stand at the fucking stove and make dinner for them to eat late in the evening."

The rage was back, like an old friend who got you in trouble whenever they were around.

"I kept it all inside. All of it. And it nearly killed me."

She came to rub my back, slowly, with kindness, taking me in as she did. It reminded me of when she consoled me about my college prospects; her hands soft and kind. What I remember most about our conversation is she listened and came over to touch me, attempting to open a piece of me closed for a long time.

Four days before my sister's wedding, two planes went into the Twin Towers. Everything about our world changed as we watched the silver towers crumble to the ground with thousands of souls in them. That day, my brother, living in New York at the time, emerged from the subway to see a tower on fire and a young man dressed in khakis, an outfit matching his own, jumping to his death. Jack ran for his life and didn't stop for miles. It would be hours before we heard his voice on the other end of the phone.

He had been the first to call my sister and say he couldn't make the wedding. Linda, having grown up on the East Coast, watched the attendee list diminish by half. Planes were grounded, and people were terrified. The crashing of the planes would play on the news for weeks leaving it imprinted in our consciousness forever.

The photographer, singer, friends, and family slowly called to say they couldn't get to California. Her fiancé's family lived in Rochester, NY. After the attack, they let twelve hours pass before renting a minivan to drive the six of them across the country to make the wedding on time. They showed up three days later. We would nickname them "The Little Family That Could."

My plan was to show up at her wedding a few days late. Before I arrived, our eldest sister Beth called me. She hid in a bedroom and spoke in a whisper. "Lin's in a bad place; she's heartbroken. Half the wedding party isn't coming; we need you to come cheer her up. Bring some of your energy."

Arriving at the house in Pebble Beach my father rented for the event, I found my sister sitting on the floor doing a crossword puzzle at the coffee table. One hand held her head as she stared blankly at the pieces in front of her. Her sorrow was palpable. I knelt down, wrapped my arms around her and hugged tightly.

"It's ruined. Everyone is calling and saying they can't make it."

"Look, the wedding is going to be smaller, but we can still have fun. We're not going to let these assholes win. Get up, a damn puzzle isn't going to make this better. You need a glass of wine. Me, too."

The wedding came together like the puzzle she gazed into several days before. My mother became a bridesmaid. A friend passionate about photography captured the weekend. Friends who could play instruments became the band. The party cut in half, our collective hearts were broken by what transpired in New York, but love and hope conquered that complicated weekend.

The man I was dating accepted my invitation to the wedding. Having just met my date, my sister went to him and gave him a hug. "I heard you sing beautifully. Do you mind filling in for the wedding singer?" My date had a voice like Nat King Cole, and when he took to the microphone, my friends swooned.

"Where did you meet him?" they asked me.

"The airport."

It would be the first time my mother and father were in the same room since their divorce. My father brought his girlfriend of several years, Lily, while my mother arrived alone. As my mother stepped into the house, it was clear she went to great lengths to look her best. She appeared ten years younger and absolutely stunning.

"Jesus, Mom, you look great, what did you have done?"

"Oh, Jennifer, stop," she said taking in the backwards compliment.

Always a beautiful woman, the divorce took some of her lightness away, but that day, she floated in like a woman in her thirties. I knew she was tormented inside.

I greeted my father with a cordial hello, and we kept our distance, as he played the role of father of the bride. While we grew to a place where we spoke, collateral damage still existed and would take years to overcome. We were rebuilding our relationship brick-by-brick, but time was the cement.

My mother insisted I stay by her side during the reception. "With your brother unable to make it, please don't forget about me. This is hard for me, seeing your father again. And with *her*," she added venomously.

As the dancing and drinking took over, I became absorbed into the party with my friends, family, and new man. As the sun set over Monterey Bay, I saw my mother sitting beside Lily on the patio. Their body language and look on their faces set off alarm bells, so I ventured to another room. Not long after seeing them together, my mother tapped me on the shoulder, stress enveloping her face.

"I'm leaving," she said, marching to the driveway, and I followed her.

"Mom, please stay. Don't go yet."

"Oh please, Jenny. You left me at the party all by myself. This was a hard day for me, and you just went and hung out with your friends. Typical." She waved her hand in the air and rolled her eyes.

"It's my sister's wedding, Mom. I brought a date I'm excited about. Please, stop, come in and have fun."

"Oh, no. You go be with your friends, your father, and his girlfriend. The one who ruined my marriage," she sneered.

For a moment, I wanted to correct her, to remind her that the marriage was over long before Lily came on the scene. I wanted her to understand that being around him was still awkward for me, too. The divorce happened to all of us. But her eyes were wide and darting like a wild animal. She was a mix of angry, hysterical, and heartbroken.

"I asked her when they got together. Guess when, Jenny? Just guess. 1992!"

Nothing about the date concerned me. That was the year I graduated from high school, and it made perfect sense since it was clear my father had moved on years before. Didn't she remember the pictures of his trip to Australia?

"I asked her, 'Did you know I was an orphan?' She didn't seem to care."

"Oh, Mom, no. Please tell me you didn't say that. Being an orphan has nothing…"

"Enough. Go, go be with your friends. That's all you ever cared about." Her hand was waving wildly, her ever-present red nail polish flickering in the night. A taxi pulled up, and she got in and slammed the door without looking in my direction.

I reached in my purse and pulled out a cigarette, a habit that helped me cope over the years. I took a long inhale that burned my throat and washed down the tears that wanted to rise up and spill over. It broke my heart to see my mother in such pain again.

I stood under the white light in the dark, empty driveway for some time. I realized that not only had my mother showed up at the wedding, the little girl inside of her did, too.

The next morning, I called to check on her, my guilt darkening the joy of the night before, but she didn't answer.

Over time, and with separation from those I was closest to in my childhood, I began asking myself different questions.

My dark teenage years had been my father's fault, hadn't they? Wasn't he to blame for wanting to leave and trying to abandon my mother and me? It had become my story, but as the years went by, it was a narrative that seemed to have holes.

Living with my sister and watching her blossom into raising a family, I began to suspect what I believed to be true about my parents wasn't the whole story. My father hurt me with his words and coldness, but there was some truth to what my sister was saying, wasn't there? I was made to believe divorce, my parent's dissolution, was one person committing all the mistakes. Yet, separated from them, living in my own world, I began to sense life wasn't like that. I had grown up in a black-and-white point of view. Wrong and right. Good and Bad. Quiet and loud. Abandoned or present.

Yet, in front of me was my sister, living the definition of gray, waving her wand of introspection in my direction. I began to wonder if I examined and questioned my long-held beliefs about the people who raised me, would that reflection change how I saw myself? Was that where freedom lived?

PART THREE

RECKONING

CHAPTER TWENTY-TWO

LIFE STARTING

Anna, 1962

Once Eve had her one-carat diamond from Bailey Banks & Biddle on her finger, Preston began his process of molding Eve. She enrolled at Penn University, where she took history and literature courses. At dinner parties, he ensured she could express her comprehension of the classics while reciting passages and possessing intricate knowledge of the characters. She had a new wardrobe, and Preston placed well-appointed jewelry on her ears, neck, and wrists. In preparation for their European honeymoon, he created a summer reading list.

"Come with me to class, Sis, you'll love it. I'm loving the books most of all. Oh, and that Dickens, it's as if he was writing about us. That was our life."

After several months of shaping his masterpiece, Preston married Eve.

The first ceremony was at City Hall in the office of a close friend of the Wilks', a federal judge. The second celebration would be a large party at his mother's sprawling estate in the Main Line two weeks later, a nod to his mother's society friends.

We were getting ready in our cramped rooms in the Coles House. The girls who lived with us descended on Eve like a flock of birds with a flurry of questions that sounded like wings flapping. Where would she live? Was Preston wealthy? Would they "sleep together" that night? She answered the questions she wanted to with enthusiasm, sparkling under the attention. I sat to the side, watching as every girl envied her; Eve lived the dream we were told to want.

She slipped into a pearl white skirt suit and let me borrow one of her dresses adorned with large green flowers. With our hair curled and gloves on, we took a last look in the mirror before grabbing our purses and walking out to the waiting car Preston had sent.

As we sat in the black leather seats, the air conditioner blew cold air on my face.

"Anna, just thinking about being with someone. Married. It seems so unreal. And frightening."

"Is anyone ever ready?" I wondered aloud, while reaching to shut the vent that chilled my skin.

As we pulled up to City Hall, the building revealed itself as a castle would. Preston stood on the sidewalk looking demure in his black, perfectly tailored suit. As Eve exited the car, I watched his face swell with pride. I wondered if anyone would look at me in that way. My brothers stood to the side, looking awkward and uncomfortable in their rented tuxedos, cigarettes dangling out of their mouths.

Walking toward them, I pondered what I would do without them.

"Guys, ready to give her away?"

"Sure, Toots. You look nice," Howard said, stamping his cigarette on the dirty concrete.

Jim and John followed.

"If giving her away means getting out of this monkey suit, then yes," John said.

Eve approached with Preston, hugged my brothers, and I noticed her white glove was shaking.

"Where...where is Mommy Wilks?" she asked.

"Already inside speaking with Judge Wimmer. You'll love his office; it's the perfect setting. He's a supreme court justice, so it will be official."

The office reminded me of a gilded library. Mahogany bookshelves surrounded the judge's desk and stretched to the ceiling. It seemed there were thousands of books, their spines wrapped in various shades of leather and fabric. A chandelier hung in the middle of the room, with a maroon sofa and green chairs. I stood to the side, shifting my feet back and forth.

After the brief ceremony, we walked three blocks to Vesper, a private dining club where Preston was a member. The restaurant was bustling with beautiful men and women laughing, drinking, and smoking. Walking through the crowd to our table, I felt clumsy in my heels, my thin ankles wobbling.

My brothers sat frozen and wide-eyed at the revelry around them, their eyes locking on the beautiful women scattered throughout the room. After champagne toasts and a meal delicious and decadent, I didn't want it to end; Eve and Preston announced their departure.

Mommy Wilks became tearful as she toasted the couple one last time. "To love and marriage. I wish your father was here."

Preston nodded, the hint of a tear in his eye, which was surprising considering how stoic he was. He signed the bill that came in a small leather folder.

I swallowed hard, trying to stop the emotions that threatened to spill out of me. I wanted to hold on to Eve like a child watching my mother exit.

Eve rushed toward me and wrapped her arms around me. "This doesn't change anything. We are still sisters. Always." She kissed my cheek, her perfume remaining as she shuffled after her new husband. My rock was gone, and a piece of me went with her.

"I guess it's just the four of us now," John said as he reached into his pocket for another smoke.

"This fabric is killing me—worse than the altar boy gear?" Howard replied.

"I just wonder how much that meal was. It was so good. I wish I could have ordered two," Jim added, his fixation with food causing us to chuckle. He was known for his ability to eat three servings in one sitting, grunting happily as he did.

"One down, one to go." John leaned down and kissed my forehead.

"I'm not getting married. I just want to work," Howard said. "Two years in the Navy, and then we're starting a business, boys."

Walking home in a trance, I wondered what I would do about my future. Living in a boarding home for young girls wasn't where I wanted to be for long. I thought of Henry with mixed emotions: a tinge of doubt and a speckle of hope.

$\sim$

The grand party for Eve and Preston at his mother's house on the Main Line was announced in the form of elegant white paper invitations written in calligraphy. For Preston, City Hall was sufficient for the paperwork, but he wanted to reveal his masterpiece—Eve—during a lavish affair.

The event would be full of mysterious and charismatic people my brothers and I would be frightened to engage in conversation. We shied away from socializing except for a small group of friends. We never said it, but we all feared we had nothing meaningful to say to strangers.

Panic settled in before the party. I called Eve on several occasions to discuss the details of the event. She lived in the Penthouse with Preston but had moved to his mother's house for the week to prepare for the party. I called her at the number she had given me.

"Wilks' residence," I heard an unfamiliar voice say.

"Eve, please." The person told me to hold, and I listened to noises in the background for several minutes.

"Hello, Anna? I only have a few minutes." At the sound of her voice, I wanted to ask how she was, but I knew that would only irritate her.

"Two questions. What do I wear? And other than the boys, will I know anyone?" I heard her sigh on the other end.

"I can have someone bring several dresses for you to try on, okay? As for the party, yes, just you and the boys."

I saw myself standing in the corner of a crowded room, in Eve's dress, speaking to no one.

"Sis, anything else?" she said in a breathless voice.

"Could I invite someone to come with me?"

"Like a date? Of course. Will it be Henry? Any other prospects these days?" I heard her hand go over the phone as she whispered something to someone. I hesitated.

"No one else."

"Well, then don't be shy. Call him. Stop hesitating! Love you." The line clicked.

Henry and I had started going on dates nearly once a week and talking at night on the phone. He had left the Home at the same time as Howard and was working as a mechanic. After a drink or two, the conversation would focus on his parents, how his mother and father drank too much and eventually turned their children over to the state. His little brother was adopted, leaving Henry alone at the orphanage.

"Do you want a family one day?" I asked him.

"I suppose one day, maybe," he replied. "But those aren't great memories for me."

"I absolutely do. I would like to have what I lost," I said.

I liked the way he smelled, masculine and strong. A mix of soap, grease, and after-shave. As he opened the car door, I sat down slowly, certain to grab my skirt and adjust it like a lady.

We kissed on our fourth date. It was a simple kiss on the lips. Smack. I didn't know if I was doing it right or if I should have kept my lips on his longer. There were more kisses, and I let my mouth linger longer. Counting the seconds in my head, I was proud as the numbers climbed but relieved when our lips parted. After each date, I would return to my room and fall on my bed, emotionally exhausted.

One night, my voice nearly breaking, I heard myself ask him, "Would you like to go to Eve's wedding party in the Main Line?"

"Of course; I thought you'd never ask. Are we staying somewhere?"

His question stopped my heart. The Main Line wasn't far from downtown, so was he asking if we would stay in a room together?

"It's just—Anna, I don't like drinking and driving, and I know I'm going to celebrate with you," he said.

"Let me call you back." I wondered where we would stay. I was unprepared to be with a man alone in a hotel room. I wrestled with the voice in my head for several minutes. I was reminded how unprepared I was for being with a man, but how a gentleman was essential for my survival—for the life I wanted.

After calling Henry back to tell him I would get us a room, it took several minutes before my hands stopped shaking.

A few days later, the girls and I watched through the curtains as he approached our door. He was handsome in a rugged sort of way. Messy brown hair, pale skin, and big brown eyes. His smile was more like a smirk.

At the sound of the doorbell, I straightened my skirt and opened the door. He kissed my cheek and said, "You're beautiful."

We barely spoke on the hour long drive. Henry kept one hand on my leg as he steered with the other. He turned up the radio and started singing; I mouthed the words to the song, missing every other word. We pulled up to a brick inn, its exterior wrapped in ivy. Plastic candles flamed in the pane windows, and the front had a bright red door.

This could be a fairy tale enough for me.

We made small talk until we reached the front desk. After a few minutes, the man behind the counter asked how many keys, and Henry replied without hesitation, "Just one, please."

Our cramped room had a large mahogany dresser and bed, and the furniture was decorated with doilies and small ceramic figurines.

After spending several minutes in the bathroom while I sat erect on the single chair in the room, Henry emerged in a suit.

"Good for the party? Borrowed it from a friend." He was wearing a bulky blue suit that was two sizes too big. "I'll be at the bar downstairs. Come when you're ready."

I spent the next hour putting curlers in my hair that I set with a noisy hair dryer. After applying makeup, I positioned my pantyhose and bra perfectly. Then, I slid Eve's dress on with a pair of new heels from Wanamaker's. Observing myself in the standing mirror tucked in the corner of the room, I turned to my right and left, observing myself from every angle, sucking in my already flat stomach as I did.

There, that's the best you can do.

I found Henry sitting in the bar, bellowing to the bartender. His voice was raised, and a boisterous laugh occurred every few seconds. I cleared my throat and called his name. He turned with a big smile on a face red from drinking and talking.

"Anna, you are gorgeous! I told you she was gorgeous, didn't I?" He motioned to the bartender.

He threw down cash and grabbed my elbow to walk me to the car.

"Excited for the party, Anna?"

"A little nervous, actually," I fretted with my skirt. "Do you think I'll wrinkle on the seat?"

He opened the car door to let me in. "It'll be okay, Anna. It's just a bunch of rich people. They won't notice us anyway."

Henry was right; we were just Eve's siblings from an orphanage.

On our drive, I witnessed the grandest houses I'd ever seen. Green lawns gracefully rolled to each home. Driveways wrapped around the front of the mansions like an elegant mink wraps around a woman's neck. Their beauty and size took my breath away. According to Eve, Preston's mother, Mommy Wilks, lived in a home that could "house a thousand orphans."

As we drove, I thought of the "clothing ladies" who bought me my outfits over the years. I was sure some of them lived in the homes we were passing. I let out a sigh, remembering I was free from ever having to shop with a complete stranger again.

Henry's voice broke my concentration.

"I was thinking. Looking at these stunning houses and all this money, I realize I won't have all this, but I will make it. Like your brother, Howard, I plan on being successful."

"Henry, look at that house. It's so big it resembles Rohrman Cottage. Does a family live there?"

"Anna, I'm trying to tell you something. I've been thinking. We know each other so well, and we come from the same place."

"Not exactly the same place," I raised my voice. How dare he think we were not wanted by our parents. "My Daddy died before he could get us. We were there for different reasons."

The air in the car shifted. Sometimes when people came too close, I liked to push them away.

"I'm sorry, Henry, I didn't mean that. All of this is a lot right now."

"I know, Anna. Don't let the money scare you."

"I don't. I just see everything these people have and wonder how any of it is even possible. Even a little bit of what they have."

"That is what I am saying to you. I was thinking. What if we got married?"

I turned to see his face. He was looking at me perplexed, full of worry and fear. "I love you, Anna."

"You...you love me?" I prayed to reach the house at that moment. "Should we talk about this later, Henry?"

We had pulled into a U-shaped driveway, and a man in a tuxedo reached for my door. There were a dozen valets in front of the beautiful brick home. I turned to Henry, put my hand on his, and smiled.

He came around the car and made his arm available. I looped mine in his and beamed as we walked through the front door. Realizing what Henry just said and what it meant to my life and entering the gorgeous doorway of a mansion made me dizzy. I was floating in, using Henry as my stability, when I saw Mommy Wilks smiling at me. Barely five feet tall, she had a plump face that always had a broad smile spread across it. She wore a well-appointed dress and a strand of thick pearls; her head adorned with a mound of perfectly shaped gray curls. I introduced her to Henry, who politely cradled her hand as he thanked her for having us.

"Anna, dear, could you do me a favor. Eve is needed soon, and we have been unable to get her out of her room. A case of nerves, I guess. Do you mind fetching her from upstairs for me? I know her dear sister will do the trick."

I turned to Henry, and he smiled. "On your way, Anna. I'll locate the bar."

Mrs. Wilks—someone of her stature—needed me. "Last door on your right," I heard her say. A waiter handed me a glass of champagne, and I tip-toed up the stairs. Naturally clumsy, I feared spilling my glass on the beige carpet, which was so thick each step left a mark.

Everything about the house looked ornate. Oversized paintings in gold frames lined the hallway. There was a series of endless white-painted entry-ways with gold trim. Coming to the end of the hallway, I knocked, nervously looking back to see if anyone would tell me to leave.

I knocked again and put my face on the door.

"Eve," I said, careful not to raise my voice. "It's your sister, Eve."

I heard rustling and the door swung open. As I entered, she walked away, her back toward me. I noticed she wore a beautiful robin's egg satin dress that matched the colors of the room. Even from behind, she looked like Grace Kelly from *High Society*.

I began talking like a typewriter going seventy words a minute.

"You won't believe what happened on the way over. Henry said he loves me and wants to marry me. Can you believe it? Me? Maybe we'll both be married this year. By the way, your party is huge and beautiful. And this house, Eve, is the size of Rohrman Cottage, even bigger."

I went to the other side of the room and found myself looking out on the backyard. There were dozens of tables and candles everywhere.

"This party is like a scene from an Audrey Hepburn movie."

I turned to see Eve sitting at her vanity and staring at herself in the mirror. She turned to look at me, and pain was carved in every corner of her face.

"Dear God, Eve, what is it?"

I watched as tears slowly rolled from her eyes down to her cheeks.

"Heavens, Eve, there are hundreds of people out there waiting for you. I came to get you."

I searched the room for a clue of what might be wrong. No clothes were flung across the room, indicating turmoil about her outfit. She looked radiant, but she also looked broken. I noticed a single twin bed.

"Is this your room?" She nodded. "Where does Preston sleep?"

"Down the hall. In a king bed."

"Have you been intimate with him yet?"

She nodded. "It's not real. He doesn't love me; he only wants to keep me."

"But the wedding? The party downstairs? It's all wonderful, no?"

"He came in here tonight and said how happy he was we're married. Something about being impressed by me and wanted the world to see my brilliance and beauty. Then he gave me this necklace," she ran her hand across a string of diamonds around her neck. My mouth fell open at its beauty: a thick gold band full of diamonds.

"Earrings to match. It's so incredibly beautiful; I cried when I opened it. Then I lift my hair for him to put it on, and do you want to know what Preston said?"

I became distracted by the glimmer of her engagement ring. The one she picked out of by herself, in my company, after he proposed. The light hitting the gorgeous stone created rainbows on the wallpaper. She was unhappy, and I couldn't understand why. The beautiful house, clothes, and jewelry. The lovely mother-in-law. The successful husband. She had it all, and now she was unhappy? Distaste rose in my throat. I had found a man in Henry, a mechanic, but knew I could never achieve something as glamorous as she had.

"Did Preston say, 'You're welcome'?" She threw her hairbrush onto the vanity.

"I'm sorry, what did he say? Please tell me."

"He put this necklace on me, and he said, 'It's so beautiful, I bought two more.'"

"For his mother and sister?"

"No, you nitwit. He bought them for other women! There are other women. He is a Svengali, and I am his Dickens bride like in *David Copperfield*."

I wanted to ask who Copperfield was, but I knew I upset her already.

"I'm a kept woman. This is my room to come out of when they're ready for me. I am perfectly poised, coiffed, and educated to bring to the party when the time is right. He wanted to mold me because he wants to own me. Poor little orphan girl Eve! I'm not going."

She threw her face powder at the wall, and it exploded like a bag of flour.

I saw her there, the sister I envied for so many years. Despite her revelation, I still envied her. The enormous, beautiful home, the lavish party, the attention. Someone thought she was worth it all; he wanted to give her his world. She felt sorry for herself while the beautiful diamonds hung around her neck. Having other women in his life sounded horrible, painful to accept, but what did we know about relationships? What did we know about love? We just knew how to survive.

Was I seeing pity in Eve? The one thing I couldn't and wouldn't accept from anyone.

I would never live in a home like the one I was standing in, wearing a dress like she was, or own a necklace so beautiful. For so many years, I had chosen to be the silent girl in the corner. The one no one noticed in the shadow of her sister. She had everything we were told to want, and she claimed unhappiness.

"You know, Eve, I'm sorry you're hurt. Look at your life. What did you expect? Perfection? He made an honest woman of you. He's taking care of you. Hell, he's taking care of all of us. He might be flawed, but I'm thankful he is in our lives. You should be, too."

Her face distorted, and she looked at me as if to say, *Is that you?*

"And what's more, I would give anything to be in your position. Having someone invest in me and want me to see the world. I'm happy Henry wants to be with me. It's a relief in many regards. But trust me, I know there is more to life than a simple guy from the Home with a drinking problem. But what am I going to do about that? It's me. It's what I can get in this world. Let's be real here, the Home never promised us much. If we didn't marry, then we would end up like the housemothers who raised us. Can you imagine? And look at you, you exceeded everything they told us was possible. I'm fairly certain there's a price for such greatness."

She continued to stare at me with wonder and shock. I had never been so firm with her. Never in my life had I been this tough with anyone. I liked the taste of the frustration pouring out of me. It was a compilation of all those years, lonely in the Home, surrounded by random girls. I knew Henry would be my husband, and I would live a simple life, nothing that looked like the opulence Eve had married into. I saw Eve in her royal chair, and she wanted my condolences. I wasn't going to ask anyone for pity, and I certainly wasn't going to let my sister beckon it from me.

"No, Eve. Get up and walk downstairs to your husband," I said and turned to the window where voices, music, and the clink of glasses filtered in through the pane.

Then, very slowly, Eve began to smile.

"Love looks good on you, Anna. It makes you spunky." She paused looking at her reflection in the mirror. She looked around the room. After a few minutes, she wiped her eyes. "I need to touch up my makeup. Would you mind brushing my hair for me?"

I stood behind her and made small brushes against her hair as she dabbed her face and reapplied her mascara. Two sisters, putting her back together in silence as guests clinked glasses and ate appetizers delivered on silver trays.

Whatever realization Eve came to that night, whether it was about what I said or not, she accepted the life she married into. Perhaps she recognized

Preston was saving all of us by ensuring our lives were going in the right direction. He wasn't just caring for Eve, but taking care of all of us. Putting me in the right living situation and job, sending Howard to the Navy, and eventually giving all the boys money to start their fencing business.

I followed Eve as she descended the staircase to wondrous applause. It was a room of gorgeous people, and they wanted her. She turned to me and mouthed "thank you" before being immersed in their embrace.

Shortly after Eve's entrance, I left with Henry. I waited until we got to the inn and were seated at the bar for a nightcap to address the comments he made in the car. I thought a lot about his proposal and came to a conclusion. First, I would tell him that, yes, I liked the idea of getting married. Then, to avoid confusion, I would remind him I was saving myself for marriage.

"Henry," I said, "I've been thinking about what you said, and I think marriage sounds lovely. First, though, I want you to know that I am not that kind of girl. Tonight," I took a sip of my drink, "I'm not prepared…" I couldn't bring myself to say it.

"I understand, Anna. I know where you come from. It just means we need to be married sooner rather than later. You are much too beautiful to wait long for."

As soon as we were in the room, he lay on the bed, fully clothed, and fell asleep. I wasn't sure if it was his snoring, or the fact we had just agreed to marry, but I didn't sleep one minute that night. I watched the moon rise and fall. As the sun crept over the hillside visible out our window, I wondered if Eve slept alone that night. And if, in some way, she was okay with that.

Against all odds, we both found men to marry. But despite that, we would remain isolated, no matter our circumstances. For us, companionship was terrifying, and we would always keep a safe distance from the people closest to us. Even the ones we married. Because to get too close to someone would reveal what lived in us, an inescapable sorrow for which there was no cure.

CHAPTER TWENTY-THREE

RUNNING

Jennifer, 2002

"Mom, you should go to therapy. You've been through a lot in life; it would help to talk about your experience."

There were a few sessions by herself, even one with my father, before her relationship with the therapist, Anne, ended. One day, she returned from her appointment and tossed her oversized purse on the kitchen counter in frustration. "What's the matter, Mom?"

"Therapy. It's ridiculous. I don't know how going there and talking about all the bad things that happened are going to help. Why would I want to do that? I know what I lived through. Plus, all the therapist did was tell me to go read a book. I'm not paying someone to tell me to read a damn book."

The recommendation, *The Women Who Run with the Wolves*, would stay half-read and deserted by the side of my mother's toilet. She refused to see herself in the female archetypes.

It wasn't the only time I witnessed my mother bristle when a person wanted to reach her pain points. When asked what she felt losing her parents so young, she would shake her head and change the subject. There were times she seemed downright angry at curiosity directed at her childhood.

"I don't want pity, that's for sure. At the Home, they told us to forget about what happened to us. They would say, 'It's in the past. Move on.' So, I just kept moving, and that's what I've done. It's worked for me."

She did not want light in her wounds.

As I built a single life in my twenties, I sensed I needed help working through what I carried. I knew several things to be true: I mistreated my body. I struggled to care for myself, food being an easy weapon to express my dislike. I carried a nagging feeling of not being good enough, of wanting love in peculiar, barren places. The other cross to bear was the absence of truth; dishonesty was a central theme in my youth. Truth lived behind closed doors I wanted open.

My eldest sister, Beth, went to therapy for years, and I witnessed how introspection influenced her; where before there existed angst, in its place was a sense of calm. She held a personal wisdom I gravitated towards.

I needed help; there were my sisters' inferences. But most of all, it was the nagging desire to constantly punish myself for being me—people noticed.

On a monthly visit to the hair salon, an outrageous expense I never shied away from, no matter how broke, the flamboyant owner asked me to be in his ad campaign. Flattered, I blushed at his insistence. "Honey, I've never understood why you have always thought so little of yourself. You belong."

Leave it to the sassy, gay San Francisco man to call you out on your shit.

I was accustomed to calling my mother when I needed an emotional lifeline. My calls she happily took, her ears eager to take me in. Even as I tired of my merry-go-round complaints, she always said it was her pleasure, "I like feeling needed."

"Mom, I need to go to therapy to sort through some things. Do you have your lady's number? The one you visited a few times. Maybe she knows someone in California."

Separation improved our relationship. We talked frequently, and she came for visits, happy to retreat from The City after spending a few days with me. Yet, she knew, during my calls, I carried a sadness with me, one I couldn't shake.

"Oh, Anne? Yes, I can get her information for you. You okay, Jen?"

"I need to talk to someone."

"I will call her, but well, just be careful. Those therapists like to burn hours and your money." She paused for a moment; I could feel the tension in her body release on an exhale. "I can help you a bit, financially, too, if you need it."

A day later, I hit the flashing red button on my answering machine and heard Anne's voice, "Jennifer, it's Anne. Susan is who I recommend; she's wonderful. I met her at a conference a few years ago. I hope you're doing well with your new life in San Francisco."

As I wrote down the woman's number, I thought, *I'm well. And I'm not.*

Susan was a tall giraffe of a woman with unruly gray hair collected at the top of her head. Her office was in Hayes Valley, one of my favorite neighborhoods. Weekly therapy became a date night for one. After finding a spot and performing world-class parallel parking, I would sit in a cafe next to her office and journal until my appointment.

If there existed a word to describe Susan, it was consistent. She welcomed me into her office the same way every time. Her hand gestured for me to sit on her worn, discolored sofa as she flopped into the chair across from me. Crossing her legs and resting her hands on her knees, she would smile and take me in. For a while, not a sound left our mouths. Then, after an awkward silence, I heard her voice say, "So, how are you?"

The question annoyed me. Tremendously.

I didn't know how to do therapy, so I would stare through the gaps between her blinds to the light shining in the vestibule. I searched for my thoughts in that space where window faced window. A few recurring themes would float to the top; my job I was grateful for but with a strange boss I tried to avoid, my long-term, very on-off dating relationship with the Wedding Singer and his ambiguous ways, and friendships. Mostly I ruminated on the boyfriend who didn't like commitments. Susan and I did this conversation dance for a while.

After a few visits, the air became stale with the same topics. It was time to admit something I carried with me that brought considerable pain.

"I have a horrible relationship with food. I have for a long time."

She nodded for me to go on.

"After starving myself in my senior year of high school, I was down to 110 pounds, maybe less. I was ecstatic. I barely ate, so when I finally started eating again, food stuck to me like glue. I panicked and purged. There was a sort of relief after doing it. A confirmation. It wasn't all the time, but it came in waves and would take over at times. It was its worst in my parents' house before I left for college—when life felt confining. Inescapable. I'm afraid of going back there. I feel like I am progressing, but sometimes it calls me back. I don't want to hurt myself anymore."

She kept nodding.

"I look in the mirror, and I don't like what I see. The truth is, I want to like myself, feel good about myself, but I don't know how to do that."

"What was happening in your life when it started?"

I read enough self-help books to know what she wanted—the shame. The teenage accident, the parents. I gave them to her. Each one of them.

"I just want to feel *enough*. I never felt enough."

"You deserve that, and you deserve for the people who love you to make you feel good. That's how healthy relationships work."

It sounded annoyingly easy, but I knew it wasn't. I began to sense that wasn't the legacy I was born into.

"How can you do something good for you?"

"I've started running. It seems to slow that negative voice in my head."

"Then keep running," she said while nodding and smiling her approval.

It seemed so simple. Could running really be the thing that ended the vicious cycle?

After about a dozen sessions, I became frustrated with Susan's therapy style, which was reserved and relaxed. I wanted her to poke and prod me more, to dig deeper. To turn me inside out. Not only was I losing patience with her, I was losing patience with myself. Each session, it felt like I was saying the same thing.

"Susan, I need you to push me more. I need more of a breakthrough."

At the next meeting, we did our familiar welcome dance. Only this time, she leaned over and handed me a copy of *More* magazine with a heavyset woman on the cover. I looked at the glossy front page and immediately turned it face down on the cushion beside me.

Our banal conversation continued until she intervened.

"Why did you turn over the magazine, Jennifer?"

"I don't know; something about it makes me uncomfortable."

"Why?" she asked.

"I don't want to look at it for some reason."

"Do you think it says something about you?"

"That photo is how I feel. Too much and not enough. God, I sound like a basket case."

"You don't."

"I feel so wrong sometimes. I feel like I can't escape it. My body can make me feel flawed as if it's the reason I can't be loved properly. If I was perfect—"

"Then what?"

"Then none of this would have happened."

"What's *this*?" she asked.

"If I'd been perfect, then my parent's marriage wouldn't have failed; I would have a better relationship with my dad. I would accept love from nice people, not assholes."

"Nobody is perfect, but I can assure you that you weren't the problem in your parent's marriage."

I found myself angry about the magazine now.

"During high school, I couldn't do anything right. My father wanted to leave, and I wanted him to go. But he stayed, and he was awful to be around. I rebelled, pissed my parents off as much as I could, and still they did nothing but sit at the table drinking and having dinner, pretending their marriage wasn't over. I knew what was happening with my father, but my mother refused to do anything. Even when he brought pictures home, and it was clear he was with someone else."

As a child, I would hyperventilate, and in this moment, it took me several deep breaths to catch air.

"Even worse, she wanted me to hate him with her. And I did. What mother wants their child to hate their father? No matter how bad the marriage."

She nodded as if to say, "Go on."

"My God, I weighed almost a hundred pounds at one point, and nothing—I mean *nothing*—was done. As I disappeared, I received positive feedback about how I looked. Something was finally right about me. I was thin—the elusive prize in my hands. I was told I was doing something right, but I was breaking down inside, and they couldn't see me standing before them. Always a good student, when my grades dropped, they said nothing. I mean nothing. I wanted to do sports, play for the symphony, every inch of my desires was snuffed out. In the end, it felt like if I disappeared, then they would be happier. One less issue for them to ignore."

"Do you want to disappear now?"

"At times."

"What does it feel like?"

That familiar rage rose. Wasn't she the one who would make the connection to my childhood and where I was now? I was nearly glaring at her. I held my lips together tightly, resisting her question until I felt the release.

"How does it feel? If the adults owned their shit, I wouldn't have to carry it. I fought for my mom because she was utterly frozen."

"What was it like in your home back then? Describe it."

I closed my eyes for a moment and remembered my house. The front door with a sailing ship engraved on the face. The decks my father built. The piano in the corner of the living room. The small kitchen with a sliding door and a round table shoved against the wall under the window. The table with its two chairs always present, the third tucked in the corner of the room that held books and newspapers meant to be read someday. My father's brown swivel chair in the living room near the fireplace where secrets were revealed.

"It was loveless."

Her familiar nod.

"There was no love. Rare hugs. Few 'I love yous.' We didn't do anything together as a family. Just cold. Quiet."

"Was there yelling? Fighting?"

"On several occasions, but not frequently. I was the one who raised my voice. It was worse than that; the air was dead. Then, I'd retreat downstairs to my room and close the door. The house felt empty as if it was abandoned."

I felt my voice rise, taking over the room.

"There were two chairs at the kitchen table, not three."

Her head tilted toward me, "Sorry, what do you mean?"

"They only had two chairs at the kitchen table. That's where they ate dinner after drinking for hours. The dining room used only when family was around. Our table, just two chairs. That's all."

The memory of my mother putting live crabs in a boiling pot of water on our stove emerged in my mind, and I tried to shake it off.

"Do you want to know the worst part about it? *I* was the problem. Not them…me! I started to rebel, so then I was the issue which I invited. 'You aren't helping my marriage,' is what my mother said to me. As if I had any control over that! They put their entire mess on my shoulders. I was their problem, so I gave up on everything. I gave up trying at school. Didn't attempt activities other than work. At least working I was paid, some sense of reward. Hell, I gave up on trying to live. There were times I just wanted to leave this world."

I hit my emotional vein.

"My father wanted to send me to Outward Bound. He scheduled it, and at the last minute, my mother called it off. The night before, she said, 'No,' and that was that. You know what I wish they'd done? I wish they'd sent me away. I wish I'd gone to Outward Bound. I wish I'd been anywhere but where I was. It wasn't until college that I was able to start putting myself back together."

I looked at Susan, and her eyes were full of tears. "I'm so sorry," she said.

I felt her sadness, and it was an invitation. My emotional onion, the one peeling open, burned the eyes in the room. Tears robbed me of words for several minutes.

"Yeah, me too. It should have been different. All of it. I could have been so much more than what I was then."

"It isn't right what happened, but you will heal. It's going to be hard for you to find people to trust. It will take time, but what you're doing right now is how you heal."

"Doing what?"

"Acknowledging your experience. Facing your past," she said with a warm, encouraging smile. My feeling of dislike for her turned to warmth, and I thought about brushing her unruly hair.

The light on the wall I faced had gone from orange to gray as the sun set to the west.

I was grateful for the conversation but done sharing my thoughts as the blood drained from my veins.

"I think I'm going to run a marathon."

Susan smiled with a hint of pride.

"Good. I know you can," she said and glanced at her clock. I knew our time was up.

In San Francisco, I started running short distances. The City, its pavement, dirt trails, and sandy beaches became the open spaces where I added miles. At first, I could barely run two miles; my lungs seemed the size of grapes as I moved forward in clumsy, hefty steps.

The place I loved became the landscape for finding a rhythm within my body I never knew I had. With each attempt, I fell into a cadence as my arms rocked back and forth. My mind cleared as I heard my breath flow in and out. The sound of my feet hitting the ground and the vibration through my legs made me feel alive. Something awakened inside. Painful and negative thoughts were replaced with clarity and certainty. My internal dialogue shifted from a dark *no* to a sunlit-fueled *yes*, followed by euphoria.

I ran hundreds of miles around The City and Marin County. The dirt and gravel became my companion as my muscles burned and pulled me farther along. Among the flowers, dirt, and swaying grass, I ran through eucalyptus trees and eventually to the crash and crawl of the Pacific Ocean.

As I ran along a trail past the Golden Gate Bridge and snaked my way along the cliffs and back again, I realized I found my religion, my way of praying.

My body transformed. Muscles appeared, and I became leaner. I no longer punished my body; I was feeding it. Using it for good. In my decade-long search for clarity, the cobwebs that clouded my thoughts were clearing. I was seeing myself differently.

After recruiting a friend to join me, I signed up for the Chicago marathon. We ran from our apartments in San Francisco to Sausalito and back, taking in the majestic city and headlands as we did. As people passed us, we whispered to each other, "They aren't running as far as us," and we would eventually pass them as they stopped. At first, I would return home, my body so worked, a nap was necessary. Eventually, running fourteen miles became something I could do without being exhausted afterward. In the thick of training, my body had transformed to something I didn't recognize or ever think it could be. My body became my friend.

After four months of training, on a cold winter day, I ran 26.2 miles through Chicago. With each mile, I felt the power of the work I had put in. I didn't doubt for one moment I would finish, even as the ache and fatigue set in, blisters formed, and sweat crusted on my exposed skin.

Running the difficult last two miles, I came to a quiet tunnel. On the other side, music played, and a sea of people cheered runners to the finish line. Joy grabbed my throat as I realized I said goodbye to the hurt girl who didn't treat her body well. I was running to the place where I belonged. Though every inch of my body ached as I crossed the finish line at a respectable ten-minute-mile pace, I never felt better.

CHAPTER TWENTY-FOUR

BROKEN DREAMS

Anna, 1966

W hen I was a young girl, my dreams were my lifeline. When I imagined the man who would rescue me, I saw his face, like a blurred mirage, and the baby I would hold in my arms. To love the child and to have them love me back, to be the mother I never had, was the dream. If I started a family, I could experience everything I lost. I could be whole again. I could hold my infant, close my eyes, and remember Mommy for the brief time we had her. There would be a husband to walk through the front door every night as Daddy had, until he didn't.

A few weeks after Eve's wedding celebration, Henry put a small gold band on my finger. The proposal was delivered simply, like us. We stayed in his Chevy, listening to music at a lookout point where couples "parked." Lost in the music when he leaned over, kissed my neck, and took my hand and put it on his thigh, I recoiled quickly, alarmed by the feeling of his flesh under his pants.

"Anna, darling you have to loosen up." He pulled my chin to him.

"Look at me," he said. "I want to marry you, let me give you a ring."

The skin on my ears burned. I looked at the simple circle he placed on my finger.

"It's lovely, Henry. Yes, yes, I will." Suddenly, almost drunk with relief, I kissed Henry longer than ever. Then, I pulled away as a recognizable taste of fear rose in my belly as our kiss became more passionate. He sighed, leaned back in his seat, and pulled a flask from his jacket pocket. He offered it to me, and I took a sip that left me coughing.

"Let's get married soon. Nothing fancy, since we don't have much money. Just a few weeks are all I'm willing to wait." He took another swig, turned the engine on, and started the drive to return me to the Coles House.

"I'd like to marry when Eve returns home from her honeymoon in four weeks. My sister needs to be there." He nodded. "I'll start planning next week."

As the words left my mouth, my insides dropped as if I were on a roller coaster.

We had agreed to marry a month after Preston and Eve returned from their honeymoon. We talked on the phone every night. A level of excitement had entered my life that I had always dreamed of, even though fear lived in the corner of every room demanding my attention.

"I want a child, Henry."

"I know, Anna." At the sound of his words, my heart froze in euphoria. A child, the thing I always wanted.

"I love you, Anna."

I struggled to say the same to him without having it come out in a whisper. There was something about love and expressing it out loud that cut off at my vocal cords.

"Anna?"

"I love you, too, Henry. It's just,,,it's hard for me to say those words at times."

Each weekend we went to a drive-in movie as our date. We picked up burgers and fries, and I ordered a milkshake, even though I was eager to be as thin as possible for the wedding. Since deciding to marry, I limited myself to eating just one meal a day. It meant that during my work hours at the bank I was sometimes so dizzy I saw stars. Ten pounds thinner, I loved seeing my slim frame reflected in the shop windows as I walked to and from work. On occasion, I caught men noticing me, but dismissed the idea of being anything other than an average girl.

On date night with Henry, I allowed myself one cheat meal. As the greasy burger and smooth ice cream went down my throat, blood was returning to my veins. After Henry swallowed his in several quick bites, he took several large draws from his flask, a familiar slur coating his voice the more sips he took.

As I methodically ate my meal, caught up in the daydream of its taste, Henry took a long drink and declared, "I can't wait, Anna."

"For the movie?" I asked, wiping the grease on my mouth with a napkin.

Leaning in, he reached for my neck and pulled me toward him with force. This time, his kiss was hard, more determined. He seemed to have more experience than he was supposed to coming from our background. His body began to press me against the seat and my food fell to the side.

"Jeez, Henry, my burger."

Even though I understood his restlessness, I was eager to get the act over with as well, but it couldn't happen in a car with Henry smelling like the alcohol he carried with him.

"Henry, stop now," I nearly yelled.

I put my hand on his chest and pushed him away. "You spilled my food all over me."

"Jesus Christ, Anna, why are you so prudish? Is it because of that ridiculous place we grew up in? We're getting married in four weeks, why can't you just let me make love to you? What is with you? This is the sixties, Anna. I've been with women, and no one is like you. It's as if you're scared of being touched."

Women? Who were the other women?

My heart deflated like a balloon.

I never witnessed his anger in such a form. Why did my fear make him so upset? I was a good girl, simply following the rules we were raised with, Henry included.

He pushed me away and turned his attention to the movie.

I felt like an egg that someone had just broken in a bowl: fractured and spilling open. I began to cry, and then my tears turned into a guttural wail. Never in my life had I cried this hard. Something was coming out of me, something foreign and so obscure I thought I could no longer breathe.

I didn't stop sobbing when Henry turned the car on or when he started driving away, even though the movie was only half done. He refused to look in my direction, as if some monster entered his car, and if he ignored its presence, it would just disappear. As we drove through the familiar streets, my tears continued to flow, and I bent over in pain.

I opened the car door without a word, walked up the front stairs, and let the front door slam behind me. A few girls were home watching TV. They looked in my direction, but I went straight to my room, collapsing on the bed and crying into my pillow until sleep took over.

I woke the next morning and went to the kitchen to see if Henry had left a message. He hadn't. Through my exhaustion and confusion about what happened the night before, I decided to stay in bed the rest of Sunday. I didn't want to talk to the girls. Even though I wanted to, I wouldn't call Henry. I wasn't prepared to explain because I still didn't understand my emotions. He would have to call me; he needed to apologize. He was the man, after all.

On Monday, I went to work with red eyes and tears waiting to appear at a moment's notice. I feared a sad song or casual word from someone would send me into a puddle on the floor. I bit my lip as I worked the teller window and found solace in the counting of money throughout the day. Working with one customer after another reminded me there was a rhythm in the world, even though I was drowning under the weight of my feelings.

By Wednesday, Henry still had not called. I began to worry something happened to him. Had he drank too much and driven? As terrible thoughts raced through my mind, I promised myself I would call Howard after work and have him check on Henry. My continuous thoughts of Henry were interrupted by an alluring accent coming across the other side of my teller window. Standing in front of me was a handsome man with olive skin wearing a Marine uniform.

"You look preoccupied." If only it were Henry's voice, I thought. "I would like to make a deposit in my account if you have a moment."

He smiled at me; his intense green eyes focused on mine.

"Sorry, I'm a bit distracted. Do you have a check or cash?"

"I would offer you a date if that would make you feel better." His eyes did not move as I lowered mine in embarrassment. I noticed the hands that held his wallet; they were perfectly manicured.

"I'm engaged, sir, but thank you." My shoulders softened at the word engaged. I was weeks away from marriage, and I hadn't spoken to Henry in four days, but that did not change the ring on my finger.

"Here, cash for deposit, my dear. If you ever change your mind about the marriage, I'll be sure to come to your booth every day when I'm in town, just in case."

While looking down at the green bills in my hand and slowly counting them, I thanked him and realized I didn't know what I was thanking him for. Embracing the familiar rhythm of hearing myself say, "twenty, thirty, forty, fifty…"

"Until next time…your name?"

"Anna." I looked at him again and my face flushed, which made his mouth turn upward in a smile.

"Anna, beautiful name." He took my hand across the counter and kissed it gently.

I wondered if what had just happened was a fantasy. It was nearly five o'clock, and the bank was about to close. How could this be? A handsome man in uniform just flirted with me.

"Wait, your receipt," I called after him.

He turned, smiled, and tipped his hat. "Save it until I see you again," he said before walking out the door. The security guard locked the door behind the man. I held the deposit slip with his name, Harry Anderson.

I started closing my teller window when I saw a familiar face staring at me through the bank's front door.

"Howard," I waved to the security guard to let him in.

How did he know I desperately wanted to speak with him?

The teller next to me, Nancy, leaned over and said, "Who is *that?*"

"My brother."

"He's gorgeous, can I meet him?" I wanted to tell her to get in line. That women loved my brother and were constantly falling all over him. I chose to ignore her request in the hope she would drop it.

Howard came over to my booth with a smile on his face, but buried below his warm hello was a look of pain. I was familiar with this look; it was the expression people have when they had bad news to deliver.

"Howard, what is it? Is it Henry, is he—?"

"He's okay. It's just…can you close up and meet me at the park down the street?"

As I walked down the street to the park, I looked down at my shoes, heard the familiar click of my heels on the sidewalk, and found the sound reassuring; at least I was moving towards knowing Henry was alive. Howard sat on a bench smoking a cigarette. Even though I hated when he smoked, he offered me one, and I took it.

"Toots, I love you. I want you to know that. I want you to be happy."

"Come on, Howard, please tell me. Is he okay? We haven't spoken in nearly a week, and the wedding is three weeks away."

"There is no easier way to say this." He took a drag, and I did too, letting the smoke burn down my throat. I began to cough.

"Toots, do you remember Gladys from the Home?"

My mind searched all the girls' faces. There before me appeared the face of a very troubled girl whose story we would eventually piece together: she had abusive parents and was turned over to the state, but not before her stepfather did awful things to her.

"Toots, Henry has been in a relationship with her for months. His brother, too."

The words knifed my heart. I closed my eyes and listened to birds call from the trees as the world began to swirl. I sat for a moment taking the sounds in, hoping the words Howard said meant something different than what I understood them to mean.

Maybe this is what happened before marriage, similar to Preston with Eve. Men experimented with other women. But, after the ceremony perhaps, Henry would be loyal.

"I can fix it. I mean, it isn't like he's the first man to cheat."

"Sis, it gets worse. She's pregnant."

I felt the wooden bench sway beneath me. All my life-shattering moments lined up like books on a shelf and toppled me over.

"He's my friend, and I love him. But, Toots, he's broken. Look, all of us guys from the Home are, but Henry is truly broken. He drinks too much, just like his parents did. Don't let him break you, too. You deserve better."

"When did you know this, Howard? Why didn't you warn me?"

"I am sorry, Sis. I just…we just wanted you to be in a good place, married like Eve."

He put his arm around my shoulder, and I leaned into him and cried. It was the first time I'd felt safe in a man's arms since Daddy. I wrung myself out, twisted out water and pain until I went silent. Howard walked me back to the Coles House and sat with me at the kitchen table as I called Henry.

"Hello." I heard his voice on the line.

"Henry, it's Anna." There was a clearing of his throat on the other end, then the sound of him crying. He waited for me to speak. "We can't get married, as you know."

"Yeah, I know." I heard him take a drink from something.

"Well, that should be it then." The silence on the other end of the line was deafening. I pressed the phone harder to my ear, relishing the warm pain on my skin.

"Howard will bring the ring back to you."

I handed the phone to Howard, stood up and walked to my room, falling on my bed in defeat. I was no longer getting married. The one salvation available to me had faded to black. Henry was gone. He left me because I was unable to give myself to him. I held onto my virginity, my purity, and it had cost me the hope of a life different than the one I was living.

My mind was a flurry of questions so violent in their pace they rendered me still. Was I ever going to make it on my own? Was I ever going to have a husband, a house, and a baby? Or was I going to be forced to live in homes with strangers for the rest of my life?

I thought of Eve and what she had. Isn't that what I deserved, even if I wasn't as glamorous and beautiful?

Perhaps the crying in the car with Henry indicated more than fear; perhaps it was desire.

My voice was a calling: *Want more. You must want more.*

Quiet knocking interrupted my thoughts. "You okay, Anna?"

"Yes, I will be. Leave me be for a bit."

"I'll be back to check on you later. I'm sorry, Sis. You had to know."

I grew tired lying on the bed thinking about it all. I watched as the last light of day crept through the curtains. I welcomed the darkness the heavy fabric afforded me. I could hide in the shade and forget about the world outside and the troubles waiting at my doorstep.

As I closed my eyes and welcomed sleep, I saw Mommy and Daddy's faces. I saw the house in Manayunk, and then the buildings of the Home. I heard the sound of Mrs. Harting waddling down the cement path with her ring of keys shaking in her hand. Was my misery linked to her somehow? Had she not prepared me for what was to come?

I could see her face so plainly it was as if she were saying to me, "You're special, Anna. All of the Rangnow children are special. Don't forget that. You'll thank me one day for what you were given here."

CHAPTER TWENTY-FIVE

WITNESS

Jennifer, 2003

In 2000, the dot-com bubble burst after a wave of unbelievable growth that made working in technology seem easy. It's not. The era overflowed with wild launch parties, insane compensation packages, huge valuations, and loads of capital with little profitability. Then, someone took a needle to the balloon, and it all came crashing down. As hordes of twenty and thirty-year-olds in San Francisco lost their positions, they packed their bags and went home. I did everything I could to find a full-time job and hold on to the place I loved. Like many, I became unemployed and desperate to pay the bills. I scratched and clawed my way through part-time jobs in search of a place to land. At some point I resolved to move back home, something that made my mother ecstatic.

Before I did, I would find a stable job making a third of what I earned before, but the role meant I could stay in The City. After months of living off the kindness of others, I had my own apartment again. At the time, it was three years since I left the comfort of my studio in Seattle. I found an inexpensive unit on the corner of Bush and Gough, one of the busiest intersections in San Francisco. I met the landlord in the small lobby with a mirrored wall, a large stack of mailboxes, and 1920s Mediterranean tile on the floor. When she handed me the keys, I was unlocking something larger than a place to live; it was confirmation I could make it against the odds.

A few pieces of furniture were being delivered from storage the following day. With me, I had a yoga mat, purse, and a large, clumsy cell phone. I walked several blocks to Whole Foods and ordered a massive burrito that lasted me three meals. Returning back to my empty apartment, the smell of fresh paint was prominent, so I opened all the windows. The noise of traffic filled my empty space, horns beeping occasionally. I sat cross-legged on the wooden floor eating the meal that weighed several pounds: there was no other place I would rather be.

My phone rang mid-bite. It was my mother.

"How is it? Are you settled?"

"My things come tomorrow, but I'm sleeping here tonight. I'm too excited not to." My voice echoed in the hollow room.

"I'm happy for you, Jenny. You sound so pleased," I could tell my mother wished the new job didn't happen and the call I was making was from the 15 on my way back to her.

"I am, Mom. I have my place, and I'm on my own."

"Good for you, Jen, good luck with the new job."

Not long after our call ended, I unrolled my yoga mat in my miniature walk-in closet and fell asleep, a towel serving as my blanket, my purse a pillow.

Weeks later I would meet the man known as The Wedding Singer, and on one of our first dates he sang for my friends and family at my sister's wedding.

Falling for The Wedding Singer was like driving down a deserted road littered with potholes, never knowing what is coming your way. He was dynamic, playful, and kind. He had wonderful friends, ambition, and was frugal. My sister, Linda, nicknamed him Ping-Pong since he bounced around life like a wayward white ball. On dates, our evenings were rarely planned. Instead, he would pick me up and drive around neighborhoods waiting to see if a certain restaurant appealed to him. The car would spin around city blocks until my hunger turned to exhaustion. At first, I found the unpredictability of those evenings exciting. There was a sense of adventure as he bounced through life curious as to what was going to come. He was consistently inconsistent. Sometimes he would call, sometimes he wouldn't. On occasion he would do the right thing, and I felt the solidity of a relationship forming; then he would leave glaring hints that told me to run in the other direction.

Warnings included how much he talked to and looked at other women and spoke of his dating escapades. There was the ballerina in New York and the actress in LA. The previous girlfriend whose picture was still in a frame on his end table.

"What happened?" I asked knowing the importance of understanding prior relationships.

"She got tired of waiting," he replied.

He didn't speak of monogamy or family, but seemed more like an orphaned single man living on his own. I identified with him in that way. We were both living in The City trying to make it.

The job began like any other. At first, there were accolades and "that was incredible." My star rose, my professional ambition was recognized, and the opportunity to rebuild my tech career promising. In any situation, you look for the good, especially after holding on for what you want, to make it on your own. The environment could be intense, a mountain of work for little pay and being available at all hours. The work itself was interesting, I was learning, and my efforts were valued. There were signs of something not being right, of an environment dangerous to women. Some women. The perpetrator was someone I called The Unwanted.

As my time there lengthened, The Wedding Singer took note of oddities, specifically, The Unwanted's behavior. "That's not right."

"What can I do? I need this job."

Driving home on the 880, the beginning of my hour-and-a-half-hour drive from Fremont to San Francisco—a long, painful commute—my two-pound cell phone rang, and I saw his number. I always hoped it was The Wedding Singer, but most of the time it was The Unwanted demanding something urgent.

"Jennifer, you need to come back to the office right now," he demanded. I'd grown to hate the way he said my name, the sound of his voice.

"I'm driving. You can tell me over the phone." In the year of working under his demands, I grew prickly to the frequent abuse of power.

"You need to come back now. It's important." This was not a new request on his part for me to drop everything and sit with him. Only this time he sounded deflated, which was rare.

My coworker got on the phone, "Jennifer, you need to come. It's bad, and it's going to be all over the media tomorrow. You will need to take the calls." I went back to the office where I learned about a sexual harassment lawsuit filed against my boss, The Unwanted, by a woman who preceded me. I heard her name mentioned many times, always in the tone of a quiet whisper.

The three of us sat in his glass office as I watched him pace and say things like, "We will fight. This is all a lie."

I observed him roaming the room. He was no longer a stealth predator with bony shoulders and a slow, measured stalk. His back hunched, and the color had left his face.

The following day, I read the affidavit she filed, and my hands began to shake as I went through a young woman's journey working for The Unwanted. She finally spoke her truth, and it was terrifying. Everything I felt, feared, blocked, and tackled in my year working for him so clearly outlined in the worst-case scenario.

What he had done to her, he tried to do to me. At times he had succeeded with me, others not. But with the plaintiff, he had triumphed after nearly every attempt. Reading her complaint was like reading his playbook. As my eyes scanned her accusations, nearly every questionable interaction I kept secret played as a movie in front of me. I had been able to outsmart and out navigate him more than she had, but it didn't mean the battle wasn't fought.

Why is it that professional women had to face this onslaught in so many areas of our lives? I knew I was a capable and hardworking, but throughout my career I always took a seat at the side table. I purchased Gail Evans's book *Play Like a Man, Win Like a Woman*, which helped me to manage the gender gap, but it didn't specifically address when your womanhood was what the men at work wanted. The male hands that went on your back discreetly at events. The comments on your looks. The promotion suggested, but only if you traveled with them, attended dinners alone, and met them in their hotel room to work. The unwanted gifts that were left on your desk.

This woman's affidavit read like a Hollywood horror movie. You couldn't craft her story if you tried, and that was the most horrifying part: these things transpired. They were real. I knew people doubted her, the media lambasted her as a gold digger, but I knew the truth because I had seen the trailer.

I became a witness.

If you observed something horrific, would you have the strength to speak up? Even if you knew the experience of taking a stance would hurt you?

I made a phone call to the plaintiff's attorney's office. A cordial woman answered, and I cryptically introduced myself. My hands shook with such violence I worried I would drop my phone.

"I read the *New York Times* article today and the affidavit. I want to say everything she said is true. He ran that entire play on me with different outcomes. If she needs my help, I'm willing."

Through the line I could feel the woman's energy shift to frantic. "Wait, one second—your name? What is your number in case we get disconnected?" I listened to the scratch of her pen as she took down my number.

"The team is not here right now, but I know they will want to speak with you. Very much so."

We hung up. An hour later my phone vibrated, and a fatherly voice asked to speak with me.

"My name is Dan. We received your message and would like to speak with you. Can you meet in person? Phones can be tricky in these situations."

"I live in The City." Without hesitation he promised to be at a restaurant on Fillmore Street in an hour.

In a large meeting room high above San Francisco, a dozen attorneys in ironed suits sat around a large mahogany table under the guidance they would be finalizing a settlement agreement. Before they did, Dan and his team asked to play something for the opposing party. In that room was a TV where a video of me played. I spoke of the playbook I ran my defense plan against The Unwanted. When her suit was filed, I had already submitted my resignation to the company because the toxicity had threatened to destroy me. The timing of both events was auspicious.

When I picked up the phone to offer my story, I stood on the shoulders of women rendered voiceless for decades.

The men in suits who sat at long tables and pushed paper didn't know the truth. I did. I chose to speak up about something wrong, to blow the whistle on bad behavior. To be deposed, to be a witness where there are sides—yours and theirs. The opposing will do everything they can to break you, to destroy your mind and spirit. If you consider yourself a survivor of something, in their eyes you've always been unstable. Your word means nothing. I was called to speak about my experience, but with that, I invited so much more. Ridicule. Accusations. Embarrassment. Labels.

On a particularly hard day of depositions, I recounted an awkward moment where I was requested to be alone with The Unwanted and to practice golf with him. A game I didn't want to play, but was made to do on a weekend as part of being invested in my job.

"Tell us how he touched you. Stand up and show us," the man in a crisp white shirt with a Rolex asked as the court reporter's fingers punctured his keyboard capturing every word.

I broke down in sobs with shame and embarrassment, sending me out of my seat and into the other room.

Dan, who had been seated next to me followed, "This is hard and what they are doing to you is awful, Jennifer, but you need to let them see you cry. They need to feel it. This is the game."

The game is this: they take your dignity in hopes of robbing your voice. You have a choice: continue to speak and declare your story, or cave to the madness they say you are inflicted with, rendering you silent.

I went back into the room, stayed seated and told my story, one awkward detail after the other. I wondered if Rolex had a daughter, and if he did, would he want her future boss to demand a golf game on the weekend as part of her "future role," so he could touch her and spend time with her.

I was deposed for five days, which in the end was a battle for self unlike any other I've experienced.

I learned something valuable from my parents. The truth might be uncomfortable, wrapped in shame, and hard to share, but if you own your story, each word builds an armor around you—a knight's shield. What we witness shapes us, changes us. Makes us who we are. What breaks us makes us in many ways, too.

I emerged from the legal experience convinced of one thing: if I could survive such grueling testimony, I could survive anything.

I was not a victim; I was a voice.

Even though The Wedding Singer's behavior was inconsistent throughout our relationship to that point, he was there for me during a job that became about so much more than work. He took my calls when I felt being a witness had broken me. He held me when I cried and shook from the offense being fired my way. He was *my* witness. He was my friend. He was my ally when I felt I had none. Speaking out is a lonely endeavor that others don't understand. Few offer their support because most people "don't want to be involved."

The Wedding Singer stood by me like no one else. The inconsistencies he displayed that drove me mad were disappearing, consistency in its place. I began to rely on his support to keep me going and to help me live through the experience. Traumatic events cause us to seek comfort in strange places. So, when he asked me to marry him, although I hesitated, it seemed like the silver lining I deserved.

Wasn't love going through the trenches together and coming out the other side?

CHAPTER TWENTY-SIX

HARRY

Anna, 1968

Lying in my bed, I would stare at the ceiling, willing the clock to turn backwards. As I glanced around my room, observing the few things that were mine, I wondered if anything had changed from the night before. I observed my dresser standing at attention, an aging mirror attached to the top of it. Next to it was a narrow closet holding a few dresses, a pair of boots, and several pairs of shoes.

Since my engagement to Henry ended, I spent every night after work reading in bed. I would go to the kitchen and have a bowl of cottage cheese, barely able to get the contents down. Then the exhaustion of having to work eight hours that day washed over me, and I retreated to my perfectly made bed with a book I borrowed from the library. The only way I could quiet my mind was retreating to the black words typed on the white page, waiting for sleep.

Each morning, I rose early and watched the sun rise against the wall of the building next to the Coles House. I imagined the people inside the narrow row house: a family with two children and a dog. Were they happy? What was happiness anyway? Weren't we all just surviving? I waited until the last minute to rise out of bed, the sound of the other girls in the house reminding me I couldn't lie there any longer.

Standing in front of the mirror, I could observe my extreme weight loss. As my frame grew thinner, I thought about how my wedding dress— the one tucked in the corner of my closet—might look. For a moment I contemplated putting it on, but shook my head as if to shake the idea out entirely. Pulling my hair back in a ponytail, I put on a jacket that hung off my shoulders as if it were on a coat hanger.

"Anna, you look fabulous. Look at your legs. Henry sure made a mistake," one of the girls said to me as I walked into the kitchen.

The sound of his name took the wind out of me.

"Thank you," as I bit my lip hard enough to draw blood. "See you later," I said to them as I exited out the front door.

I walked to work with my head down, my chin nearly touching my chest. Entering the bank, I felt grateful for the familiar space. I ventured back to the vault where the manager handed me a bag of money for my teller drawer. The smell of the musty bag rose to my nose. I counted the money and put each denomination in its place. I slid my divider to the side and waited for the customers to come in. As I waited, I breathed deeply, trying to hold down the emotions that were swirling inside of me, threatening to rise up at a moment's notice. I focused my attention on the oversized clock above the front door as it clicked by slowly, second by second.

You are still here, Anna. You are still here.

As someone approached, I let my smile extend so far it made my cheeks hurt.

After a few hours of work, inevitably one of the girls would ask me to lunch. "Let's go have lunch, Anna. Some fresh air will do you good."

Occasionally I would go with them, but most of the time I sat in the back room eating the lunch I brought for myself. What I didn't tell the girls was that, while I loved their company, I counted the days until my sister came home from her honeymoon.

A few months into her summer honeymoon trip to Europe, I had sat down on my bed and written Eve a letter. In it, I explained that my relationship with Henry ended because he was unable to stay committed to me and would have a baby with someone else. I kept the note short, choosing to spend more time letting her know I missed her, not dwelling on the tragedy of my situation.

I went to the post office and gave the man behind the counter the address where my sister would be staying in Italy. A villa in Tuscany, the place she and Preston would stay for their last few weeks.

I imagined her there in a white dress with a scarf holding back her hair, a glass of wine in her hand. She would open my letter, and pity would take over for a few minutes before she took a sip of wine and then got distracted by conversation.

I received a postcard a few days before her return.

"Sister, I will be home on September 5th. I am sorry to hear the news, but you will survive. I promise you. With love, Eve."

When I laid eyes on Eve for the first time in months, she took my breath away; her face tan and relaxed, her walk almost regal. She floated toward me as I stood waiting for her outside the bank. She smiled as she came near until she noticed me and her face fell, her expression one of shame.

"Oh, dear heavens. Look at you—skin and bones." She opened her arms and hugged me hard. I buckled under her embrace. The lid that held back the overwhelming emotion broke. I cried until the fabric on the shoulder of her jacket was damp.

"We're going to get you back in shape. You must remember men are men. Marriage, well, if I have learned anything, marriage is a business deal. Let's get down to business." With her words, she placed her hand in mine and led me down the street to her penthouse several blocks away.

Eve was the closest thing to a mother I would ever have. No good reason existed in fighting that reality; I embraced it. I needed her. I needed Preston.

As the doors of the building slid open, a tall man wearing a coat and hat smiled at us. "Welcome back, Mrs. Wilks."

"Clarence, this is my sister, Anna. She will be staying with us for a little while. Could you please have someone get her things from the Coles House on Ninth and Clinton."

He tilted his hat and said, "Yes, ma'am." Something about his way made me want to fall into Clarence's arms, too.

Riding up the elevator to the top floor, we entered their penthouse. We turned left and walked down a long hallway to their guest room.

"This will be your home for a few weeks. Until you feel better."

My eyes darted around the large room. In it were two twin beds, a large dresser, and two closets with mirrored doors. The space was adorned in blue-and-green wallpaper with matching comforters.

Eve sat on the edge of one of the beds and began talking about her trip, the decadence of it all. As she spoke, I wondered how two sisters, sitting on beds opposite each other, could live such different lives.

"Is this your room, too, Eve?"

"No, my room is down the hall. I can be with you if you want me to." I nodded, grateful the obscure dynamics of Eve and Preston's marriage meant that I got to share a room with her again.

An hour later, Preston returned home with the smell of whiskey on his breath. Eve and I sat next to each other on a sofa in the main room and watched as he poured himself a tall serving of brown liquor in a crystal glass. He elegantly sat down in a fabric chair that swiveled. He looked at me intently.

"Anna, you don't look well. Can you tell me what happened?"

Clearing my throat, my voice was hiding in the depths of my stomach. Yet, I knew I couldn't hide from the powerful man seated across from me. I had to tell him the truth. I owed it to him after everything he had done for me. For us.

"As I was telling Eve, everything seemed to be going okay. We were engaged and wanted a small wedding just as you had."

Then I giggled at how preposterous that sounded; my wedding was going to be nothing like Eve and Preston's.

"And, then, well...I don't know, he seemed to want more from me and...I...I didn't."

"He didn't hurt you did he, Anna?" Preston tilted the glass of liquor to his mouth.

"No. No. Henry's a good man. He just...there was another woman, and she's pregnant."

Preston placed his glass on a small table next to his chair and leaned towards me.

"I understand. Times are changing. The rules are changing. People are much freer in the physical way, but that isn't how you were raised. And quite often, that's not the type of woman men want to marry. Single unwed mothers are not accepted by society; Henry has to marry her, to correct his wrong."

I glanced at Eve, who sat motionless and attentive. Her husband speaking appeared as if she were listening to a pastor at church.

"Anna needs to get healthy. Certainly, marrying someone from the Home isn't the ideal situation."

It was the first time I heard her opinion of my potential union with Henry.

"Stay as long as you like. You can keep Eve company," Preston said as he leaned down, kissed her cheek, and sauntered down the hallway. I heard the master bedroom door shut with Preston on the other side.

Living with Eve was like living in a hotel. The chef prepared our meals, sometimes twice a day. I was dressed in Eve's high-end clothing and went to dinners in elegant restaurants. Her joy was infectious as she dressed me up and watched me participate in her world. A doll for her to play with. At first, the process of being social felt awkward and painful. I forced smiles to make conversation, but after a bit, I settled into the glamorous routine. I found a stiff drink or two made the evening more fun, and it was my first introduction to alcohol as a source of relaxation.

We sat on Rittenhouse Square sipping cocktails watching people go by. I began to notice men, and slowly they began to notice me. As I flirted, I felt myself coming out of my invisible shell.

One night over dinner with Preston, I could sense my time with them neared its end. "We have enjoyed having you, Anna. Living with all of those girls in the Coles House isn't sufficient for you anymore. You need to be with your family. Your brothers are all living together, and it's time you joined them."

He took a sip of his martini.

"Thank you, Preston. I think that's a good idea. I would love nothing more than to be with my brothers again, living under the same roof for the first time since Daddy put us in the Home."

Preston smiled toward Eve, and she returned his glance with appreciation. As the mother to us all, I could see her relief in his ability to guide her siblings. I imagined he listened to her fret about our futures for hours on end, long ago deciding to be the steward of our wayward ship.

The sense of someone influencing our lives was a familiar feeling. I always had the impression something guided me, even in the darkest moments of our childhood. That there were helpers among us, not some celestial being ruling our fate. Looking at Preston, I felt gratitude he was one of the helpers.

Feeling healthy again six months later, I began to enjoy my interactions with customers at work. No longer terrified of my reaction to their presence, I welcomed conversations. I didn't forget Henry, but I saw the finality in the decision he made. A woman was pregnant, he was the father, so marriage was inevitable.

One morning while looking down at something on my counter, I heard someone say, "Hello, Anna."

I recognized the deep and seductive voice, a distinct accent hard to forget. Standing before me was Harry, the man in uniform.

"I let several people go before me, so that I could be in your line."

I heard myself say, "Thank you," in a trembling voice.

"Cash, please." He handed me a withdraw slip.

As I looked into my drawer for the cash, I noticed the slip of paper with his name I kept in my drawers from months before.

"The last time you came, you left your receipt. I kept this for you." I smiled and handed it to him along with the cash he withdrew.

The expression on his face changed, and his eyes locked at me with an intensity that made my spine tingle. He wasn't much taller than I was, but his shoulders were broad. His clothes perfectly pressed.

"I see. You didn't forget me either. And the fiancé?" Harry looked at my ring finger.

"It didn't work out,"

He didn't say another word. He just smiled, that intense unwavering gaze, put his hat on, and walked out the door.

"Careful, you're vulnerable," Eve said to me when I called to let her know he came to the bank twice that week, and on the second visit I'd accepted a date. She nursed me back to normal while telling me to be tepid.

"I know, Eve, I'll be careful. I just need to…"

"Get out in the world?" she found the words for me.

"Yes, I need to experience life, Eve. Who's going to want me if I am thirty and still living with our brothers? I'll be turning twenty-six soon. My lord, I am almost an old maid. I could turn into one of those housemothers from the Home if I'm not careful. I want a husband and a baby."

"Family? Hmph. We all know how painful all of that can be."

"Well, Eve, it might not be what you want, but I want a baby, and to have a man who helps me navigate this world. Is that too much to ask? After all we've been through?"

"Just be careful. We're different from the others. And Jesus Christ, Toots, be careful with men. Mrs. Harting didn't prepare us for this world. They didn't tell us about real life. They raised us to be nuns. Little good that does any of us now."

My first date with Harry was promising. He opened doors for me, asked me questions about my work at the bank, and shared stories from the military that convinced me of his strength and reliability. Soon we found ourselves in a pattern of seeing each other once a week. We went to dinner, saw movies, and began spending time at each other's homes.

I moved in with my brothers to a small house with a fenced-in yard. With help from Preston, Howard started a fencing business, and John and Jim were working for him. When they came home, I liked to make them dinner and listen to their stories as they popped open cans of beer and watched TV. Harry loved to come over and join them as I cooked in the kitchen.

In the mornings, as I made my bed, sometimes my breath would stop short realizing nearly twenty years before my brothers and I lived under the same roof with our parents. I straightened the bedding even tighter to force the thought from my mind.

We are here now.

Life started feeling normal. I was living with my family, and there was a man interested in spending time with me. Harry was affectionate and loving, but as we kissed, I began to sense he wanted more.

You've been here before.

Suspecting something was going to have change, I called Eve.

"Jeez, Anna, I guess you have to give it up before marriage now, these days. It's 1968, and the world has changed. The world is not what the Home taught us. Look around, women are burning their bras and having sex, making love, whatever. Lie back and relax, just be careful you don't get pregnant. You heard Preston; single mothers are still considered outcasts. That hasn't changed. Your life is over if you are single and unwed—your babies', too."

"How do you not get pregnant?" I asked her.

"When you're sleeping with a man, relax as much as you can. Lie on your back and let him do it. There comes a point—oh dear, I don't even like talking about it. There's a point, a point where he's finished. Let him finish, but not when he's inside of you. You'll see. That's how you get pregnant, if he stays *in* there."

"Sounds terrifying. How come they didn't tell us about all of this stuff at the Home?"

There was long pause on the other end. "Because Anna, they were trying to keep all of us from getting pregnant. Think about all those girls, so many broken girls who could have found themselves in trouble if there hadn't been rules and the church."

"I see. Well, I'm not sure I'm ready for all this."

"Do you really love him, Anna? Is Harry the one?"

"He's intense, but I like that he's in charge. I think the military does that to you. Makes you wild." I heard her sigh on the other end of the line. "Sometimes, Eve, he does frighten me. The other night, we were driving, and he thought someone was following us. He really did. But then I just think he gets spooked based on all the things he's seen. I can't blame him for that, can I?"

"Just be careful, Toots."

Several more dates after my phone call with Eve, Harry and I found ourselves on his bed kissing. His hands began to move to foreign places, parts of my body that had never been touched. I thought of Eve's words and did everything I could to relax. I thought of Mrs. Harting and all of her rules, how her presence turned up in the strangest places and refused to leave my consciousness.

Perhaps, I wondered, that is exactly what she had wanted.

I felt myself float away as Harry did things to me, no longer able to feel the sheets beneath my skin. He whispered something in my ear, and I simply nodded as my mind drifted to the orphanage, my parents, and my small house in Manayunk. I felt a tinge of pain. Something had happened, an intense sensation. It was quick and then it was over, a lingering warmth took over my lower body.

"Harry, what are you doing, you promised you would…you would… not stay," my voice panicked.

Was that making love? I wasn't feeling love from his actions; I felt anxiety and pain.

"Anna," he said as he wiped the hair from my forehead, "I love you."

He spoke the words I waited to hear from someone ever since Henry, but I felt hollowness and fear stirring inside me. Was this what love felt like? It felt most like the pain of regret.

"Stay the night, Anna?" I heard him say. Every bone in my body wanted to be somewhere other than where I found myself. Shaking my head, I turned away from his hands and raced to the bathroom.

My reflection in the mirror gave me nausea. I didn't recognize the woman I saw gazing back at me.

No, Anna, this is not the person for you. You need to run from this.

Harry dropped me off at my house; as he walked me to our doorstep, he said, "I love you" again.

"Okay, thanks." I turned the key, slipped through a narrowing opening, so he wouldn't follow me and fell against the door with him on the other side.

My brothers stared in my direction, their eyes wide, then turned back to the TV.

Harry continued to pursue me, but I cut him off. Something about that night, the way he had taken over my body left me confused. An overwhelming sense I didn't want anything to do with him took over. I began ignoring the phone when it rang in the house. If the boys answered, I instructed them to tell him I wasn't home. "Everything okay there, Toots?"

"Yeah, it's just…I need a break from him is all." I was grateful he was working in New York.

After our regular weekly dates stopped, his intensity emerged in other ways: flowers arrived at the bank, and he left random gifts on my doorstep. After several weeks his phone calls and drives by our house slowed.

Six weeks later, he called, and I answered. His voice was high, desperate sounding. He told me he was deployed to the Middle East.

"I might die out there, Anna," he said several times.

"I wish you a safe trip," I said and let the quiet take over the static on the line.

At the sound of his words, a strange wave of relief washed over me at the idea my problem might be permanently solved. I wanted oceans between us.

CHAPTER TWENTY-SEVEN

YOUR OWN DAMN FAULT
Jennifer, 2006

We had a beautiful, joyous wedding, bought an old house we remodeled, and began a life with a view overlooking the Golden Gate Bridge.

Everything in our relationship had changed and nothing at all. He lived his life, and I lived mine, which for someone who is fiercely independent had the appearance of working.

We had parties and hosted dinners. My mother, well-settled into her aloneness, would visit us on holidays. We cooked Thanksgiving dinner and decorated our Christmas tree that stood tall in our large window facing the Bay. The sunsets would provide a fire to the night. Always a green thumb, my mother helped me dig up old, tired looking plants in our yard and replace them with flowers and shrubs that brought vibrance to the midcentury house. In my new marriage, we had created something beautiful, a house.

I started a new job at a technology company that opened doors I waited ten years to appear. Things had turned around freeing me from the things that weighed me down for years—mentally and emotionally. I was coming out the other side, clearer and stronger. I found my voice in a variety of ways—artistically, physically, and emotionally—and my voice rang strong.

My sister, Linda, once reflected on the impact of my childhood and said, "You lost ten years putting yourself back together."

At this stage of my life, those ten years were up. Her timing was on point.

A book emerged in my life, one that would knock my consciousness off its safe seat. Someone else's words, their story was mirroring my own. Just like Kate Chopin's *The Awakening* awoke something in me during my senior year of college, as I read Elizabeth Gilbert's *Eat Pray Love*, her words mirrored my inner most voice. I, too, found myself on the bathroom floor only weeks before, in a ball, crying because I knew the horrible thing I needed to do. I knew the mistake I made overcommitting to someone I was finished with, but I had yet to say the words out loud.

I don't want to be married anymore.

This author was laying my overdue declaration out in page ten of a book I could not put down. I wasn't the only one seeing the irony. A friend reading it at the same time messaged me, "This must be hard for you to read." She knew, deep down, too, I had yet to finalize my transformation. My pilgrimage to self contained one more excruciating step.

My mother is someone who can have moments of intense clarity. In the midst of tragedy, or trouble, she can see through someone's pain and call out the straight line.

After two visits during Christmas, she heard me sing the same tune as the year before. The unhappiness in my relationship spilled over from one year to the next. I married a dear friend, not the makings of a life partner, even if he tried to fill that role. Driving her to the airport, we sat in silence. I could tell something bothered her, but I didn't probe. Enough was bothering me. I pulled over to the concrete sidewalk. Our doors opened to the sound of engines, and the smell of dirty air swirling around us. Grabbing her suitcase from the trunk I put it on the sidewalk next to her; she had the ever-present large purse tucked under her arm as if about to be robbed.

Her back straightened, and I noticed she was on the verge of tears.

She gave me one of her awkward hugs that I began to realize came from someone who wasn't touched much as a child; there was a pat on the back and a loose grip.

I didn't want to see her go. I couldn't speak as I knew she held the truth to my regret and was about to take my secret with her.

"Jenny, if you're in this same place a year from now, it's your own damn fault."

She muttered, "I love you," grabbed the handle to her bag with a fierceness, and turned to the glass doors that opened as she approached them. Her words were harsh but left me shocked by her strength. I had witnessed her mother mic drop moment. She was gone, but not before she punctured my heart, trying to bring me back to life.

Fifteen years prior, she left a note on my bed that read, "You are on your own." As my life reached another "Y" in the road, she left the marker for me to see.

I was reminded of my father all those years ago, "I don't want to be here anymore." That was his marker. My mom had hers. Fate ensured I would never forget those moments; they defined our relationship. Their words were branded onto me like a poorly chosen tattoo.

My father had spoken his truth then but chose to bury it. My mother had listened and chose to ignore it. What was I going to do?

I pondered how to extract myself from a man I didn't want to hurt but whom I was harming by not being honest. I knew I couldn't carry on the way my father did. I knew better because I lived with the pain that exists when people don't declare their truth.

This reality, this knowing what I had to undo, threatened to break me open.

Jennifer, you've been here before, but you're stronger now. You're stronger than your parents were then.

I hadn't seen Susan in several years. Her pantsuit hung off her tall frame as she motioned me to sit down minutes before. Her office was still in Hayes Valley, just a different location. The furniture in her room changed, but her demeanor remained the same. Consistent. I longed for consistency, it seemed to be the prize for healing.

Sitting in front of her, parts of me had evolved, but other aspects remained stagnant. Through running I found a way to stifle the voice of self-abuse that chased me throughout my adolescence. I ran several marathons, and each time I crossed the finish line with raw feet, sore legs, and a body damp and salty while spectators cheered and music played. Proof not only of my aliveness but of my strength as well.

The sessions began around her usual question, "How are you?"

"Life has progressed. I have a job that I love. My father and I have a relationship again, and he comes and stays with me when he's in town. Becoming a grandfather really changed him. He's softer now, happier. I can see how miserable he was when I was young, and in a way, I understand it. He just wanted to be free."

"Why is that something you understand now?"

"He had my eldest sister, Beth, when he was nineteen. He worked tirelessly since then, taking nine years to go to night school while raising a child and working full-time. Once I was a teenager, he was burnt out. Cooked. He worked so hard he had a heart attack before forty. Life was telling him to slow down."

"So, you have come to accept what happened?"

"I don't like it, but I can see why things were the way they were. I'm married to The Wedding Singer, and I can see my father's dilemma. You want to do right by people and be dutiful, but you also know you should blow the whole thing up. That's how I feel. The Wedding Singer was there for me when I needed him most. But..."

"Yes?"

"I can see, slowly, I deserve to be happy. Truly happy."

She smiled her crooked smile.

Just say it, Jennifer.

"I'm not sure I know what love is,"

"You say you don't know what love is. What do you mean?"

"I don't know what a healthy family looks like. Even a healthy relationship. What I've created all seems so familiar."

"What's familiar?" Susan had changed her style with me ever since I confronted her on being too easy years before; she was no longer afraid to explore a place that made me uncomfortable. I liked prodding.

"The other Saturday I was standing in our house—he was out golfing like he is every weekend—and I was alone. The house was quiet. Standing in the dining room looking out to the Golden Gate Bridge, I saw one of my father's ships go by, just like when I was a little girl. Only now I'm in California. In my house. I had this overwhelming realization that I recreated what I knew. That I was standing in a house that felt like my childhood home on Upland Terrace."

"Is that a bad thing?"

"Yes, yes, it is."

"Why?"

Didn't she know already what the issues were with my adolescence?

"Because it was awful to be there. That quiet house. The absent parents that were there, but off in their own world and rarely engaged with me. My house now is still and quiet…an absence of love surrounding me. It feels the same."

"And that doesn't feel good?"

"NO, it feels awful. My mother came to visit for Christmas again this year. She could tell I was miserable and had grown tired of listening to me lament about the state of my marriage. As I dropped her off at the airport, do you know what she said to me?"

Susan let her head say, "No."

"She had tears in her eyes and said to me, 'If you are in this same place again next year, it's your own damn fault.'"

I saw Susan smile. I sensed she was pleased by what my mother said to me.

"What do you think I should do? You've listened to me long enough."

"Professionally, I'm not supposed to tell you what to do in your life. I can simply guide you."

"Look, I won't hold you to it, but you've been listening to me for years. I sound like a broken record. What should I do about this relationship? Tell me, off the record. Just tell me what you see."

Susan looked at me. I could tell she was struggling between her oath as a professional and as someone who had listened to me for countless hours. She paused and let out a large sigh and leaned forward.

"I think you should leave the relationship, Jennifer. It's been too many years of challenges and feeling like it is less than what you want and deserve. It's clear to me you know how you feel. You're just afraid. Understandably so, but you will be okay. I'm certain of it. Look how far you've come."

After hours of counseling sessions with her over the years, Susan saw me sitting in front of her. I recreated everything I saw with my parents. I was reliving my life on Upland Terrace all those years ago, even if it looked different from the outside. Inside was the absence of genuine, real love, and it was my fault. I let it happen.

I was holding on to the idea of love rather than the warm pulse of a relationship that worked. I held on to what I had seen as a young girl. Only I knew better now; I did the work sitting for hours on a worn sofa across from a woman who took the time to listen.

"Be kind to yourself, Jennifer. Let your life be full of what you deserve. You've had enough of what you don't deserve. You have the power now."

She was right. Since moving to San Francisco, I healed my eating disorder and found self-love through running. I repaired my relationship with my father—even came to a place where I understood him. Despite real struggles at times, my career survived the trauma of speaking out in a world that wanted women to remain quiet. I was on a path to somewhere professionally after years of grinding and holding on.

The truth was, I didn't need to eat in Italy, pray in India, or fall in love in Bali. My odyssey was fleeing home, building a life in San Francisco, and learning to love myself. It was then I realized I deserved something different than what I witnessed as a young girl. We had all deserved something different then.

To truly break free, I needed to summon the strength to do for myself what my parents hadn't done for themselves.

Hurt sticks you in a moment of time, a place of pain that fossilizes your being until there is a moment when you take a hammer to the hard shell around your heart and break it.

CHAPTER TWENTY-EIGHT

THE GIRL WHO DISAPPEARED
Anna, 1968

"Preston and I are going to the Jersey shore for the week. Why don't you join us?" Eve said on the other end of the line.

"Oh, yes, please. Anyone else going? Eligible bachelors?"

Since Harry left for the Middle East months before, I felt lighter. He was no longer on the same continent to pursue me, which alleviated my stress but didn't erase the shame I felt from giving myself to him. The distance allowed me to breathe and to forget my lapse in judgment although I didn't understand the experience in the moment.

The summer air was hot and sticky, and the beach was full of people spreading baby oil on their bodies and turning their skin the color of leather. I loved being on the shore, listening to the crash of the waves and the sound of gulls spinning through the air. Not one for crowds, I could do without all the people, but at least the beach felt peaceful. We arrived early with our bags, blankets, and umbrella, so we could be close to the water. Stripping down to my swimsuit, I noticed a few men glancing at my red bikini. I came to realize I had a good body: long legs, a tiny waist, and large breasts that men liked to take in.

Eve was sitting next to me in a rainbow-colored chair covered by an umbrella.

I glanced at her to notice she had a look of alarm on her face.

"Jesus, Anna, your chest! You're thin as a rail, and your boobs are huge."

"Good Lord, Eve, you don't have to shout it."

I looked down at my top and realized they were larger than normal. Grabbing at my chest to ensure it was on correctly, something occurred to me—my breasts were bigger, but they also hurt.

As if a cloud covered the sun, everything around me went dark. My eyes blurred, and I was faint. A movie played before me, the grainy negatives whizzing past my view. As if watching myself from a distant place, realizing my period had been absent for months. My knees buckled and my stomach somersaulted. There in my mind, I saw it like it was yesterday, Harry lying on top of me, panting and whispering, "I love you," me not saying it in return.

A seagull screeched, and I felt the earth rumble beneath my feet.

Eve reached for my arm and looked me over for signs of illness. Her green eyes were searched my face and noticed the fear in my eyes. "Oh, dear God, Anna. Are you pregnant?"

I fell on the blanket with my hand on my heart, unable to catch my breath. Preston rushed over from his conversation nearby as I folded on the ground gasping for air. Eve grabbed a glass of water and dumped it on my head.

Preston was holding my arm and looking intently in my eyes. In that moment, I realized I had grown to love him.

"Did you faint?"

I shook my head.

Please Eve, don't get Preston involved. He has done so much for us. Please don't tell him the mistake I might have made.

"Preston, I think we have a problem. Let's get Anna back to the hotel. We need to speak in private."

After Preston and Eve guided me back to the hotel room and laid me down on the bed, she went to the store to get a pregnancy test. It seemed like a useless exercise since I already knew the answer. It all came together in a crashing reality, like dominos falling down in a line, an awareness that swallowed me whole. I took the test, and the answer was clear.

"Oh, sweet Jesus, Anna, you are pregnant. How could you let this happen? You're going to have to marry that man." Eve was frantic.

She left the room, promising to return after speaking to Preston. I was alone, lying across my bed like Jesus, arms outstretched and ready to be nailed to the cross. I stared at ceiling, willing it to show me something, but it remained blank and solid. Like my choices.

I could have the baby and live a life of shame and ridicule, a poor single mother with little prospect of landing a decent job or anyone wanting to marry me. What little family I had, other than my siblings, would disown me. I would be one of those compromised girls. I had seen those women before, the young mothers holding their child's hand but lacking a wedding ring. People staring at them with judgment, then turning their heads as if the woman and child didn't exist. What good would that be for my baby?

My hand went to my stomach, and I felt its expansiveness, the possibility of what lived within me; I felt my heart flutter for two.

"I want this baby," I said aloud to the empty room, silent except for a fan turning.

Then it came to me.

Harry. Oh, God, Harry.

I didn't love him, I knew that. I thought of him, and a moment of fondness turned to anger. I hated how he smothered me and terrified me with his wild ideas and ways. I thought of the day he thought people were chasing us, or how he insisted on sitting in certain spots in a restaurant for "better visibility." Fury raced through my veins as I realized what he did to me. He knew my vulnerability and took advantage of me. The little orphan girl who knew so little had so much taken. What little freedom I possessed stolen from me, again, just as my parents were taken from me.

I will never forgive you.

Eve and Preston forced me to shower, get dressed, and join them for dinner. I sat motionless, except for the sound of my fork and knife scratching the plate as I pushed my food around.

"Anna, I'm disappointed, but you're not the first girl to find yourself in this position. What you must consider is that if you don't marry, and you go ahead and have this baby, your life will change dramatically. Your child's, too. Unwed mothers are treated differently in society."

"Preston, let's be gentle with her," Eve said, her sisterly hand touching my lower arm.

"I can't marry Harry. I don't love him, and I want to love someone. I want to be in love like our parents were. His intensity scares me at times. I'm fearful of the type of father he'll be."

Pausing to take a drink of water, I felt the fury again. The heartbreaking anger about what he did to me. "He did this without asking," I said, loud enough for patrons to hear me.

Preston lowered his voice to a whisper even though we were in a corner booth with a red candle and maroon leather cushions.

"Anna, it's important to look at your options. First, you could pursue something illegal and terminate the pregnancy, but that's a risky and dangerous choice. Second, you can have the baby and marry Harry. Third, you can raise your baby on your own, but suffer the consequences."

He paused, sipped his martini, and looked at Eve.

"Fourth, you can have the baby, and we will raise it as our own."

The sound of my fork dropping on my plate caused a few heads to turn nearby. "You and Eve, raise my baby? You don't want children."

"No, I didn't think I wanted children, but perhaps this gives Eve something to do. A child could be good for us. Also, we have the means to support a child and give it the life a single mother like yourself could not."

Eve's face half contorted. Months before she had told me they weren't having children, but now Preston wanted to give her my baby as a project. Seeing Eve's face, the look of confusion, I knew it was a terrible idea. I closed my eyes for a moment and imagined them pushing a stroller down the street with my baby inside. I would see them at the park and notice my sister and her husband with my child and be forced to extend my gratitude and love.

"I appreciate that, but absolutely not," I said.

Their voices became muffled by the dizziness in my head that took over.

"Anna, for option one you might be out of time. It's a horrific procedure, and there is some risk to it. This is a decision you'll need to make soon after seeing a doctor. Don't decide now, give it a few days. We'll get you a doctor's appointment in Philadelphia early next week."

The doctor's confirmation of my pregnancy was as cold as the utensils he used to examine me. I was roughly four months pregnant based on the last time I'd been with Harry. No wonder my belly had grown firm, and my usually flat stomach protruded slightly.

"No father, I take it, as you are here alone?" The doctor looked at his notepad with judgment etched on his face.

Of course, Preston's well-to-do doctor would judge me. "Yes, there is a father in my life. He's overseas," I lied. *The truth will set you free, Anna.* "It's not a relationship that's going to work."

"Now, let me be straight. I don't agree with what ladies like you have gotten yourselves into, but I do need to give you a warning."

Ladies like me.

He knew nothing about me. He didn't know where I came from, how ignorant I was about sex while society and men were demanding it before marriage. What did the doctor know about my parents dying and being raised in a Baptist orphanage with a priest and his wife who told us to save ourselves? How nobody prepared me for being with a man, just told us to find one to marry and then let him have his way. What did this man know about Henry—a man I loved although simple—and his impatience with my purity? Did he know Harry didn't protect me; he did what he wanted with me? What did this doctor know about what I survived?

"I've seen young women come in here after getting an illegal procedure, and I've seen how horrible it can be. Women who were pregnant and alone like you. Those women had abortions and are scarred for life. Most can't have children now. Don't do it if you want a family under better circumstances someday. And I'm certainly not the type of doctor who knows of anyone who does such things. You'll be on your own."

On my own? I wanted to laugh in his face. I was on my own for years unlike this judgmental man who had a wife who cooked his meals and poured his cocktail every night.

He pulled a pamphlet from a drawer and handed it to me.

"Florence Crittenton homes are adequate. They are homes for wayward women like yourself. Safe, clean, and they ensure your baby is adopted by a wonderful family. You will have staff who direct you to upbuild your self-respect and character. Women of your kind will be together. Once it's over, you can return to your life and try to make good on your mistake. Perhaps then, you'll have a chance at a normal life."

He turned and let the door slam behind him.

A family. My baby would have a family.

After the conversation with the doctor, I walked aimlessly for hours, sunk in the hopelessness of it all. I made sure to wrap my jacket around me tightly and to cross my arms to hide my protruding belly. How could I face the judgment of society if I were to keep the baby and not marry Harry? Who was going to want me? Preston said it himself: I would be an outcast.

I thought of Harry. He wanted me, but I didn't want him. Everything in my body told me he was wrong for me and to flee his presence. Look at what he had done to me, to our baby.

As I walked, the pace of my steps slowed down as I grew tired. I sat on a bench and breathed heavily. A voice not unlike the one that spoke to me in the Home spoke. *You have choices. You always have.*

After a deep sleep unlike any I've ever had, I woke up with my decision. The right choice for me. The right life for my baby. I called Eve and told her I was leaving for Miami to live out the last five months of my pregnancy.

"Once I give birth, I will be giving up my baby for adoption," I declared as my voice shook in dread.

Eve didn't oppose my decision despite suggesting they could raise the baby. I knew, even as they were offering the solution, that it wasn't the right choice.

As I hung, up the voice appeared again.

Anna, this is your familiar; don't be afraid.

I located Harry and told him I was pregnant. After a few moments listening to his enthusiasm, I told him my decision. "I'm giving the baby up for adoption, Harry." He resisted over the sound of a grainy phone line but eventually relented, knowing I would disappear.

A month later, just as the waist on my dresses were getting too tight, I packed my things and vanished. I told my brothers I was going on a trip with a friend for a few months. They didn't ask many questions and told me to have fun.

That morning, Eve picked me up and drove me to the airport.

"You're doing the right thing, Anna. I know Preston said he might want the baby, but our marriage...." She paused for a minute, staring off into the distance. "It's barely staying together. A baby wouldn't help us."

"I know, Eve. I know it isn't what you want. What I'm doing isn't even what I want. What choice do I have? It reminds me of Daddy's decision to put us in the Home. It's not what you want to do, but it's what's right at the time. Isn't this what we do, us Rangnows?"

"Did you tell the brothers?"

"No, Preston is right; only the three of us should know."

She nodded, leaned over and gave me a hug; as we embraced, our shoulders trembled in unison.

"Take care of yourself, Toots. I'll be thinking of you."

I grabbed my suitcase from the trunk and walked toward the entrance that said TWA. As the automatic doors opened, I turned to see Eve watching me as she leaned over the steering wheel of the car. She waved loosely, and I realized we were both heading to a place where we would be letting go of something profound; we were both venturing on a path to loss.

Once the plane landed in Miami I hailed a taxi. "8909 Southwest 94th Street, please," careful not to say the name of my destination. The driver attempted to make small talk on the thirty-minute drive, but eventually, my one-word answers silenced him.

We pulled up to a stately white house situated in a quiet, suburban neighborhood. The Florence Crittenton home was inviting with vines growing on the walls, a covered deck, and bright white walls. Tall green trees surrounded the property as did a wrap around fence. As I got out of the car, a warm ocean breeze swept through the palm trees lining the street. I thought how nice it would have been if the trip were a vacation.

The driver got out of the car, "Help with your bag?" he said, and his eyes went to the bulge of my belly under my jacket.

"I see," he said as he took my cash, and quickly got into his car and drove away, hitting the accelerator as he did.

I opened a small white gate in order to make the short distance to the front door. For a moment I wondered if I were in the correct place until I noticed the curtains were drawn on the lower floor. Despite the beauty there was an overwhelming feeling of sadness, it protruded, just like at the Home. Those beautiful buildings that carried so much sorrow wrapped in hope. I was about to disappear into a world I could not escape.

I knocked on the front door, my hand trembling as I did. Entering the house, it all felt familiar, joining an institution full of complicated truths hidden from the outside world. A place where the kindness of others would be my salvation and my undoing.

CHAPTER TWENTY-NINE

THE ORPHANAGE
Jennifer, 2006

I f you plan on breaking your own heart, more than likely, you will end up breaking someone else's. At the age of thirty-three, I learned the lesson many parents fail to teach their children. It's about failure, but not the "don't be afraid to fail" adage. This one is much harder to comprehend. That often in life, we are afraid to say, "I'm finished with someone," because we think that means we failed at a relationship, but the failure is in not speaking your truth.

My father tried to live by this wisdom. He wanted to leave for an unknown reason; I doubted I would ever have the answer to his disassociation from family. As an adult I began to wonder if people inquired about his pain? Did a caring hand rest on his shoulder to ask what weighed him down?

On his knees in a church somewhere in Philadelphia, my mother's father prayed for his five children's fate after their mother died. His burden: how would he care for his kids when he had to work and had little money? Within the cement walls of that church, his pain was heard as a nun asked, "What is bothering you, my son?" That moment of curiosity would lead to an orphanage where his children, in the end, would be saved.

Where had the curiosity gone in my nucleus of a family? Why wasn't it a home where someone asked, "How are you?" For all of us then, it would have been a question that salvaged relationships, years, and ultimately decades of hurt.

I knew this to be true, because a tall lanky woman spent hours, then years, asking me just that. Although her question annoyed me at first, it forced me to say what I felt about my own story.

We retreated to our hurt corners then, each convinced their pain mattered most. As a child, I deserved better, but the climb to claiming agency made me stronger. I could see that on the other side. While I needed to undo my life in some ways, with every cell of my being, I knew this shift was where my power lived.

Looking out the porthole on our descent into Brazil, I noticed a sea of *favelas*, concrete and cinderblock masses that appeared like waves rippling under the plane's shadow. I was astounded by the density of the seemingly makeshift but intentional living spaces crammed together. My awe was soon taken over by excitement, knowing I would spend the next week volunteering at an orphanage nestled deep within the mass beneath me.

With me on my flight were three coworkers. We were on a volunteer trip organized by our company, one of the many reasons I would forever be indebted to the place I worked. Amid my brief and declining union to The Wedding Singer, the company felt like the refuge—and reward—I'd been seeking.

Several months before my volunteer trip to Brazil, the universe sent me signs that told me to move my life in another direction. The first was my mother and Susan declaring my need to do something about my marriage. The other was on a flight home from a business trip in Seattle. I was standing in SeaTac's notoriously long security line. In front of me was a petite woman in her fifties.

Moments before, I watched her kiss a nice-looking, bespectacled older gentleman goodbye. When she entered the roped maze ahead of me, she waved to him as he stood to the side by the ropes that separated them. As we snaked along, he appeared again, moving several feet each time, so that when she came to the turn, he was there. They chatted, and she stepped forward as if on an assembly line. Then, after we made another turn, he appeared waiting for her to return to the edge of the barrier. This happened several times, and I began to wonder why anyone not flying would linger in an airport longer than necessary.

I observed them as they spoke, parted, and came together again. Each time he saw her, he wore a warm, loving smile, and they exchanged a few words. While observing them and in need of entertainment, I cooked up several scenarios. The first, they were in a torrid love affair and only saw each other once a year for a weekend of lust. Better yet, they were an older couple having found love for the second or third time. He lived in Seattle, and she lived somewhere else, a golden-years type of arrangement.

Seeing them piqued my ongoing curiosity about love. After one of their brief interludes, as I watched him smile in her direction, I leaned over to the woman and said, "Excuse me, I hope you don't mind, but I have to ask how long you've been together. I've never witnessed such sweetness between two people in the security line."

She laughed, and we both looked down the lane to see the man standing there, waiting again, to greet her at his place by the barrier. He was genuinely happy to linger in the chaos.

"We've been married for thirty years. We raised two children, and he has always been this way with me."

I felt my mouth drop open. "Wow. I didn't expect to hear that. You seem so connected and in love."

"We are."

I pondered how I could count on one hand the times a boy dropped me off at the curb in an airport. I was witnessing some next-level sort of love.

"What's your secret?" I asked.

"We give each other space, and we love each other when we're together. I've always done my girl trips, which is where I'm going now. The most important thing is to be independent and free but together at the same time."

A few people around us began listening. It was truly remarkable witnessing him gaze at her, completely in love, as if it was the first time. When we reached him, she told him my question, and he smiled. "I've always known how lucky I am to have her. I miss her when she's gone, but I want her to enjoy life without me as well."

With my eyes full of tears, I said, "You both gave me something to aspire to in life. It's beautiful to see; thank you."

We said our good-byes, and I noticed people around us after listening to our small exchange had furrowed brows as they questioned their own relationship.

What they shared seemed so simple, but I knew it wasn't. It was work. It was intention. It was commitment. It was consistency. It was love celebrated even in a crowded airport, a place where compassion seemed to disappear. Two people, married for decades, shown a light amongst the gray tension, and it was beautiful because they were clear.

While in Brazil we stayed in a dorm with Cross Cultural Solutions; we slept in bunk beds, ate rice and beans, and every morning loaded into buses that took us into the heart of the favelas to an orphanage. The van bumped up and down over the fragmented streets. Before our trip we were given a shopping list of things to bring for the kids: coloring books, crayons, balloons, and balls, but avoid candy. We played with the children all day, leaving at three. Throughout our time there the children would say in unison, "*doce tia*" so often we asked the guide what they wanted—only to learn they were asking for candy. Oddly enough, the thing the children loved most was to have their picture taken; they wanted to be seen.

I spent a good portion of my day taking turns holding a two-year-old boy we called "Little Old Man," because of his pensive, solemn demeanor. I wondered what he had seen in his young life, and why he wore such reserve on his face as if he had lived decades. Where were his parents? I wondered what it was like for him to feel something from me during the day and then return to his cot in a concrete room surrounded by other children at night. When would he be held again? Would it be enough love to carry him through?

As he leaned into me, I closed my eyes in appreciation and love. With his warmth in my lap, I felt a shift in my soul, a confirmation I wanted children. I let Little Old Man's head rest on me until he fell asleep. I breathed in his sweet smell and asked the universe to send both of us something miraculous.

During the week in Brazil, I thought of my mother and how she called an orphanage home for ten years. Children amassed in a place with one another; strangers thrown together in shared spaces dependent on the kindness of others. Children with nowhere else to go. Children who wanted nothing more than their parents, no matter who they were, but for some tragic reason they could not be together.

How could my mother teach me about relationships, family, and motherhood when it was something she was seeking, not something she understood? She knew the absence of love far better than she understood a healthy, present one. This was her painful legacy to me, to pass on the knowing of love and holding on to a vision of its presence long after it had gone.

I thought of my brother. How my mother had chosen to give him to another family to raise, and how in some ways, that was better than what happened to her as a child. For her generation, providing him with a stable home and family was a life lived better than the one destined for a single mother raising her child alone. Mothers forced their pregnant daughters to relinquish their babies. Society told them being pregnant was their mistake, even though often it was something done to them.

I wanted children, but I didn't want them with the person I was with. I knew that to be true from the deepest part of my soul. I had been finished with The Wedding Singer for some time. Yet I finally understood it was not failure, but clarity of a new kind—freedom from what was then. Among the dust and barren home of the orphaned children, it no longer felt like such a struggle to declare my truth. Who was I to complain about what I had and where I was going? A failed marriage was recoverable. There were options. The children I colored with, hugged, and made laugh as they wore my sunglasses were stuck. I wasn't.

With Little Old Man in my arms, I was holding my family's secrets. The things we rarely talked about. The truths my mother ran away from at times. The orphanage. The adoption. The divorces. The betrayals. The marriages that should have never happened.

These were the legacies gifted to me, and as I began to accept myself, the fear of owning them dissipated. These familial secrets were mine now, too. I had a choice on how to hold them. Would I keep them as shameful secrets or understand them as hardships that were overcome?

Knowing I needed to do something different with my life, first I had to accept the mistakes I made. I'd chosen the careful route by trying to stay in a relationship for the long haul. I found myself crying on the bathroom floor while reading Elizabeth Gilbert's *Eat, Pray, Love* and felt an instant kinship with her experience. Curious by my devotion to the book, The Wedding Singer picked it up and started to read, then said to me, "Wow, we should get divorced."

In that moment, I appreciated him because he wasn't afraid of those brutally honest moments. Although it hurt to admit I had gotten us there, we'd also done it together. He opened the door, and we began to walk through it.

On the eve of my thirty-third birthday, I wrote a list of intentions. I got up from bed with the familiar angst another year brings and said to myself, "No more. It's time to manifest this life on my terms." I wrote down the eleven things I wanted from a relationship. I was also prepared to live life solo and have a child on my own. The process of writing my wish list was prescriptive, like a doctor's note diagnosing what you have and how you will get better. Something I'd never done for myself. For the first time in my life, I was documenting what I deserved.

I made my wishes simple, allowing for life to fill in the color: consistency, passion, similar interests, stability, family, deep understanding, similar life goals, spending time together, planning for things, active lifestyle, and a deep bond.

I hid the piece of paper in the top drawer of my dresser and let fate do the rest.

CHAPTER THIRTY

WHAT LOVE FELT LIKE

Anna, 1969

"You must forget this place and what happened to you here," the counselor said as I shifted in my seat, trying to find a comfortable position. My belly was growing, and everything on my body was swollen. On a near-daily basis, our counselors coached us on how to rehabilitate from the place we found ourselves.

"Forget the father, your child, forget it all. You are doing the right thing giving your child to parents who can love them and give them a better life. A life not based on sin. The girls here are not people you can know after this experience. They're not your friends, so don't share any contact information with them."

Shamed robbed me of my voice.

At the orphanage I learned to be obedient, to be quiet and submissive to the rules that kept us in motion. My time in the Florence Crittenton home had nearly silenced me completely.

There was a part of me that wanted to remind this strange woman that I lived by other people's rules for years, that this was just a continuation of the familiar for me. Where there was compassion and care at the Home, the place I found myself in Miami was void of it. To remain inconspicuous was the goal.

As young, pregnant, single women, we spent our days in the living room watching TV, reading, and learning to knit. The curtains remained drawn on the bottom floor to hide us from the outside world. We slept upstairs and were allowed to open those shades. I breathed in the fresh air as if it were cool water after a day in a dry desert. Knitting became my salvation. The constant movement of my hands while watching spools of yarn turn into a scarf, a hat, or a blanket was a welcome distraction as my belly and discomfort grew.

Despite the counselor's recommendations, we bonded with one another. We shared our stories in hushed voices and silent tears. Looking around the room, I marveled at how young and beautiful all the girls were. Women full of life, despite being isolated in a house until we were transported to a hospital to deliver children in our bellies.

During my stay, we left the grounds twice. On these rare occasions, we were driven to a shopping mall and quickly shuffled through in the hope that no one would realize what we were—pregnant, unwed women. Our guardians followed us around closely, ensuring we didn't speak to anyone. We were given fake wedding rings to wear in case anyone asked a question. While it was a taste of freedom, the pain we carried with us stripped any joy from the experience.

Occasionally, at night, I would hear a girl begin to gasp and cry. I knew it was her time, my eyes widening in fear as the counselors rushed to quiet her. A car would start up at the back of the house, and I would hear the engine fade into the darkness as she was driven away. She would return, her belly deflated and her face even more so.

"Tell us, how bad does it hurt?" we asked.

"Nothing can prepare you," they would say, and it would be the last time we ever saw them.

I soon learned the sensation the girls experienced was like a deep burning, followed by a ripping pain as if someone was taking an ice cream scooper to your insides. As I was driven to the hospital, the shock overwhelmed any emotion threatening to spill over. As we pulled up to the hospital, a nurse rushed over with a wheelchair.

"This is Anna from the Crittenton House," I heard the counselor say. The nurse nodded and didn't say a word to me as I winced and bent over clutching my belly. They brought me to a room with no windows at the end of a hallways and left me alone for some time.

As the process moved along, and more mind-numbing contractions came, the counselor began walking me through the process. I had forgotten her name and didn't care. I was supposed to forget about all of this, wasn't I?

"Anna, we recommend you don't hold the baby. It makes it too difficult." I nodded, unable to comprehend that someone was going to take my baby.

Another contraction came, and I screamed.

"You're getting closer, dear. I'll grab the doctor."

Entering the room was a handsome man, his white jacket flapping like a cape, followed by two nurses. They didn't look in my direction. It all felt so familiar. I was invisible before, a statistic among children, only now I was the mother.

You can run, Anna. Leave this place now and take your baby with you.

The thought was quickly snuffed by the reminder that the people waiting for my child were better than me, more deserving. What life could my baby have with a mother shunned for her bad decisions?

"The baby is coming. It's time." The doctor's eyes continued to avoid me as he looked toward my counselor. "We're going to tell her to push, and she needs to push hard."

My child was coming into the world, into existence, while I was disappearing. I was dispensable. I continued to push, but I had something to say.

Leave me alone. All of you get out of here and leave my baby with me.

As the room filled with sounds of my delivery, there was a shift. Released into the world was a baby boy whose cries quieted mine.

My baby. My God, my baby. Give him to me. Give him to me. Oh, dear God, someone please let us out of here.

The nurses rushed over and grabbed the squealing infant out of the doctor's hands.

I looked to the counselor who summoned the compassion to pat my arm. In the first sign of empathy, her eyes were full of tears, but I imagined they weren't for me, they were for him.

"What is it? A boy? A girl? Can I just hold them for a minute, please?"

"A boy, dear. A beautiful baby boy. He's perfect." Her hand went to my head and pushed me down. "Relax. You did a good job."

My giving birth was a job. The delivery of my first child was a transaction. My body tangled in fatigue, relaxed into the stiff sheets. I felt every organ crash into knowing it would never be the same again.

There was no natural light in the room, just four sterile walls with paint the color of mints and white tile. A steel table held medical equipment. My heart was the cold temperature of steel.

My son's cries were carried out of the room. I never even saw his face. They finished working on me and left without a word. I was alone in the metallic, cold room with a stranger. She wiped my brow, and I was grateful for her touch.

"Here, take this," she said, handing me a small paper cup with a pill in it. I swallowed the large oval shape down without a single question, and then the world went dark.

I woke up hours later feeling sedated in a small room with a window. The sky appeared black, and the clock on the wall said five. *Is it morning or night?*

I stood up, and everything inside me hurt. My stomach, still swollen, looked smaller now. I pulled open the curtains, grateful for the sound breaking the stillness in the room. My view faced a parking lot. I stared at the cars and noticed the hum of a fan and the ping of an elevator.

He is here, Anna. He is in the building. Find him. Take your baby and run out of here.

As I stared out the window, I realized I had no car. I had nowhere to go. Where would I take the baby? None of these people would let me leave with him. I had nothing to offer that sweet being, his face unknown to me, his cries playing like a soundtrack in the distance.

You are nothing to him now. Forget about it like they told you to. Remember, this is the sacrifice parents make. Remember Daddy? Isn't this what he did for you? Didn't he let you go so you could have more?

I lay back down on the bed and let my eyes grow heavy. Nurses came in and checked on me, muttering a few words as they did.

After resting for two days in the hospital room by myself, the nurse from Florence Crittenton came to get me.

"Pack your bag; it's time to leave now."

On the drive home in the car, the counselor sat next to me.

"Remember, forget what happened to you here. Try to make a life for yourself beyond this. Forget the girls, forget everything. Get married and have a family, like an honest woman."

I sat in silence as she spoke to me, my eyes transfixed as buildings passed by our car in a blur. I saw my belly still extended from where my baby once lived. I thought about what she was saying, and I wondered if a new life was possible.

As we got closer to the place where I would collect my things and leave the next morning, I noticed waves rolling on the beach in the distance, shifting forward and backward as if timed to music. In my head, I heard Rachmaninoff's "Prelude in C-Sharp Minor," and my fingers began to move against the swell of my legs as if they were on piano keys.

Letting go of my first child is where my life ended but also where it began. Of all the things that could have destroyed me, hearing his cries being carried out of the room broke the little girl Anna inside of me. I realized that nothing in my life could have been worse than that moment. Not even losing Mommy, being placed in an orphanage by Daddy, and losing him two years later. Nothing undid my soul the way giving up my baby did, a hurt so vast it remained difficult to comprehend, one that would remain a secret.

Surviving the decision meant I had to rebuild myself all over again. I returned to Philadelphia and refused to accept anything less than what I wanted out of life. I would pursue the "more" I ached for in life. Love. Normalcy.

I put one foot in front of the other, waiting for my spirit to repair itself. I told no one what happened, not even my brothers. How could life take so much from me and not give me what I deserve?

At the age of thirty—at a time when many women were considered old maids—I took a new job as a secretary at Sunship. The company was a bustling shipyard connected to Sun Oil, where many eligible young men worked. My job was simple, and at times I was so bored I sat at my desk reading a book.

I had taken to wearing modern clothes, short minidresses with knee-high boots to show off my legs, and tight sweaters to emphasize my ample top. I started to walk with my head held high. Men began flirting with me, and I started to have a sense of hope.

One month into the job, a newly divorced, single dad of two girls put his tie over the partition of my desk and asked me for a date. I called Eve with excitement telling her about "Cutie-pie," the nickname I gave him.

His name was Richard; he was driven and determined. He focused on work and seeing his children on the weekends. Our conversations flowed as we connected on the complicated truths of living. I knew I could not accept a man who didn't know what happened to me, so I told him about relinquishing my firstborn.

One night, sitting on the red-painted steps of his small house in Boothwyn, martinis in hand, he asked me what I wanted out of life.

"A dog and a baby," I said.

A year later we married. We found common ground because we were both starting over in many ways.

My dream of having and holding a child came a year later. I held my little girl and never a day went by that I didn't feel the overwhelming warmth of being a mother. From the moment she was born, I focused on giving her the one thing I'd wanted so much in my childhood, a mother's love.

As I looked into her eyes, I told her she was the best thing that happened to me, even though every time I looked at her, I knew there was a piece of me missing. Somewhere out in the world was my firstborn.

I always wondered what happened to my little boy. I thought of him from the moment I woke up till the time I went to sleep. I promised myself that, when I could, I would find him. If we reunited, I would try to explain why it happened and how it happened and hope he understood.

That is what you learn when you lose so much at such a young age: there is loss in love. There always is. But to love, even if for only a brief moment in time, is worth it.

CHAPTER THIRTY-ONE

THE BIRTH

Jennifer, 2010

Nearly two years after writing the list of qualities I wanted in a partner and tucking the list in my top dresser drawer, I was being driven from Berkeley to CPMC hospital in San Francisco at four-thirty in the morning. In the driver's seat sat the man who personified the characteristics I wanted.

We met at work. He walked on my floor with a cowboy swagger and a story. At first, we had a friendship, and that soon developed into a connection that couldn't be ignored. He was like my father, a divorced dad of two young kids, determined not to let his early life's mistakes rule his future. A man determined to make the most of what he was given and to have the life he'd always wanted. But he was different from my father in that he was open and unafraid of showing vulnerability.

Upon hearing about our engagement, my father called with concern, "You need to be careful; you don't want to deal with all of that." The knife of my father's words continued to live, but they didn't take me down as they did before. In fact, I began to understand his love language. His cryptic words were referring to my fiancé's divorce, and what it would mean to help raise his children.

"Dad, come on, you see he's similar to you, right?" My sister Beth would echo the same to him when he brought up his concern. My father knew that marrying someone like him was complicated. The irony of my decision was not lost on me. Being in my mid thirties when single again, I knew the chance of meeting someone divorced was likely and children from a previous marriage probable. However, I wanted someone who had experience and who learned lessons when things didn't work the first time.

I met my match, someone who saw and moved in the world as I did. Someone who was not afraid to show me love and appreciation. He embodied consistency. A man who might drop me off at the airport from time to time but not stand with me at the security line.

Over the years our marriage would be tested by outside influences in ways I never imagined possible, my father's foreshadowing. Eventually, I would realize that fundamentally, you are never stepping into a parenting role as a second wife; you are living with someone's divorce, and that can be messy. Downright ugly at times.

My marriage would be a series of lessons in seeking agency all over again. However, love wrapped the pursuit. The lens was slanted, a different view, but there would be one thing that held us together when times felt unsurvivable. We loved each other, and our union began when we were two complete individuals. We didn't need to be together; we wanted to be.

We were married in a modern glass rental house in front of a handful of friends and family four weeks before my delivery. It was a surprise pregnancy early on in our engagement that we immediately learned was high-risk. "You'll be lucky if you keep this baby," was the painful warning. For decades I suffered from debilitating endometriosis, and when I learned of my pregnancy through an ultrasound, they discovered my severely separated uterus shaped like bunny ears.

Keeping my pregnancy was my only concern until a month before the due date. Once I knew the baby would make it, I decided I didn't mind a more permanent union made with my extended belly between us. I was finally having the child I always wanted with the person who was right for me. Convention no longer mattered. I knew a happy wedding wasn't an indicator of a successful union.

Only a few people attended the small ceremony in our house on a Friday night after receiving an invitation the week before: my sisters, my parents, my husband's potpourri family, and a few friends. At the reception, I found my mom and dad sitting together on our sofa. It was the first time they'd had a conversation since their divorce. The room stared in their direction, whispering about their reconnection after decades of quiet.

I took a seat in between them. Our fractured family unit, together again after twenty years, with the swell of my belly as the anchor.

My mother appeared nervous. "I don't know why you get worked up because we're talking," she said.

"Mom, relax; people are just happy that you're having a conversation at my wedding."

Their words were short and brief and solely about the little boy due a month later.

Someone took a picture of the three of us. The first photo taken of us since the awkward dinner after I'd graduated from high school, and it would be our last.

A month later I awoke at three in the morning with an overwhelming sensation of having to go to the bathroom. Remembering what the nurse told me at one of my many ultrasounds, I realized what was happening. The night before we hosted a friend, and as she and my husband drank red wine, I declared, "That's it, I'm done being pregnant."

They laughed, "It doesn't work that way. You don't declare you're ready, and it happens." Well, I did.

Twelve hours later, I was nearing the end of the delivery. Since my epidural, I'd been pushing for hours, living in that strange sensation where you are exerting yourself, but you can't feel the pain. The nurse at the end of my bed coached me when the air in the room shifted. Several people huddled near her whispering to one another. My attending nurse called out something that caused someone to rush to the wall beside me and push a red button. Within seconds the door to the room flew open, and a team of nurses dressed in blue with masks on ran in. One was pushing a table with surgical materials; the rest were racing around the room grabbing items.

In an instant, I had gone from pushing and counting to a flurry of activity at the base of my bed. I looked toward my husband whose face was void of color. Before I could ask why the energy was changing, the blond nurse with blue eyes, who was asking me to push, turned to me.

"Jennifer, you might need to deliver via C-section. I don't want you to panic, but the baby's heartbeat is dropping, and we need to act."

She sounded like the teacher from *Peanuts*.

My husband put his hands on my arm.

"What? Why?" A machine beeped as my blood pressure skyrocketed.

My doctor raced in, her white coat floating behind her like a superhero.

She pushed the stressed nurse out of the way. I watched her eyes dart in every direction, assessing the situation.

"Why didn't you tell me this was going on? You're supposed to call me."

The attending nurse's head dropped, and she skulked to the corner of the room.

I observed my doctor take a deep breath, then her eyes turned to me with intensity. I had chosen her as my doctor because of her demeanor. "Can you shift on your left side?" I moved my body, barely feeling how I was shifting except for the sensation in my shoulders. Her hands were going places within me I couldn't feel.

"Turn more to your left. There, that's it." My entire body leaned to the left, including my hips with my feet still in stirrups. A beeping sound I hadn't noticed before changed.

"We're okay," she said to everyone in the room. Her shoulders lowered. She said something to the crew that raced into the room several minutes before. They gathered their things and left at a slow pace, unlike the running from a few minutes before. A few looked at me and smiled.

My doctor was in charge now and spoke with tranquility and command, "Your baby has the cord wrapped around his neck. I'm going to cut it, but I want you to know he's going to come out purple."

After another push, there was the sound of a snip, and blood splattered across the room reaching far away walls and the ceiling, some hitting her in the face.

I felt utterly helpless. "I'm sorry," I said as if I had any control over the expulsion of my blood.

"Nope, that's my job." She smiled at me. "You can lie down flat again."

I noticed my husband making weird hand gestures, as if he could help in some way, but he only reminded me of a clumsy puppy.

In the moment of stillness after chaos, I thought of my mother and how scared she must have been when she delivered my brother. Alone, judged, and completely at the mercy of others. No one familiar by her side. Like me, she was in a room giving birth, but that was where the story changed. She was alone. No one loved her. No one cared for her. She was shameful; someone to be dismissed. They wanted to take her baby, and they wanted her to disappear. To be forgotten forever. Somewhere in that hospital, the parents who would raise her son were eagerly awaiting his arrival. Papers would be signed, money paid, and then he was their child. Not my mother's, theirs. She spent hours delivering her baby, only to hear him carried away before she even saw him, his cries haunting her forever.

My God, how did she survive such a horrific experience?

My thoughts were broken by my doctor's voice.

"We have a few more pushes." She began counting by threes. When she hit three, my upper body lifted, and I exerted with all the energy I had, falling back in exhaustion seconds later.

"Okay, on the next one at the count of three, I want you to sit up and grab your baby."

What did she just say?

"What? Grab my baby?" I said, looking at her, but her eyes were on her work.

"One."

"Did you say grab my baby?"

No classes, magazines or blogs had mentioned this.

"Two...hurry, or I have to...three."

With little sense of what was happening, I sat up and reached between my legs spread open on the table and grabbed the infant I spent twelve hours extracting from my body. His warm, wet, and bloody body was in my hands, and I pulled him to my chest and laid down. There was no rule book or thought process to what I had just accomplished.

What lives in my mind of this moment is not a memory, but a scene that split my life in two—then and now.

A nurse rushed to my side.

"We have to take him for a moment to make sure his vitals are okay."

"He should be fine," my doctor said. She was smiling at me, proud her "grab your baby" surprise had worked.

I was lost in the euphoria. I turned to see my husband in tears next to me, the camera frozen between his fingers, speechless.

"Hon, take pictures, GO. Did you not get that on film?" I knew those feelings and sensations would never leave me, but I would always have the hardest time seeing the blur of the room. How such a dreamlike weave could have been my reality. The sensation of pulling my son close to me and having him carried away was like levitating. Within minutes he was back on my chest wrapped in a blanket printed with blue and pink feet.

"He checked out fine. The cord issue didn't affect him. There he is. A beautiful boy with a full head of hair," my doctor said as she smiled and left the room.

As he lay on my chest his eyes met mine. He was quiet, almost serene, exhausted from his journey into this world. My hands were still red with blood from grabbing him the moment he emerged into the world.

Gazing into his face my center shifted to a place of belonging and clarity I had yet to experience in life.

"Hello, Drake."

He gazed back at me.

Then, I promised him I would never let go.

Giving birth can be a reckoning. A culmination of who you are, hope, and the breaking open of a love you've never known.

Three months after our son was born, we flew to Seattle to visit and introduce him to friends and family. My mother hosted a brunch, "To show off my grandson."

"You can invite your father if you want," she said in a strained voice. It was the same uneasy tone she used for twenty years whenever she spoke about her ex-husband. It was mixed with sadness, hurt, and longing.

Despite living three miles from each other, my parents barely spoke except for brief "hellos" at parties or events and a brief conversation at my wedding.

My father harbored both personal and financial resentment toward her. My mother, in many ways, was still waiting for him to love her again.

"Dad, we're hosting a gathering at my mom's house on Sunday. I want you to know you're invited, but I also want you to know I understand if you don't come. I know how you feel about everything."

Two months earlier, my father had flown down, along with my sisters, to meet Drake when he was only a month old. Pulling up in his rental car, he marched up our steps and said, "Let me have him."

Once in his arms he proceeded to pull down his diaper to see if he had a "winky-dink."

"Yup, it's a boy," he said as my sisters and I giggled. My father was a man who had three girls and four granddaughters before my son finally came around. My oldest sister, Beth, referred to his only grandson as "The Golden Ticket."

My phone call to invite him to my mother's house was made after it had taken me decades to understand my father and finally see him for who he was: a man who had worked tirelessly since he was a parent at nineteen and spent nine years going to night school to get a college degree. By the time I was a teenager, when he announced he wanted to leave our family, he had been raising children and providing for others for nearly thirty years. He built a company from nothing, nearly raised all three of his kids, and wanted a break. He was a man who did well in life, not because it was handed to him, but because he was gritty. Despite my disappointment in his decisions then, I was beginning to see where his anger came from; he wanted to be on his own and then denied himself that gift out of duty. Being a husband was a job he no longer wanted to fulfill. Hurtful and wrong, yes, but admitting this truth took guts.

"Let me think about it. I'll call you back." I heard the phone click. I knew he was standing at the familiar spot by the phone in the kitchen of our old house, smoking a cigarette, and thinking hard about walking into his ex-wife's home.

He called me back two minutes later.

"I'll come. I'll come because of that little boy."

There was the beautiful and harsh truth of my—our—story. Decades later, we healed from what happened in my family through the hope that emerged with the birth of my son. He gave all of us something absent from our lives for so many years.

My mother was given a second chance. I afforded her the thing she lost all those years ago. She was able to enjoy her grandson after making the painful decision to let her firstborn go.

My father found a reason for acceptance.

For me, light existed where there had been cold, dark, and lonely shadows. Hope emerged; there was distance from what was then.

EPILOGUE

I was compelled to write my story, to write my mother's story in the hope of understanding not only who she was, but who I am. As I grew older, I came to realize that my mother's young life, in many ways, influenced my own. Her love has been my guide but also my undoing at times. When I became a mother myself, I began to see the connection in our stories. The burden of legacy and the power it has over us. When I had my son, the stakes became higher because I was now responsible for another person's life. I needed to understand my experience and find a way to use the past—even the painful parts of it—for good.

The passing of my father allowed me to finish this book. Days before he died, he told my sisters and me the missing piece to the puzzle of my adolescence.

When we found out he had only months to live, we became his caregivers. He wanted to die with dignity, and we made sure of that. We leveraged the Washington State law to give my father the power to choose the day of his passing. An engineer by trade, he planned to leave on his terms versus suffering unnecessarily. He bestowed us with the honor of walking him to the other side, and he was determined to leave this world as elegantly as possible.

On the heels of his illness, my oldest sister, Beth, received a diagnosis for an aggressive cancer. The doctors gave her a year to live unless she received a stem-cell transplant. As my father declined, she was having chemo in preparation for her life-extending procedure.

My sister Linda took on the majority of our father's care as she lived nearby. I flew to Seattle often to relieve her and spend time with him. We had repaired our relationship over the years and finally came full circle. I like to say my father and I grew into ourselves and grew up together in some ways.

With a few weeks left to live, Linda and I moved in with him. Decades later, I was back in the house I'd been raised in. The house my mother got in the divorce and then sold. The house my father bought back from a stranger.

At first, discomfort took over in this familiar, yet unfamiliar, place. There was the sliding door in the kitchen where my father stood at attention near the phone. The floors that creaked under the carpet. The house with a view of the sound, and the ships, including my father's, sailed past throughout the day. The massive engines created a vibration in our small village. I was in the house with the basement bedroom and bath where I waged war on myself during my adolescence.

I refused to stay in my old room, never wanting to return to that dark place where merely being within the four walls brought back the sad terror I carried as a teenager. I chose to sleep in the guest room near the kitchen. As an adult, the kitchen felt small and cramped, not large and foreboding as it did when I was a child. The small table tucked against the window, looking out over Commencement Bay. A different table from the one where my parents had dinners late at night after drinking for a few hours. Something other than the one where I browsed through cookbooks while denying myself food.

We took care of my father during the day and prepared a meal of his choice at night. I made him his nightly martini with crushed ice and olives. We sat at his feet and read to him. We watched *Jeopardy* together.

"Jennifer, you make the martini. Linda, you cook the food." It was a wise choice on his part; Linda is brilliant with food, and I'm better at mixing a drink. There were no requests for Beth, who sat quietly on the sofa next to him, experiencing her own dance with death.

After his perfectly curated evening came to an end, and he sat in his recliner to fall asleep, the three of us would sit at the kitchen table and talk. We were bonding in a way none of us knew was possible. We talked about our father, who he was, and who he wasn't. We drank his wine. We talked about how we weren't done with him yet but knew he desired to leave his body but not his life. We discussed how different our childhoods were and how they shaped us.

"It wasn't right, what happened to you in this house, Jen," my sister Beth declared. My muscles softened at her recognition of my truth.

"No, Beth, it wasn't. He said he wanted to leave when I was fourteen, and for some reason, he stayed. It was hell. It really was. I know you both wanted more of Dad when you were younger, but living here wasn't ideal. He was so tortured then."

Their heads nodded. They lost him when they were young, too, but in a different way.

We agreed as he faced the end of his life, my father was soft and open. He held our hands in the car rides to the hospital. He cried and shared. He invited us into his many friendships he had kept separate. He let us know he was the happiest during the last five years of his life: retired, traveling to see his grandkids, proud of us girls and what we had done with our lives. "I like your husbands; go figure," he chuckled.

A few days before he died, breathing oxygen through tubes in his nose, he sat the three of us down at the kitchen table and said, "There is one more thing I need to tell you. I'll be right back." With authority, he took his walker and the oxygen tubes in his nose and made the long trek back to his bedroom to retrieve something. He returned with a black folder and sat down at the table, out of breath.

"There was a woman. She was the love of my life. Her name was Maya."

My sisters and I exchanged glances. All our eyes confirmed what the other was thinking; we had never heard the woman's name.

He opened the small folder in his hands and pulled out pictures of his trip to Australia those many years ago, the ones that gave me a hint of his affair when I was a teenager. There were dozens of pictures of him with Maya. They were the pictures missing from the stack he'd left on the kitchen counter for my mother and me to peruse. He also pulled out his expired passport with the country stamps and dates for us to see. The dates were in 1988, the year he announced he wanted to leave. My blood raced and caused me to sit upright at attention.

Are you kidding me? This happens now?

At last, I knew why he said to my mother and me, "I don't want to be here anymore." It was nearly thirty years later, and I finally had the answer.

Linda looked at me and mouthed, "Are you okay?" I nodded despite feeling the weight of the reality my father had just gifted me.

Before me, I was staring at the proof of what we had all suffered then. All I could think was how sad it was for him that he never realized his relationship with this strange woman, even if later that night, my sisters and I concluded it was most likely lust personified.

My God, why did I have to wait so long?

And there it was, the catalyst I needed to put the puzzle together. By the time I was fourteen, both my parents were absent, caught up in their own fantasies—their own lives at crossroads. My mother had found her son. My father had found a new love.

How could they have guided me through my adolescence if they were lost themselves?

"Now there is nothing left to tell. You know everything." He got up, tore up the pictures, and threw them in the trash.

My father died two days later in what was a peaceful and beautiful grand exit layered in nothing more than love.

My sisters and I held him as he took his last breath.

Before he left this world, as I sat at his feet like I did each night, there was something I needed to tell him about his revelation.

"Dad, you didn't need to stay. I'm sorry you felt like you had to." He was always about duty and responsibility. I now understand that when he wanted to go years before, it was because he knew he could no longer fulfill his role as a husband. It was a difficult realization he shared and then chose to ignore. As an adult, I identified with his dilemma; I had done it myself in my first marriage.

I looked up and found him with his head tilted upwards, his eyes closed, the pain melting from his eyes. In the weeks before he died, I would see him do this often when he was facing a truth that was permanent now—his life was ending.

"Thank you," he said and let his head fall against the pillow on his worn rocker.

One of the last things I said to him before he died was, "Go see Maya and your parents, Papa." I would like to think he did.

The truth of the matter is I lost my father when I was fourteen and then at forty-two. His departure from this earth was a gift on so many levels, but most of all, it was the purest form of love and grace I've witnessed in my life.

It was through the truth he bestowed on me at the end of his life that I finally understood the catalyst for the trauma I'd faced as a teenager. Also, through writing my mother's story, I have come to realize why she couldn't let go of her marriage even though it was irreparably damaged.

My father was the one thing she always wanted in her life. He was the security and stability she craved for decades. To let my father go would have been like saying goodbye to *her* father all over again. Her life's foundation was about losing the people she loved. For her, to love was to hurt. To let go of my father would have been giving in to the legacy of pain she had endured. If she could, she would make him stay, and she did. The agreement was made under the premise it happened for my benefit, but I have said to her it would have been better if he'd gone. She still doesn't see it that way.

My mother, the survivor, the hero of her own story, tried to reverse something already done. My father left by the time he announced his desire to leave. Reflecting on those dark days, she said, "It wasn't all that bad; we weren't throwing plates or anything like that. It was more like a cold war."

"Mom, *Red Dawn* was scary. Those were the days we were hiding under our desks at school in case there was a nuclear war." The analogy is lost on her.

I have tried to understand how she doesn't see the dysfunction in that, but again it is not something she is willing to face even though she survived it. It is my belief that her life in the Home was the reason she could live in such a painful existence for all those years. The Home, and her life in it, is the center of her emotional being.

"Despite it all, I did have a good experience in the Home. All we wanted were our parents, but we were well cared for and had a good childhood," my mom says often.

Eventually, my mother would tell Mrs. Harting she was grateful for her, just as the woman who ran the Home said she would. Not every child from their orphanage feels that way. But the Rangnow children see the positive in their experience. They realize the good in their father's insistence on keeping them all together. In the end, they have always clung to each other, like he intended.

Eve would play the role of mother to my mom. They would remain close throughout their childhood and adulthood until one day, after a visit to my aunt in Lake Tahoe when I was nine years old, they didn't speak for nearly ten years. My mother says that, despite the grief from the separation, it was a break that gave her clarity.

"I needed that time out of Eve's shadow to see who I really am. It was the first time I felt beautiful. Free."

They would never discuss the reason Eve stopped calling her or why, but upon hearing about my mother's divorce, she decided to pick up the phone and call my mom.

My aunt would play an interesting role in my life. As a young girl, I idolized her. She had nine cats and two dogs and lived in a house on stilts. Later, she became a steward of truth, especially toward the end of her life. She was diagnosed with myelofibrosis, and it was taking her slowly. I asked my mother if I could document her life.

"I'll ask, but she's guarded."

After a few phone calls, Eve relented. She agreed to a lunch where we could talk about their childhood.

"Go slow, Jenny. Eve doesn't like to talk about the past."

A month later, we were seated in front of Eve, sipping wine. At first, she sat rigid like an emotional brick wall. I had a lot of convincing to do.

"I want to know about your life," I said. "About you. I don't want your story to be lost. I want to know not only you, but myself. Our history."

We were seated under an umbrella on the deck of a restaurant in Port Angeles. Eve wore pink, and her blond hair sat coiffed in a headband. Her eyes were bright, and she had plump, shiny skin. Even with a few extra pounds on her from her medication and an illness taking over her body, she was beautiful. To hear her speak and laugh, you could sense what a stunning young woman she had been: the type of person to take over a room just by entering it.

After a few minutes of hesitation and a few sips of her drink, Eve began to sing. Much like my mother does when she has a glass of wine or is in the car for a long drive.

"Well, Jenny, you have to forgive us as we fucked and fumbled through our lives. We weren't prepared for the world we were thrown into when we got out of the orphanage. The orphanage was like a convent. Hell, it *was* a convent. They kept us away from boys, under curfew, and then sent us out in the world terrified of sex. 'Wait until you get married' is all they would say. We were thrust into the world when women were burning their bras, and the sexual revolution was happening. We had no idea what to do."

I thought of my mother pregnant with my brother and alone. How terrified she must have been, knowing society thought of her as an outcast given her situation but witnessing the world's view on sex slowly changing.

As Eve drank more of her wine, she became more impassioned.

"You know, Jenny, we could have been something. I could have had a career, but instead...*nooooo*. We were raised to get out of the orphanage and find a husband. That marrying a man was our hope in life. That as women, we should cleave to our husbands. Pshaw!"

I loved her more with each sip and word.

"So, that is what I did. I married Preston and let him walk all over me. We were married for ten years; he made me go and buy the ring on my own when we were engaged. The final straw for me came ten years later. We were sitting down for breakfast. Preston sat crying, begging me to console him because his mistress left him, and she was such a wonderful lover."

She saw my mouth hang wide open.

"Yes, he said that! My husband!" She took a large gulp. "After that, I was done with him. I had the strength to leave him after that."

"I called Howard and told him get me with his pick-up truck. I left with a twin mattress, some jewelry that I'll give you, and my clothes. That was it."

"Decades later, I called Preston and told him what an asshole he was." She was beaming with pride, having staked some sort of dignity from that situation.

The lunch with Eve was like putting together a puzzle whose pieces my mother laid out on the table but failed to put together. Eve completed the vision I had of their young life. I could feel the closeness of the two sisters and how at times they were in conflict with one another. Almost too dependent on each other for survival.

Before she passed, she had taken the time to identify the things she wanted to give people.

She wrote messages on Post-its attached to each item. A few weeks before she died, I received a package in the mail. Inside was a beautiful gold diamond necklace with matching earrings. Along with it was a note written in Eve's elegant handwriting:

> Here is the infamous necklace and earrings Preston gave me. Upon opening it, I was thrilled to receive them until he said, "It's so beautiful, I bought two more." I was heartbroken, but they really are beautiful, aren't they? Now they are yours. Just know there are two more out there in the world. Love, Eve

In one of their last moments together, lying in bed succumbing to the end, Eve looked at my mother and said, "I never really knew myself."

To watch my mother lose the second-most important woman in her life was like watching her lose her lifeline. She charged through it as if dancing with an old friend. To love was to let go.

I began to see a familiar pattern in her life; the people she was closest to often disappeared. Still, she marched forward.

My mother and brother maintained a relationship for many years that slowly faded to something distant and cordial. They had good times together and were able to reconnect after lost years, but something happened. Something that will remain between them.

For my sisters and me, Jack is the brother we don't see often enough. The one we wish we had in our lives much sooner. He's as good as people come—funny, playful, loyal, and hard working. Something about how we blended as a family will always feel beautiful but limited. For me, the experience of learning about my brother will always feel like gaining and losing something at the same time. I will never have enough of him because our relationship began with loss; his heartbreak is something I can't comprehend.

Five years before Eve's passing, their brother Jim died in his sleep. His siblings had always fretted about him, the youngest and most vulnerable. He had said to them often, "If I pass away, it's okay. Don't be sad for me; I'll be relieved in some ways."

My mother's two remaining brothers live a mile from each other in Oklahoma. They are as entwined now as they were in the years at the Home. During a tornado, Howard raced to John's home, so they could survive it together. They gathered in John's storm shelter with a dog, a cat, and a bunny. They held down the door with all their strength as the sound and fury of the tornado rampaged above them.

"It sounded like a train running us over," they told me on a phone call.

When all went quiet, they opened the door to see everything around them flattened. They endured, rebuilt their homes, and continued to live as a team. They faced the storm together as they always have.

I have come to realize that despite the losses, despite the trauma she experienced, my mother is the hero of her own story. She never gave up when most of us would have. It was her stubbornness, her conviction, and her quest for normalcy that allowed her to endure. It was the reason she was the only one of her siblings to have children; despite it all, she believed normal was possible.

When people asked about the book I was writing, my mother always squirmed. "Is that the book where you complain about me?"

"No. I am writing your story, my story, so I can better understand myself."

"Yeah, well, I like that. I never knew my mother, and I feel cheated. I would like to have known who she was."

Those words are the statue of her existence. The driving force in her life. The foundation of how she mothered me. She mothered from a place of loss and from a void she was trying to fill. My mother always saw me through the filter of her own experience. She was never just my mom; she was the mother she never had. She cared more about being the mother she lost than about being *my* mother, which meant that simply being there and living the fantasy of her childhood equated to enough. And there was the harsher reality of our relationship to absorb; I was the child she kept. The one she wasn't forced to relinquish because society told her she was bad, that her child's only hope was to have parents different than her. I was never going to be able to fill that hole in her heart. I would never be enough because I was just one child. How could I be? It was impossible.

I have also come to realize that I would eventually disappoint my mother. That my love and my father's love was never going to fill the empty spaces in her soul. Towards the end of their marriage, my father—along with my cousin—helped locate her parent's unmarked graves. Incredibly poor, they didn't have enough money for the markers when they died. My dad, already on his way out, purchased headstones, so their resting place could finally say who lay there. Her parents were no longer resting in unmarked graves; they had names. They were somebody. Looking back now, I realize this was part of my father's mental checklist to leave his union honorably.

"If I look at my childhood compared to yours, I was the perfect mother to you," she has said. I have tried to remind her there is no such thing as a perfect mother, but she doesn't want to believe anything different. If I am not there for her in the way she wants, I've heard her say, "I wonder if you love me at all." This while she is seated next to me at a family function that I've ensured she is attending.

For my mother, in many ways, her broken parts have never truly healed. She comes at life from a place of what was taken from her and what life owes her back.

For me, the adage that we become our parents is not true. We echo them in some ways, like our reflection in a pond with ripples. Yet, we don't become them; we live with the legacy of their failures and successes. I've tried to explain to my mother that trauma unaddressed is trauma transferred, but she doesn't want to see the connection in our stories. I no longer need her to see my perspective; my truth lives in these pages, and that is enough for me.

I suppose all of us are trying to decode our parents in some way, to understand them, so we can have a sense of who we are, and why we had the experience we did growing up. And the hope is if we can figure out the riddle, we can do better for our children. This is my hope in writing this book. That my son can see me for the imperfect mother I am and understand the reasons why. That he can accept the ink of emotions in my veins and know I have always been trying to do better—for him—for me. That my failures are simply me trying.

The dream we all have is to rise, not to fall. It was my mother's dream, and while her story is unique, the revelation is the same. To love is the dream. To continue to get up, even after we tumble, is the ascent.

I honor my mother and her story, and I understand that what I have— what I have been given and earned—has a lot to do with who she is. My mother's tenacity—her will to achieve her dream—afforded me the chance to have the life I'm living.

My mother's revelation by the Christmas tree when I was thirteen became my reckoning nearly twenty years later. I made different choices in life, and some that were similar. The culmination of our legacy—from mother to daughter—occurred when I delivered a healthy baby boy, allowing my mother to experience the one thing she lost in life she could never reconcile—her baby boy. She often tells me my son, Drake, is the love of her life, and I believe her.

Sometimes when I look at my son and mother playing together, I see the beauty in it all.

They are a connection made, a chain broken.

End

ACKNOWLEDGMENTS

There is the process of writing a book.

Then, there are the helpers you meet along the way.

Renate Stendhal, our therapeutic conversations sparked chapters that led to this book. There is no memoir without you telling me to "step out of the way" when I finally committed to the work. Debbie Layton, for introducing me to Renate and inspiring me to write in Stinson Beach.

My first official chapter was born during a class through Stanford Continuing Education with Rachel Howard. Years later, I would reach out to her with a manuscript, and her insightful feedback uplifted the book into its current shape.

Brooke Warner and Linda Joy Meyers for the writing clinic that provided me with the formula for writing a memoir. Linda Sivertsen, you are the Book Mama and a writer's best champion. Your Carmel Writing Retreat was a dream, as were the attendees. Special thanks to Elsie Beach, who, after hearing me read, said, "Your story reminds me of a saying in my field, 'Trauma unaddressed is trauma transferred.'" Betsy Rapoport, who dug in and gave me essential editorial feedback.

Tiffany Hawk for the life-changing book proposal course that helped me reshape my pitch at the perfect time. Let's not forget the introduction to the editor who would acquire my work. I'm forever grateful.

Lastly, to Julie Barton, my husband's coworker introduced us. He came home from work and asked me, "Do you know the book *Dog Medicine?* I can get you an introduction to the author."

"Um, yeah, she's amazing."

I was so nervous when I first met you. Eventually, I would begin attending writing classes at your zinc table. To the women in my group who share the depths of your souls every Wednesday, you helped me get here, too. Julie, you were a writing hero who became my teacher, and I'm now honored to call you a dear friend. Your words, "Keep going," meant everything when I needed it most.

Teachers can alter the course of students' lives. Dr. Westmoreland your words, "Do something with your writing. You have a gift," led me down this path. I only wish I believed in myself as much as you did in those early years.

To Debby Englander, thank you for receiving my book proposal and quickly making an offer. When I imagined getting a book deal with an editor, my vision was of you. Thank you, Regalo Press, for acquiring my manuscript and to the publishing team at Post Hill, including my ever-patient managing editor Caitlin Burdette, publisher Anthony Ziccardi and Gretchen Young, Sara Ann Alexander, Alana Mills, Caitlyn Limbaugh, Kate Harris, and Rachel Hoge. Lastly, thank you to The Book Designers for the beautiful cover and for going many rounds to get it just right.

There are friends, people, and places that inspired or supported me throughout this process. In no particular order: Dave Eggers, Greg Isles, Kelly Corrigan, Matteo Pistono, Jeff Forney, Lauri Levenfeld, Jenny Hlavac, Amy Gorman, Gregg and Kelle, Sue Panico, Robert and Mario, Mer and Ray, Heidi "The Glue" Yarger, Sandra Possing, Mel Robbins, The City (San Francisco), Jackson Hole, the JH Writers Conference, and my life changing career at Salesforce.

To all my *About Your Mother* podcast guests, thank you for letting me share your stories. I've learned so much from you, especially bravery. Our conversations are some of my proudest moments.

To the women who went away—forced to surrender their children under societal pressure in the decades before *Roe*—your stories live on, and we will not forget what you endured in silence.

YaYas, you were the sisters I needed in my young life. You saved me without knowing you did. I'm so proud of our forty-plus-year friendship and daily text exchanges, mainly focused on cats, concerts, and the Seahawks.

To my husband, Mark, thank you for believing in my talent when I wrote that first chapter and for encouraging me to leave my technology career to pursue creativity. It all works because of you. Conor and Allie, you were mirrors into my past and future. Tremendous gratitude for caring despite the complicated role a stepparent plays in your life.

Beth and Linda, I am not me without you. You were the light in my world as a little girl, and you are to this day. Beth, your cancer fight sets the bar in our family in terms of strength and resilience. You are so damn clear; I learn from you every day. Linda, you are the glue, the wonderful, limber, and consistent piece in our puzzle.

For my brother, you were the greatest birthday gift of all time. Nothing tops you. Adoption in families leads to a series of never-ending questions. While I can never understand the pain of being an adoptee, I hope this book helps answer some of those questions you might carry.

Dad, for consistently showing us strength, loyalty, and commitment, even if, at times, your resilience was misunderstood. You were the steady force in my life. In the end, I realized we were more alike than different. I can still feel your hand in mine and always will.

Mom, there are no words to express my gratitude. You are not a survivor; you are a warrior. I am who I am because you fought in life, you endured, and you never gave up or gave in. Thank you for giving me your blessing and letting me write this book. I know it wasn't easy to put your story in my hands. Thank you for telling me I was a good writer, even though this memoir was probably not your desired outcome with that gesture.

And finally, for Drake, this book is for you. The greatest miracle in my life is being your mother. As my imperfections overflow at times, I hope that you understand in reading this, there are generations of extraordinary maternal survivors in our family who paved the way for me to be your mother. None of us are perfect. Because of these incredible women, your light beams in this world. Shine bright, my boy, for all of us.

SUGGESTED FURTHER READING

The Girls Who Went Away by Ann Fessler

The Baby Scoop Era by Karen Wilson-Buterbaugh

American Baby by Gabrielle Glaser

The Lost Family by Libby Copeland

The Awakening by Kate Chopin

I Know Why the Caged Bird Sings and *Mom & Me & Mom* by Maya Angelou

The Complete Stories by Flannery O'Connor

The Optimist's Daughter by Eudora Welty

Eat Pray Love by Elizabeth Gilbert

Bird by Bird by Anne Lamott

Writing Down the Bones by Natalie Goldberg

For additional resources related to adoption, familial secrets, and the girls who went away please visit: www.byjennifergriffith.com

ABOUT THE AUTHOR

Jennifer Griffith hosts the popular *About Your Mother* podcast and holds a degree in English from Washington State University. Her lived experience with generational trauma, familial secrets, and the hidden history of adoption is the inspiration for her work. In her writing and on her podcast, she focuses on honoring the complexities of motherhood, family, and the unique experiences that shape our lives.

Photo by Jeff Forney